A PEOPLE'S GUIDE TO

# RICHMOND and CENTRAL VIRGINIA

UNIVERSITY OF CALIFORNIA PRESS
PEOPLE'S GUIDES

Los Angeles
Greater Boston
San Francisco Bay Area
Orange County, California
New York City
Richmond and Central Virginia

**Forthcoming**

New Orleans
Tokyo

### About the Series

Tourism is one of the largest and most profitable industries in the world today, especially for cities. Yet the vast majority of tourist guidebooks focus on the histories and sites associated with a small, elite segment of the population and encourage consumption and spectacle as the primary way to experience a place. These representations do not reflect the reality of life for most urban residents—including people of color, the working class and poor, immigrants, indigenous people, and LGBTQ communities—nor are they embedded within a systematic analysis of power, privilege, and exploitation. The *People's Guide* series was born from the conviction that we need a different kind of guidebook: one that explains power relations in a way everyone can understand, and that shares stories of struggle and resistance to inspire and educate activists, students, and critical thinkers.

Guidebooks in the series uncover the rich and vibrant stories of political struggle, oppression, and resistance in the everyday landscapes of metropolitan regions. They reveal an alternative view of urban life and history by flipping the script of the conventional tourist guidebook. These books not only tell histories from the bottom up, but also show how *all* landscapes and places are the product of struggle. Each book features a range of sites where the powerful have dominated and exploited other people and resources, as well as places where ordinary people have fought back in order to create a more just world. Each book also includes carefully curated thematic tours through which readers can explore specific urban processes and their relation to metropolitan geographies in greater detail. The photographs model how to read space, place, and landscape critically, while the maps, nearby sites of interest, and additional learning resources create a resource that is highly usable. By mobilizing the conventional format of the tourist guidebook in these strategic ways, books in the series aim to cultivate stronger public understandings of how power operates spatially.

A PEOPLE'S GUIDE TO

# RICHMOND and CENTRAL VIRGINIA

Melissa Ooten    Jason Sawyer

with photography by Kim Lee Schmidt

University of California Press

University of California Press
Oakland, California

The *People's Guides* are written in the spirit of discovery and we hope they will take readers to a wider range of places across cities. Readers are cautioned to explore and travel at their own risk and obey all local laws. The author and publisher assume no responsibility or liability with respect to personal injury, property damage, loss of time or money, or other loss or damage allegedly caused directly or indirectly from any information or suggestions contained in this book.

Library of Congress Cataloging-in-Publication Data

Names: Ooten, Melissa, author. | Sawyer, Jason, author. | Schmidt, Kim Lee, photograher.
Title: A people's guide to Richmond and Central Virginia / Melissa Ooten and Jason Sawyer ; with photography by Kim Lee Schmidt.
Other titles: People's guide ; 6.
Description: Oakland : University of California Press, [2023] | Series: A people's guide series ; 6 | Includes bibliographical references and index.
Identifiers: LCCN 2022051973 (print) | LCCN 2022051974 (ebook) | ISBN 9780520344167 (paperback) | ISBN 9780520975385 (ebook)
Subjects: LCSH: Richmond (Va.)–Guidebooks. | Richmond (Va.)–Description and travel. | Virginia–Guidebooks. | Virginia–Description and travel.
Classification: LCC F234.R53 O58 2023 (print) | LCC F234.R53 (ebook) | DDC 917.55/4510444–dc23/eng/20221214
LC record available at https://lccn.loc.gov/2022051973
LC ebook record available at https://lccn.loc.gov/2022051974

Designer and compositor: Nicole Hayward
Text: 10/14.5 Dante
Display: Museo Sans and Museo Slab
Prepress: Embassy Graphics
Cartographer: Rebecca Wrenn
Printer and binder: Sheridan Books, Inc.
Manufactured in the United States of America

32  31  30  29  28  27  26  25  24  23
10  9  8  7  6  5  4  3  2  1

# Contents

# Maps

# Introduction

On June 9, 2020, a group of Richmond activists removed the Christopher Columbus statue from its pedestal in Byrd Park and threw it into nearby Fountain Lake. Action to dismantle the monument came on the heels of a solidarity event with members of the Richmond Indigenous Society and the movement led by Black activists to protest white supremacist violence in the wake of George Floyd's murder by Minneapolis police on May 25 of that year. Activists immediately targeted Richmond's statues to subvert symbols of white supremacy prominently displayed across the city and regional landscape, particularly those related to the confederacy, with the end goal to mobilize a large-scale coalition to dismantle racist policies and practices enshrined in the region's power structures.

The need to share, experience, and elevate these community histories, alongside

their relationship to power and place, is vital. *A People's Guide to Richmond and Central Virginia* centers these narratives, sites, and landscapes to reverse past erasures while also recognizing the power of communities to name and claim their own spaces, histories, and legacies. The guide situates the experiences of everyday people asserting their humanity in order to thrive within their own communities across time and space. It highlights the ongoing impacts and effects of these legacies throughout the region.

Richmond and Central Virginia, a historic and contemporary center for racist violence, also cultivates communities that organize for resistance and liberation. On August 11, 2017, tiki-torch-wielding white supremacists marched on the Lawn at the University of Virginia in Charlottesville before the "Unite the Right" gathering the following day. They organized the event in opposition to the city's proposal to remove confederate monuments from highly visible public spaces in town. At that rally, white supremacist

---

After activists toppled Richmond's Christopher Columbus statue in Byrd Park, 2020.

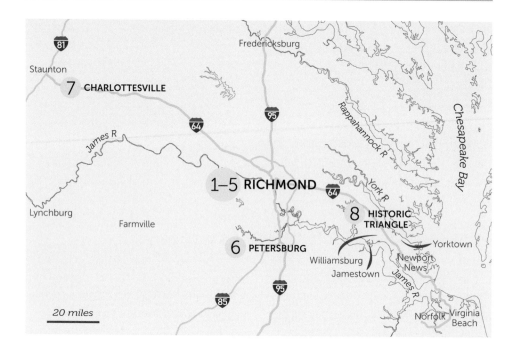

James Fields Jr. drove his car into a large crowd of human rights supporters, killing Heather Heyer and injuring nineteen others. The events in Charlottesville heightened the sense of urgency among social justice movements in Virginia and beyond. Two months before the Charlottesville events, years-long debates pushed Richmond's mayor to establish a commission to "develop context" for the five confederates statues on Monument Avenue. However, actionable plans for this work floundered until Black activists reignited the removal process through direct actions three years later.

Black-led movements reclaimed space and power often denied them in Richmond and beyond during the summer of 2020. Amidst ongoing police violence, protestors marched daily down Monument Avenue, which became a central site for community gatherings. Activists renamed the space that held the Robert E. Lee statue to Marcus-David Peters Circle in honor of a high school biology teacher killed by Richmond police in 2018 while experiencing a mental health crisis. On a meticulously manicured lawn set within a majority-white, affluent neighborhood, racially and economically diverse Richmonders decorated the statue's pedestal with graffitied slogans in support of the Black Lives Matter movement. Crowds transformed it into a space where everyday life took shape; they played basketball, sold food, danced, and created community. People curated memorials to victims of racial violence, which they placed at the base of the statue. Simultaneously, protestors demanded significant institutional change, calling for the city to defund the police and demanding that the state extend its eviction moratorium during the global coronavirus pandemic. This upsurge of resistance and protest was no anomaly; it was a continuation of four hundred years of community power and resilience.

These collective struggles are contemporary manifestations of centuries-long resistance by communities against the power structures embedded in Richmond and Central Virginia that place white supremacy, settler colonialism, and economic privilege at their core. Mired in conspicuous stories of triumphant white European settlers, first presidents of the nation-state, and wrongfully maligned confederates, the city and region today feature historic truth-telling processes as diverse communities memorialize their own histories while mobilizing to dismantle racist, patriarchal power structures. Many of these sites of resistance and survival, however, have been deliberately obscured from landscapes, historical texts, and public memory alike. *A People's Guide* seeks to make them more visible to a broad, contemporary audience.

## An "Up and Coming" City: Popular Narratives and Other Myths about Richmond

Typical guidebooks to Richmond and Central Virginia lionize the region's prominence in Revolutionary and Civil War battles, while emphasizing today's trendy neighborhoods alongside rapidly expanding craft brewery and foodie scenes. With few exceptions, guides establish two main narratives: the first centers the contributions of white economic elites, the architecture they com-

missioned, and existing sites that memorialize them. The second spotlights Richmond's tourism economy, casting the city as a hip and creative enclave that celebrates an independent, local sensibility.

The first narrative signals the tendency of guides to ignore the extensive communities of the Powhatan, the Monacan, and their tributaries that occupied this region at the time of English colonization. Instead, the guides tout the legacies of English colonizers, often with no mention of the extermination campaigns they led against Indigenous communities. Guides focus heavily on white, male, often slave-owning leadership from the region's colonial and antebellum eras. While some include significant Black history sites, they often use these sites to promote a narrative of "progress on all fronts," suggesting a city that has moved beyond its oppressive past. Only one text mentions 2020's "Summer of Protest," and it fails to link that action to the region's robust history of economic, racial, and social justice struggles. Most guides ignore predominantly African American, immigrant, and working-class neighborhoods, instead directing tourists, residents, and other curious citizens to established historic markers, monuments, and homes in the most affluent parts of the city that feature elite white history-making through a superficial lens of unmitigated progress.

The second narrative emphasized by guides promotes Richmond as a center for independent business, edgy art, hipster flair, unique charm, and economic possibility. *The Insider's Guide to Richmond* notes that the city "has the advantages of a cosmopolitan city—top-notch museums, historic sites, beautiful and varied architecture, engaged universities, vibrant arts, music, and culinary scenes, and a spectacular setting along the James River" with the advantage that "getting around where you want to go is a piece of cake." This rendering exposes a grave ignorance of a city with a high number of residents living in poverty, most of whom must navigate access to employment and housing through the region's inadequate public transportation system. It also masks historically oppressive practices related to housing segregation, community development, and other means that often determine who can occupy which spaces.

*A People's Guide* provides a critical intervention for more accurately rendering Richmond and Central Virginia's past and present. The trajectory of perennial progress advanced in mainstream guides mirrors regional branding efforts, which promote lofty narratives of economic growth that tout the region as a creative center for tourism, business, and culture. Connected to this curated image is a recent cultural and artistic renaissance that, while deeply rooted in the area's history, blurs the lines between corporate and independent artistic and cultural work. This rebirth at times serves as a harbinger of gentrification, especially in predominantly Black and Latino neighborhoods. In his 2017 newspaper column, Richmond journalist Michael Paul Williams, who won a Pulitzer for his *Richmond Times-Dispatch* commentaries during the summer of 2020, refers to this bifurcation—between a

hip, upwardly mobile city filled with accompanying amenities and a city where many residents see little change in their inability to secure basic needs—as the RVA versus Richmond divide. The divide captures the essence of a long-standing gulf in which the city's social and economic challenges remain inadequately addressed while high-end real estate development flourishes alongside national tourist marketing. Standard tourist guides only feature RVA; this guide aims to bridge the two to accurately capture the city's, and the region's, complexities.

RVA, the popular moniker for Richmond created in the early 2010s, intentionally brands the city to attract economic development and tourism. It symbolizes a culturally and economically affluent Richmond filled with craft breweries, maker spaces, and a food and arts scene rivaling those found in much larger cities. Richmond, on the other hand, is the city where 1 in 4 residents live in poverty, including nearly 40 percent of its children. It holds the dubious distinction of having the nation's largest food desert for a city of its size alongside the country's second-highest eviction rate. Due to centuries of racist policymaking, those in poverty are most likely to be Black, Indigenous, or Latino. Spatially, impoverished Black citizens are most likely to live in public housing communities that physically isolate them from the rest of the city.

Unlike traditional guidebooks, *A People's Guide* connects the origins of the nation's settler colonialism with contemporary contestations over white supremacy and connected socioeconomic and gender-based oppression that still shape the region, and the nation, today. It centers five themes that disrupt dominant narratives perpetuated in tourist material and corporate media while exposing vast gaps created by these widely disseminated sources. Each theme emerges differently across city and regional geographies, and some feature more prominently in certain chapters than others due to historic and contemporary patterns of development and migration alongside economic and racial exclusion.

The guide intentionally places narratives of resistance by Indigenous and Black communities at its forefront. Thus, the first theme articulates the country's founding as rooted in white colonization and settler colonialism, beginning with the first permanent English settlement at Jamestown. It includes people's resistance to campaigns of extermination aimed at Indigenous communities and the mass enslavement of Black people to provide labor that drove the country's economy for centuries. The second theme makes visible community efforts to dismantle the workings of white supremacy, including the disruption of Lost Cause nostalgia, an erroneously triumphant rendering of the confederacy as a heroic endeavor rather than one that sought to maintain enslavement by perpetuating racist institutions and belief systems. A third theme showcases community resistance to government-planned destruction, especially of Black neighborhoods, and the concentration of poverty by design. It highlights people working, often against enormous odds, to rectify the impacts of redlining and highway

building, the racial and geographic segregation of public housing, and repeated waves of gentrification. Centering people organizing for environmental justice encompasses the guide's fourth theme. These sites span rural and urban landscapes where people have mobilized against corporate greed and malfeasance in efforts to protect the health and long-term welfare of their communities. The final theme amplifies a homegrown artistic and cultural resurgence with deep roots in the region's history of Black cultural production, the fostering of LGBTQ artists and activists, and the use of art to cultivate and sustain community. These sites exemplify contestations over artistic production that link to broader power clashes, most of which use art and culture to provoke social change. The guide integrates these five themes throughout the text in order to investigate sites of everyday life produced by, and deeply rooted in, past and present power struggles.

## A People's History of Richmond and Central Virginia

Werowocomoco, a place of great spiritual and political significance to the Powhatan, rests at the north bank of the York River. Thousands of people once lived there, and Central Virginia was the focal point of many Indigenous trade routes stretching far into other regions of the continent. Further west, ancestors of the Monacan traded with the Powhatan and the Iroquois to the north. Archeological evidence shows Indigenous people lived in this region in both formally and informally connected communities for thousands of years before white colonization. Indigenous people began consolidating power in response to European encroachment as early as 1570. In 1607, English colonizers established their first permanent settlement fifty miles downriver from Richmond at Jamestown, and initially were unable to survive without the assistance of Indigenous communities. In a grim irony, colonizers soon pursued an agenda of removal and genocide against the Powhatan and their tributaries, the very communities who had once ensured their survival. At the same time, the Monacan actively deterred interaction with the English and continued to move west to avoid the colonizers for as long as possible. By the 1670s, the colony of Virginia had pushed the Pamunkey and the Mattaponi onto reservations, although Pamunkey leader Cockacoeske used what power she had to help ensure her community's survival. The Pamunkey and the Mattaponi still live on reduced portions of these lands today. Estimates suggest that the area's Indigenous population had decreased by 95 percent by 1700. However, their ancestors still occupy these lands, having resisted four hundred years of colonizing projects aimed at their erasure.

In 1619, the *White Lion* arrived, carrying about twenty enslaved people who had been kidnapped by the Portuguese from what is now Angola. This marked the beginning of the enslavement of Africans in the colony. Those forced into enslavement resisted the institution in diverse ways. In 1663, a Gloucester County group of enslaved Africans, white indentured servants, and Virginia Indians worked together in an attempt to overthrow their oppressors. In 1669, the colony's governing body, conceding that many enslaved Africans and indentured servants had liberated themselves, sought more stringent laws to prevent future "runaways." Enslaved people in Westmoreland County attempted rebellion against their enslavers in both 1687 and 1688; in turn, this colony also passed several new laws in the late seventeenth century to better control enslaved people and prevent their liberation efforts. By 1700, the English had exponentially increased the importation of enslaved Africans as their primary labor source to keep pace with the explosive growth of the cash crop, tobacco. At the same time, colonizers constructed and exploited racial difference. In doing so, they aimed to reinforce their control over enslaved laborers while codifying the privileges of whiteness in both law and custom, a process that the United States mirrored when the nation-state formed over a century later.

While Virginia's landowning white men readily restricted the freedom of those with whom they shared the colony, including white women, Africans both free and enslaved, and Indigenous communities, they increasingly chafed at British control. The Revolutionary War (1775–83) provided opportunities for Indigenous and enslaved communities alike to pit warring whites against each other to create better conditions for their own people. Hundreds of enslaved people joined the British army when promised their freedom, and thousands took the opportunity created by the chaos of the war to escape enslavement. Indigenous communities also made bargains and switched sides readily between the colonists and the English, leveraging competing offers of alliance to better safeguard themselves.

Virginia became a state in 1788. Agricultural and manufacturing magnates in Central Virginia prospered, with tobacco reigning supreme. Other industrial development in Richmond, the state's capital, included mining and ironworking; the Gallego flour mills, the world's largest, shipped flour globally. This substantial rise in agricultural production and industrialization fueled the market for enslaved labor. Due to its population, river access, proximity to agricultural development, and emerging industrial infrastructure, Richmond became a prominent industrial and trade center prior to the Civil War.

The slave trade was Richmond's number-one economic driver by the time of the Civil War (1861–65); the city ranked only behind New Orleans as the nation's leading site for the sale of enslaved people. The business of enslavement was deeply woven into the city's landscape; sales took place on street corners, in pubs, and in basements of the city's most luxurious hotels. Enslaved people resisted when and where they could. Urban slavery, in which enslaved laborers were hired out, lived apart from their enslavers, and sometimes earned their own money from side work, defined much of enslavement in Richmond. It enabled a small number of people to purchase their freedom or the freedom of their families. Black Vir-

ginians also organized rebellions. The 1800 rebellion of Gabriel and his co-conspirators in Richmond and Nat Turner's 1831 rebellion seventy miles away in Southampton County nearly succeeded in scaring the state legislature into abolishing slavery.

Richmond's population swelled during the Civil War, both as the capital of the confederacy and due to its location near many battlefronts. Its downtown core burned to the ground when fleeing confederates set fire to supply buildings that grew out of control in April 1865. After the war, it remained a nucleus for white supremacy, with the rise of Lost Cause mythology, Jim Crow laws, and other projects aimed at restricting the rights of African Americans. In the wake of the Civil War, Richmond's industries rebuilt not only the city but the South more widely. Its iron building industry thrived as did tobacco, especially cigarette manufacturing. Black men, newly empowered by the voting rights granted to them by the 15th Amendment, elected dozens of Black men to serve in the General Assembly in the late nineteenth century. One legacy of that interracial governance was the establishment of statewide public education. Concurrently, former confederates crafted a historical interpretation of the Civil War, known as the Lost Cause, that falsely claimed that a battle over states' rights caused the war and it had little to do with slavery. This interpretation, meant to buttress white supremacy at a time when Black Virginians openly challenged it, included demarcating public space as white, embodied by the installation of a sixty-foot-tall statue of confederate general

Robert E. Lee on Richmond's Monument Avenue in 1890.

Richmond and the region's rise as part of the "New South" created a surge in employment for industrial workers in the early twentieth century. The area featured large-scale production in textiles, cotton, tobacco, and emerging retail and clothing industries. A system of racial and gender-based apartheid undergirded these industries. Throughout the nineteenth century, Black women dominated frontline work in the profitable tobacco industry, but by the early twentieth century, white women occupied an increasingly large number of these positions. Industries reserved skilled labor and management positions for white men, with Black men confined to labor deemed "unskilled," which primarily meant those positions paid wages much lower than those paid to "skilled" white laborers.

In 1902, Virginia adopted a constitution that disenfranchised many of its citizens, most notably Black men, and segregation laws increasingly sought to treat African Americans as second-class citizens. Richmond and Charlottesville pioneered zoning ordinances as tools to enshrine racial segregation in the 1910s; other forms of housing discrimination continued into the 1970s, with projects touted as economically and socially progressive continually destroying Black neighborhoods in the name of revitalization and renewal. Segregation, however, also allowed for economically diverse Black neighborhoods to flourish. Jackson Ward became one of the nation's most vibrant centers for Black business and entertainment. This tight-knit community also initiated numerous organizing and mutual aid opportunities. When women gained the right to vote in 1920, Black women in this neighborhood organized mass voter registration drives that led to more than 10 percent of adult Black women in the city qualifying to vote in elections that fall, despite the many racially motivated barriers to voting that they faced.

As Black activists vocally demanded civil rights in the 1920s, white supremacists further honed their strategies to maintain power. They passed a law legalizing sterilization for "idiocy, imbecility, feeblemindedness or epilepsy" in 1924, which specifically targeted poor Virginians. They also passed the Racial Integrity Act of 1924, tightening the boundaries of who could exercise the privileges of whiteness. Anyone with "one drop" of African ancestry could no longer be legally recognized as white. Walter Plecker drafted this legislation, and he led the state's Bureau of Vital Statistics from its inception in 1912 until 1946. Placed in charge of official state documents including birth, marriage, and death certificates, he carried out a campaign of bureaucratic genocide against Virginia Indians. His work to expunge the existence of Virginia Indians from state documents had severe consequences in Indigenous communities' quests for sovereignty and access to public resources. Nevertheless, Virginia Indians resisted these attempts at erasure, and as of 2022, the state is home to seven federally recognized and eleven state recognized tribes.

Union organizing in support of better working conditions was strong throughout the city in the early twentieth century, despite political and industry-led attempts to use race to divide unionists. While this race-baiting hindered unionization, representation of unionized workers increased through the 1930s. After the National Industry Recovery Act of 1931 ensured workers' right to organize, workers organized against mining, railroads, transportation, and utility industries, prompting state politicians to draft anti-union legislation. In the late 1930s, Richmond saw particular union growth as the Southern Negro Youth Congress organized thousands of Black women working in the tobacco industry. By the mid-1940s, however, legislators and their corporate supporters crafted laws to curtail the power of organized labor in the state's largest and most powerful industries. Anti-labor actions also kept wages low, even as jobs became more available in the economic boom that followed World War II.

After World War II, urban renewal projects, accurately dubbed "Negro removal" by intellectual and author James Baldwin in a 1963 interview, significantly compromised nearly every Black community in Richmond, decreasing Black wealth for generations. By 1960, the city had destroyed thousands of housing units in Black communities, yet these projects predated the later destruction of the Navy Hill and Fulton neighborhoods. Similar midcentury demolition projects devastated Charlottesville's African American communities, while Williamsburg had forcibly displaced its Black residents and businesses decades earlier with the restoration of Colonial Williamsburg in the 1920s.

Communities' vitality depended on housing conditions as well as educational opportunities. From their inception in 1870, Virginia's public schools were racially segregated. They became political battlegrounds after the 1954 *Brown v. Board of Education* Supreme Court decision desegregated public schools nationally. Richmond schools' desegregation began in 1960 when Carol Swann and Gloria Mead, two African American students, began attending the formerly all-white Chandler Junior High School. In Charlottesville and elsewhere, Virginia's governor closed public schools in 1958 rather than integrate them. Persistent lawsuits pursued by Black students and parents, argued by Black lawyers like Oliver Hill, eventually led to desegregated schools. Virginia Indians (see *A Note on Terminology,* page 15) also fought prolonged campaigns with the state to receive access to rudimentary public schooling. Today, struggles for educational equity look different, but they still reveal that students of color and lower-income students often receive inadequate schooling. Black and Latino students are overrepresented at underresourced schools, and communities continue to organize to address problems like overcrowding, police violence, the need for multilingual services, and inadequate protections for LGBTQ students.

By the 1960s, power shifted in the city as white families, fueled by fears of desegregated schools and aided by extensive highway systems, moved into surrounding counties. Local organizing among Black voters maximized African American voting power until the passage of the Voting Rights Act of 1965 eliminated the many barriers Virginia had erected to curtail Black voting. As a result, city officials annexed a swath of Chesterfield County in 1970 in a move to deliberately shift voting in the city from a Black majority to a white one. In 1971, activist Curtis Holt sued the city in response. In its 1972 *Holt v. City of Richmond* ruling, the U.S. Supreme Court called the annexation "constitutionally impermissible" but allowed Richmond to keep it in place if the city changed how it elected its leaders. As a result, the city did not hold another election until 1977. The subsequent election system, alongside the work of organizations dedicated to Black voter mobilization, led to the city's first Black mayor, Henry Marsh III, and its first majority-Black city council in 1977.

The 1970s also saw women's groups and gay and lesbian Richmonders claiming public space by organizing prominent gatherings in city parks. Women's festivals, begun in 1974, eventually led to the city's first pride event at Byrd Park in 1979. Feminist bookstores, communes, and activist groups that met in homes and supportive churches allowed gay men and lesbian women to gather safely. This cultivation of community support and space became critical during the HIV / AIDS crisis of the 1980s.

In 1972, the Zajur family opened the region's first Mexican restaurant near the border of Richmond's Southside and north Chesterfield County. As a result, diverse Latino communities with familial roots in Mexico, El Salvador, Guatemala, Puerto Rico, and beyond settled in this particular area in subsequent decades. Since 2000, the number of people immigrating to Richmond and Central Virginia from Latin American countries has increased tenfold by some estimates. It is expected that 1 in 4 Chesterfield County residents will identify as Latino by the 2030s. As a result, Latin American culture has blossomed here in the form of markets, restaurants, and services, creating economic and social resources for their communities. As well, communities have organized to protect undocumented workers and address racial profiling. In the late 2010s, a group of undocumented immigrants formed ICE Out of RVA to organize against Immigration and Customs Enforcement (ICE)'s collusion with local police to target diverse immigrant communities, and parents and students mobilized at local schools to contest school officials searching for anyone who "looks Latino" to root out undocumented families. These movements showcase the ways that communities continue to organize against oppressive policies and practices while building upon past histories of resistance.

Asian and Middle Eastern communities are growing as well. Asian American residents account for nearly 10 percent of the population in Henrico County, which surrounds much of Richmond to the north, east, and west. Arabic is now the third most spoken household language in Virginia, after English and Spanish. These communities are more recent additions to the Central Virginia region, and as a result, they are featured less prominently in this guide than others. However, these new immigrant groups will continue to reshape the region's landscapes and power dynamics as they organize for humane immigration policies, multilingual educational and public services, and a host of other issues in pursuit of equity.

## Everyday Space, Place, and Landscapes of Power

A "people's guide" interrogates how power shapes people's complex relationships with space, and how people collectively remake that space to assert their humanity and dismantle oppressive systems. It highlights the ways in which material spaces and places underpin shifting and uneven racial, sexual, and economic relations that took root at the beginning of European colonization and continue to shape communities' access to economic, political, and social power. Writing on the geographies of Black women in her work *Demonic Grounds,* Katherine McKittrick notes: "Geography is not . . . secure and unwavering; we produce space, we produce its meanings, and we work very hard to make geography what it is." Just as geographic dominance and spatial colonization shape our regional landscape, residents challenge and reshape those legacies of conquest and exploitation. Part of the work of this guide is to uncover what such dominance has worked to conceal, to ask how residents of Central Virginia occupy and contest space in order to reveal how they move through and construct meaning in the spaces of everyday life.

Space negotiation reconfigures historic and contemporary routes that link communities to natural and built environments. These routes shape the movement of people and can serve as mechanisms to fortify, symbolize, and consolidate power. These historic and socially reinforced routes are often accepted as permanent fixtures in the landscape. As shown in the map on page 2, the James River bifurcates Richmond and flows past Jamestown to empty into the Chesapeake Bay and Atlantic Ocean. It has immeasurably shaped the region's lived environment. To the Powhatan and the Monacan, the river served as a critical source of food, migration, and trade. For that same reason, colonizers pushed Indigenous communities away from the James and other significant waterways soon after their arrival. Later, the river allowed Richmond to grow into a large center for the sale of enslaved people. It also enabled a vast trade in tobacco, flour, and iron that set the stage for industry-generated environmental harm that still plagues area waterways and most affects communities of color, who live in areas most impacted by environmental hazards. Today, the river attracts affluent residents and tourists alike for leisure and recreation, but the growth of green spaces along the river also threatens further gentrification in historic African American neighborhoods while failing to adequately address the ongoing pollution of the river.

Similar to how the region's waterways once shaped settlement and trade patterns, highway and interstate construction has driven regional trade, tourism, and migration routes since the 1950s. Interstate 95, the region's major thoroughfare that runs from Florida to Maine, and Interstate 64, the region's east–west artery, intersect in Richmond. Historically, this highway-building has displaced thousands of Black and working-class white Richmonders while facilitating white flight to the suburbs. At the same time, by linking Richmond to larger nearby centers like the nation's capital ninety miles to the north, these transportation nodes have facilitated the contemporary migration of a diverse group of immigrants into the city and region, who are, in turn, reshaping spaces to meet the needs of their communities.

## Research Processes, Sources, and Methods

The timing of *A People's Guide* is critical. Regional growth and tourism continue to outpace even liberal estimates. As more people move to the region and many others visit, understanding how residents organize to challenge oppressive power systems is more important than ever. While colonial and confederate histories dominated outsiders' knowledge and tourist geographies of the region in the past, a marked shift in national attention emerged in 2020. The *New York Times Magazine* ranked the transformation of the statue of confederate Robert E. Lee into a diverse public gathering space christened Marcus-David Peters Circle first on its list of "The 25 Most Influential Works of American Protest Art since World War II." *Fodor's* called the city's Black History Museum and Cultural Center "unmissable," and *Travel + Leisure* listed the city as one of "The 50 Best Places to Travel in 2021," specifically

noting the reclamation of Peters Circle, the Slave Trail, and local artist Hamilton Glass's Mending Walls RVA mural project, which calls for residents to engage in difficult conversations about racial injustice. Photography from Peters Circle appeared on the covers of internationally acclaimed *Artforum* and *National Geographic* magazines. This recognition marked a pivotal moment in centering those who have long organized for social justice as vital to the region's importance.

*A People's Guide* features more than 120 sites where ordinary people assert their humanity and dignity while organizing their communities, as well as sites where powerholders have worked to restrain those actions. The guide immerses readers in place-specific sites and landscapes of everyday struggle. It centers an inclusive and expansive historical and contemporary regional geography by archiving stories and spaces often overlooked in traditional guidebooks, textbooks, and conventional memorialization efforts. These histories of community resistance and resilience inscribed in the region's landscape work to correct an erroneous narrative—that elites make history worth knowing and sites worth visiting—by showing how ordinary people come together to create more equitable futures. The guide, alongside multiple interventions from local activists, artists, community members, and scholars, pushes us to examine what we think we know about the spaces we navigate and to question our assumptions about the origins, experiences, and power relations of institutional and community life in Richmond and Central Virginia.

The guide's methodology is undergirded by a blend of interdisciplinary approaches that combine research in history, sociology, and cultural geography. It merges archival research and extensive review of existing scholarly works with dozens of interviews and oral histories. We accessed archives and research material at the Library of Virginia, Virginia Museum of History and Culture, The Valentine, the Black History Museum and Cultural Center of Richmond, the Pamunkey Indian Museum and Cultural Center, area universities, and local historical associations. We worked through newspaper repositories like the *Richmond Planet* (1883–1938), Richmond's first Black newspaper, an incredibly important source for historical Black perspectives. We also utilized critical sources for understanding Virginia history, such as Virginia Humanities' *Encyclopedia Virginia* and *AfroVirginia,* the Virginia Department of Historic Resources, and the *Virginia Magazine of History & Biography.* Scholarly sources essential to our research can be found in the bibliography. Secondary sources and archival material did not always adequately capture contemporary histories of diverse communities. For this information, we leaned on an extensive advisory board of activists, artists, scholars, and community members, who shared not only their own invaluable knowledge but also many other community-led projects from which we drew. We used existing oral histories, and conducted many of our own, to capture a diverse snapshot of the social justice work being done in our communities.

With Richmond at its core, the book comprises eight chapters with the five themes outlined earlier integrated throughout. Chapters 1 through 5 explore everyday landscapes within the city of Richmond. These chapters include Downtown, the East End, Northside, the Fan and West End, and Southside. Three additional chapters explore area centers critical to understanding Central Virginia as a region. Chapter 6 explores Petersburg, which likely contained the South's largest free Black community prior to the Civil War, and points to the south of Richmond. Chapter 7 explores Charlottesville, perhaps best known as the home of the University of Virginia, envisioned by Thomas Jefferson and physically constructed by free and enslaved Black laborers, and points to the west of Richmond. Chapter 8 explores the region known in tourism material as the Historic Triangle—Williamsburg, Jamestown, and Yorktown—as well as rural areas that encompass Charles City County, Gloucester County, King William County, New Kent County, and beyond. Personal reflections by community members, activists, artists, and scholars accompany some sites to underscore ongoing community work.

The best way to experience a place's history and geography is to travel through it. Some sites that sit close to one another in neighborhoods like Church Hill and Jackson Ward can be navigated by bike or on foot. Despite pioneering the country's first electric streetcar system in 1888, Richmond later enthusiastically embraced highway-building, turning away from robust investment in public transportation, which remains sporadic and underdeveloped. As a result, you will need private transportation to access most of the sites.

A guidebook, by its nature, is selective and incomplete. We could not possibly represent the full complexity and breadth of the region's community history and geography, and we have not attempted to do so. We know some readers may find that a site of great importance to them is missing, and we hope these experiences spark further conversation and learning about the abundance of sites where everyday people create community, shape space, and make history. We have tried to err on the side of including stories and sites we believe to be lesser known, both in public memory and in the physical landscape.

This project has had many starts and stops across its production, which began when Melissa discovered *A People's Guide to Los Angeles* by Laura Pulido, Laura Barraclough, and Wendy Cheng on a trip to L. A. and used it to explore a city completely different from the one extolled in traditional guidebooks. As part of the larger *A People's Guide* series, this guide uncovers histories and landscapes of ordinary people asserting equity, dignity, and humanity. It seeks to counter traditional guidebooks that highlight the "best of" a particular area, which usually means "the best known" or "the most powerful." While it is the result of extensive research and peer review, at its heart this guide centers histories of community resistance and resilience not told collectively elsewhere.

Any and all errors are the authors' alone. Many of the stories we tell in a few hundred words could be explored in an entire book; in many cases, if such a work exists, we direct readers to it. We encourage those interested to investigate the sources we list under the "to learn more" sections of the sites, as they offer additional context and nuance. They often recognize an invaluable collaborator we consulted for the entry or a critical work of scholarship or journalism that deserves further exploration. Additionally, we encourage you to explore the "to visit nearby" sites listed after many entries, as they represent more formally memorialized spaces to enrich your visit. We offer thematic tours at the end, in which curious travelers can spend a day exploring groups of sites based on themes of particular significance in the region. The guide concludes with a bibliography, an excellent resource for taking a deep dive into the region's rich histories and geographies. Like the guide, the sources listed interrogate power relations by centering community resistance and survival. They served as indispensable resources in developing this guide.

As you explore Richmond and Central Virginia, we hope that it will inspire further curiosity about lesser-known histories and landscapes, as well as greater attunement to the power struggles that go into the making of *all* places. By working collectively to re-remember these sites, it can lead us to embody and expand the critical practice of historian and philosopher Howard Zinn. In *A People's History of the United States,* he wrote: "If history is to be creative, to anticipate a possible future without denying the past, it should . . . emphasize new possibilities by disclosing those hidden episodes of the past when, even if in brief flashes, people showed their ability to resist, to join together, and occasionally, to win." It is our hope that this guide builds upon this inspiration to make visible the landscapes where these events happened, why these places matter, and how they can help raise our collective consciousness to envision a future rooted in freedom making and justice for all people.

A NOTE ON TERMINOLOGY:

*We recognize the importance of using precise terminology when describing identity groups and the difficulty in doing so. As writers, we strive to honor how people name and describe themselves, while acknowledging that singular labels applied to large groups of people are always evolving, often contentious, and reflect significant power dynamics.*

*In this guidebook, we use the term Virginia Indians to identify the area's Indigenous communities because it is the term most tribes in Virginia use to describe themselves. We use specific tribal names whenever possible. Contemporary tribes that appear in this guide include the Mattaponi, the Upper Mattaponi, the Monacan, the Pamunkey, and the Chickahominy. For further information on terminology related to Virginia Indians, we recommend reading "Writing and Thinking about Virginia Indians" in* The Virginia Indian Trail Guide *edited by the late Karenne Wood of the Monacan Indian Nation, an early advisor to this project.*

*For immigrant groups from Latin America and their descendants, we use the term Latino. Central Virginia's diverse Latin American communities most often use Latino and / or Hispanic to describe themselves; they also use their countries of origin. We use Latino, the Spanish for Latin, recognizing that the term as a form of categorization remains fraught. Other community members use Hispanic, Latine, and Latinx.*

# 1

# Down-
# town
## Richmond

# Introduction

**DOWNTOWN RICHMOND HAS BEEN A SEAT** of state and city government since Virginia gained statehood in 1788. It exemplifies the deep contestations over space, dominance, and control highlighted throughout this guide. First inhabited thousands of years ago by Indigenous communities, these lands were gradually seized from the Powhatan and their tributaries by English colonizers, beginning in the 1600s. The colonizers desired control and access to the area's resources and strategic geography as defined by the James River. In the ensuing four centuries, the river has functioned as a pivot point, leading to the historic concentration of municipal, industrial, and economic institutional power in this part of the city. Today, the State Capitol grounds, City Hall, and other government buildings line the downtown core, alongside banking institutions, corporate law firms, and the extensive Virginia Commonwealth University Health System. Decisions made here directly impact communities throughout the state.

Sites in this chapter exist alongside tourist attractions and downtown landscapes flanked by centuries-old factory infrastructure, government buildings, and dense highway construction. Government procedure, commerce, and tourism overshadow many activist histories and ongoing social justice struggles here. Nonetheless, Downtown Richmond contains many sites of resistance against colonial, state, and industrial power. Salient themes in this chapter include communities' rebellion against and liberation from enslavement, collective organizing to dismantle white supremacy, and a cultural resurgence led by local artists who center social justice in their work.

The sites and stories in this chapter interrogate widely misunderstood geographies

Commerce along Richmond's Main Street, 1905.

related to histories of enslavement and resistance to it, particularly within urban landscapes. Enslavement in the city grew alongside industrialization; the city's position as the state capital and regional transportation center added to the growth of the enslaved population. Initially, slave auctions took place on street corners here, but

Aerial view of Richmond with Tobacco Row featured in the foreground along the riverfront, ca. 1960.

Vendors sell their wares at downtown's Sixth Street Market in 1908.

prior to the Civil War. Enslaved people in urban settings often lived away from their enslavers, which allowed them more freedom of movement and opportunities to organize. A prominent example occurred in 1800 when Gabriel and his co-conspirators planned a revolt to kidnap the governor and force him to abolish slavery. While the rebellion was exposed before it began, news of Gabriel's actions spread through both free and enslaved Black communities, earning him the moniker "General Gabriel."

Today, community members seek to preserve these historic spaces of resistance alongside early cemeteries, like the **African Burial Ground** (see page 23) and the Shockoe Hill African Burying Ground at 1305 N. 5th Street, sites that the city developed under pressure from Black enslaved and free residents in the early nineteenth century. However, this work challenges projects often championed by city leaders and private developers alike who see these spaces as ripe for redevelopment. Developers transformed many structures from the city's early industrial era, such as warehouses and factories used in tobacco, cotton, and flour production, into luxury residential spaces at the beginning of the twenty-first century.

as the trade increased exponentially over time, these transactions moved into taverns and then other, larger spaces. For example, the city's most luxurious hotel in the 1840s, the Exchange, hosted sales of enslaved people six nights each week in its basement. The work of enslavement infused nearly every downtown business in the decades

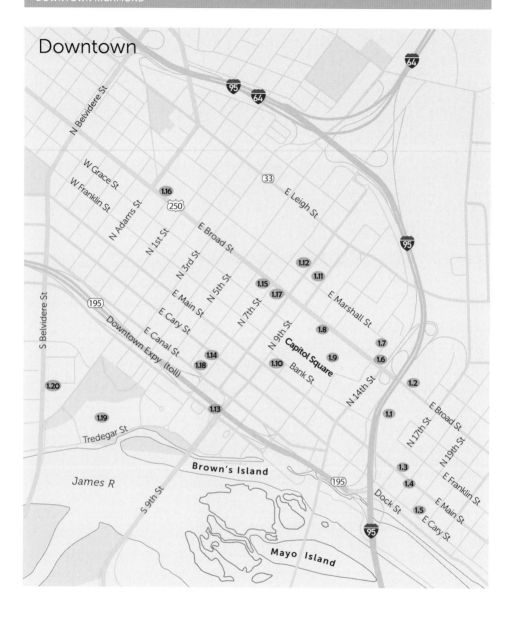

City leaders and boosters praise these projects as examples of economic growth and revitalization, while these same projects often threaten grassroots preservation efforts. Recent threats include proposals for a baseball stadium, luxury live-work complexes, and high-speed rail. Volunteer, civic, and community groups consistently resist these plans that privilege elite political and economic interests. In addition, recent development to create recreation and park space here, which includes the starting point of a fifty-mile bike route connecting Richmond and Williamsburg called the Capital Trail,

As the seat of the State Capitol, Downtown Richmond is a historic and contemporary site of protests for social change. Here, African Americans march toward Capitol Square to demand equal rights, 1981.

signals continued interest in downtown living alongside further gentrification in neighboring East End communities, like Church Hill and Fulton.

In addition to becoming a base for recreation, Downtown Richmond has grown into a twenty-first-century artistic hub, perhaps most discernible when thousands crowd into it for the city's First Friday Art Walks, which operate in galleries and creative cultural spaces along Broad Street and beyond. Downtown celebrates numerous large-scale public art projects, particularly street murals and art festivals. Arts and cultural activities often exist in tension with economic development schemes. In the 1980s, the city evicted dozens of artists from downtown gallery space to create an arts district that did not officially materialize until 2012. Some cultural events deliberately highlight homegrown artists and cultural creators while others draw in nonlocals to the exclusion of local artists. The conciliatory work

of public artists organized by Hamilton Glass and other locals who use downtown as their hub have opened racial dialogue and education in ways that highlight local efforts to address racist violence across the city and region.

These artistic and cultural efforts work in tandem with community organizing to reclaim and reimagine physical space, with varying results. During the summer 2020 protests, for example, activists pitched a tent camp in front of City Hall and named it Reclamation Square, with the intention to hold around-the-clock vigils to demand that city leaders initiate immediate police reforms. Within hours, officials had declared the assembly an unlawful one and used tear gas, pepper spray, and rubber bullets to disperse those encamped there. This action served as a vivid reminder that residents continue to contest city and state space and power in this core for government and business, as they have for centuries.

# Downtown Richmond Sites

## 1.1 Devil's Half Acre

E. Franklin Street east of 15th Street behind
Main Street Station

Behind the Main Street Station train hub sits
a parking lot that once housed a large slave
jail complex known as the Devil's Half Acre.
The jail housed enslaved people awaiting
sale in the decades prior to the Civil War.

Excavation work begins at Devil's Half Acre, 2006.

Commonly called Lumpkin's Jail after its
owner, Robert Lumpkin, Black activists call
the site by the name that the enslaved gave
it: the Devil's Half Acre.

Lumpkin operated this jail, located in the
center of the city's slave trading district just
two blocks from the State Capitol building,
between 1844 and 1865. He and his jail were
known for extreme cruelty. A tall fence over
ten feet in height surrounded it, and iron
spikes further discouraged escape attempts.
Years after the Civil War, city residents still
recalled the whipping posts prominently displayed there.

Lumpkin had a sexual relationship with
a woman he legally enslaved, Mary. They
had a number of children together, and they
sent at least two of their daughters north to
be educated, who eventually lived there as
white women. At the end of the Civil War,
federal officials caught Lumpkin trying to
flee the city with enslaved people in tow.
He died in 1866, and as his legally named
heir, Mary inherited his property, including the former jail site. In
1867, a theologian from Chicago arranged with Mary to
lease the property at what
had been the jail site in order
to start a school for freedmen and women. The school
operated at this site for a
short time before eventually
finding a permanent home
on Lombardy Street in the
city's Northside. This school
became Virginia Union University (VUU), Richmond's
only historically Black university.

Ongoing building projects have persisted
at this location for decades. While projects
change, the near-permanent existence of
wire fencing and traffic cones deters access
to the site. A small grassy area enclosed by
a low-lying fence with a few markers stands
near the interstate. These plaques briefly
record the site's history and its important
connection to VUU.

## TO LEARN MORE

Dawkins, Jenna. "Uncovering the Story of an Enslaved Woman at Lumpkin's Jail." *Virginia Humanities,* April 16, 2018.

Green, Kristen. *The Devil's Half Acre: The Untold Story of How One Woman Liberated the South's Most Notorious Slave Jail.* New York: Basic Books, 2021.

Tucker, Abigail. "Digging Up the Past at a Richmond Slave Jail." *Smithsonian Magazine,* March 2009.

## TO VISIT NEARBY

Visit **VIRGINIA UNION UNIVERSITY** at 1500 N. Lombardy Street.

## 1.2 African Burial Ground

15th Street at E. Broad Street

Just north of the Devil's Half Acre, a short tunnelway leads to the city's first African Burial Ground. This land was the first designated for both free and enslaved people of African ancestry to be buried within the city. It may have opened as early as 1799. The city gallows buttressed the lot, and it is where the state executed Gabriel and twenty-five other enslaved people for planning a rebellion against enslavement in 1800. Black Richmonders protested the poor conditions of this burial ground, and when the city refused to act, a group of free Black residents

Contemporary memorial at African Burial Ground.

purchased land in 1815 for a new, private site to the north. The city closed this site in 1816 and opened another site within view of the site established by free Black Richmonders the previous year, which became known as the Shockoe Hill African Burying Ground.

Much of the African Burial Ground lies under Interstate 95, the building of which also destroyed a significant portion of Richmond's largest Black neighborhood, Jackson Ward, in the 1950s. While this site is only two blocks from the State Capitol grounds, knowledge of its history and significance had been obscured until the turn

African Burial Ground, 2020.

of the twenty-first century. Today, the city minimally preserves the site, and even this preservation has been hard fought and won by local activists. Despite the city's development of the Slave Trail—a commemorative walking path that follows the route traveled by enslaved people, taking them from where their ships docked across the river in Manchester to holding areas like the Devil's Half Acre—this area is difficult to find. The inconsistent history of who and what city leaders choose to memorialize motivates community members to demand recognition of their voices in the process, even while they question whether the work will happen at all.

After the site's rediscovery in the 1990s, the Richmond Defenders for Freedom, Justice and Equality, a community activist group organizing for the survival of Black communities, placed signage about this site's history here, as no other memorialization existed. It served as a parking lot for Virginia Commonwealth University's medical campus until 2011 when activists, after a decade-long struggle, successfully got the property transferred to the city under the purview of the Slave Trail Commission. While its former use is clearly visible as concrete peeks out through gaps in the seeded grass and large parking lot lights soar overhead, community members continue to care for this site, using signs, offerings for their ancestors, murals, and other objects to restore and honor this space.

PERSONAL REFLECTION

## ANA EDWARDS

**Public Historian and Chair, Sacred Ground Historical Reclamation Project**

When you are aware of an area's history, you can see it, you can see what's hidden. I want to reweave Black history into Richmond's history. The impact of the transatlantic and domestic slave trades on all New World peoples and nations has been devastating on the one hand. On the other, we are here now, the result of it all, and have to figure out how to go forward. Richmonders, no less than any others, want to see that history, the struggle and the planning for a better future reflected in the landscapes they live in. Learning history empowers and energizes me and I've seen it empower others. Getting to know the early history of Black life in Richmond and its relationship to my family's journey over time through slavery and freedom, and the connection of it all to the start of the nation, was like having a hundred doorways burst open. There were young people on the streets [in 2020] who knew about the relationship between Richmond's past and present inequities because they grew up in Richmond when the work of the Sacred Ground Historical Reclamation Project, the Defenders for Freedom, Justice & Equality, and so many others was becoming common knowledge. That tells us that this kind of public history work is important.

TO LEARN MORE

The Sacred Ground Historical Reclamation Project: https://www.sacredgroundproject.net/. A project of the Richmond Defenders for Freedom, Justice and Equality, it centers Black community members' continued efforts to preserve and shape memorialization of Black historical sites in the city.

Lazarus, Jeremy. "One Woman's Crusade Brings Attention to Long-Forgotten Black Cemetery." *Richmond Free Press,* March 6, 2020.

Smith, Ryan. *Death and Rebirth in a Southern City: Richmond's Historic Cemeteries.* Baltimore: Johns Hopkins University Press, 2020.

**TO VISIT NEARBY**

**SHOCKOE HILL AFRICAN BURYING GROUND** at 1305 N. 5th Street represents the second public cemetery for Black residents, opened by the city in 1816. The city designated one acre for free people of color and one acre for enslaved people. It contains 22,000 gravesites and was added to the Virginia Landmarks Register in 2022 after years of community organizing to better protect the site from future development.

## 1.3  1708 Gallery (former location)

1708 E. Main Street

1708 Gallery originally opened at this location in Shockoe Bottom as an artist-run space in 1978. In 1990, the gallery sponsored an exhibit that included *In Memoriam* by Cuban-born artist Carlos Gutierrez-Solana. His work featured a large acrylic painting of three nude men that the gallery prominently displayed in its large, street-facing windows. The work commemorated the recent deaths of Gutierrez-Solana's friends, who had died from AIDS. Its intent was to generate support for AIDS patients while also educating gallery visitors about the disease.

Soon after the gallery installed the art in the windows, Virginia's state attorney, Joe Morrissey, arrived with a copy of Virginia's obscenity laws. He insisted the gallery owners cover the painting; they refused. Then a group of men arrived with white butcher's paper and pasted it over the windows in order to block the art. In protest, supporters of the gallery taped pictures of renowned works of classical nude art over the covered windows.

A federal judge ordered that the art remain covered until hearings could be held. In court, the state needed to prove that the work offended community standards of decency and had no artistic value. After Gutierrez-Solana testified about producing the work in grief as a tribute to his friends, the judge ruled against the obscenity charge. The paper came down, and the exhibit continued as a critical space not only for cultivating artistic freedom but also for centering AIDS awareness and education at a time when there was still much fear, prejudice, and misinformation surrounding the disease. Now located at 319 W. Broad, this gallery continues to thrive as a community gathering space for artists, cultural workers, and activists.

**TO LEARN MORE**

Marschak, Beth, and Alex Lorch. *Lesbian and Gay Richmond.* Mt. Pleasant, SC: Arcadia, 2008.

Kollatz, Jr., Harry. "Artistic License." *Richmond Magazine,* November 11, 2016.

## 1.4 Adams Express Company

18th and E. Main Streets

On this site, abolitionists operated a package service that helped deliver enslaved people to freedom in the North, including Henry Brown. Brown was born into slavery on a nearby plantation in 1816 and, as a teenager, worked in a Richmond tobacco factory. At the age of twenty, he married an enslaved woman named Nancy and paid her enslaver fifty dollars not to sell her. Brown then rented a home where they lived and raised three children. Twelve years later, Brown returned from work one day to find that without his knowledge, his wife and three children had been sold to a North Carolinian enslaver.

This sale prompted Brown to plot his escape from slavery. With the help of James Smith, a free Black man, and white sympathizer Samuel Smith, they secured a large crate marked as "dry goods" to be delivered to the Pennsylvania Anti-Slavery Society in Philadelphia. They employed the services of the Adams Express Company, a private mail service that abolitionists used to deliver anti-slavery tracts to slaveholding states, to transport the crate north. Brown was shipped out of Richmond on March 23, 1849, and arrived in Pennsylvania the next day. He soon earned the nickname Henry "Box" Brown and became a well-known anti-slavery writer and speaker. He moved to England after the 1850 passage of the Fugitive Slave Law, which endangered his freedom even though he lived in the North.

Both James and Samuel Smith were later arrested when caught trying to ship more enslaved people to freedom. James's trial ended with a divided decision; he escaped punishment. Samuel received a six-year sentence in the state penitentiary. The building that housed the Adams Express Company was destroyed when confederates fleeing the city's capture by Union forces in April 1865 set a fire that grew out of control and burned much of downtown. The city rebuilt the destroyed area soon after the Civil War, and today this area is a center for city nightlife.

### TO LEARN MORE

Ruggles, Jeffrey. *The Unboxing of Henry Brown*. Richmond: Library of Virginia Press, 2003.

### TO VISIT NEARBY

**BOX BROWN PLAZA** at Riverfront Canal Walk near the intersection of S. 15th and Dock Streets. This memorial to Brown includes a physical rendering of his shipping crate.

## 1.5 Walker and Harris Tobacco Factory

19th and E. Cary Streets

Former tobacco factory renovated into luxury loft living.

On February 25, 1852, Jordan Hatcher, a seventeen-year-old enslaved person, arrived at the Walker and Harris Tobacco Factory to

Tobacco factory workers in Richmond, ca. 1900.

nor Joseph Johnson for clemency on Hatcher's behalf, emphasizing that Hatcher had killed Jackson without premeditation and without an intention to kill him. At the same time, tobacco manufacturers cited a "growing spirit of insubordination" among enslaved workers and urged the governor to carry out the sentence, noting that examples must be made of such offenders.

Governor Johnson commuted Hatcher's sentence, instead ordering him to be sold and transported out of the U. S. This decision was unusual and challenged the dominant view of what enslavers thought enslaved people deserved for killing an overseer, as evidenced by the two thousand–strong crowd of white Richmonders who gathered near City Hall on the evening of May 7 to protest the governor's decision. The crowd threw stones at the governor's residence, threatened to break down his door, and accused him of being a Northern abolitionist. In the aftermath, the General Assembly attempted but failed to pass laws restricting the movement of enslaved people around the city. On June 16, enslaver Garland Ware purchased Jordan Hatcher for transport out of the U. S. Nothing more is known about Hatcher.

This incident illustrates the ways in which the enslaved negotiated survival amidst horrific circumstances, as well as the fact that white Richmonders did not hold monolithic views in relation to punishment

complete his daily work as a stemmer, someone who strips tobacco leaves from their stems. This kind of urban work was typical for enslaved people living in Richmond. Enslavers who lived elsewhere could find a use for laborers not needed on farms and plantations, and industrialists eagerly paid enslavers a smaller wage for the work of enslaved people than they paid their white laborers. William Jackson, a nineteen-year-old white overseer, chastised Hatcher for what he deemed poor work and began to whip him. Hatcher eventually picked up an iron poker and struck Jackson on the head with it. What first seemed like a mild wound worsened. Hatcher had fractured Jackson's skull. After an unsuccessful surgery, Jackson died. Authorities found Hatcher hiding nearby, jailed him, and charged him with murder. A court found Hatcher guilty and sentenced him to death by hanging.

Prior to his execution date, sixty prominent Richmond citizens petitioned Gover-

for self-defense. The factory was destroyed by fire in 1865, but other factories rose in its place. Today, those factories have been converted into luxury residential spaces.

**TO LEARN MORE**

Link, William. "The Jordan Hatcher Case: Politics and 'A Spirit of Subordination' in Antebellum Virginia." *Journal of Southern History* 64, no. 4 (1998): 615–48.

## 1.6 First African Baptist Church (former location)

College Street at E. Broad Street

Congregants founded First African Baptist Church here in 1841. Today, this church building is part of VCU Health.

W.L. Sheppard sketch, 1874.

Founded in 1841, the First African Baptist Church represented a major victory for former Black congregants of Richmond's First Baptist Church, who had been petitioning to create their own church for two decades. While Virginia law at this time allowed Black congregants to create their own church, the law required that their pastor be white and that the all-white parent church oversee church affairs. Robert Ryland, an enslaver, pastored the church but, in practice, Black congregants gained wide latitude to shape their own religious experience. Scholar Midori Takagi calls the independent Black Baptist church "arguably the most important institution to emerge during the late antebellum era."

Establishing their own church allowed parishioners to create structures for self-governance that challenged white-controlled systems outside of the church. For example, the church often functioned as a community court where free and enslaved Black Richmonders resolved interpersonal disputes. Even when those involved did not agree with the decisions, they often recognized the system as one that was generally fair and equitable, unlike their experiences with white-run systems outside of the church.

The church grappled with unique problems related to Black people's status of free and enslaved. Enslaved men repeatedly petitioned for the right to serve as church deacons and committee members along with the right to vote on those decisions. They noted that enslaved members constituted the majority of the church's membership and contributed substantially to the financial upkeep of the church. Church leaders maintained that given the outside restraints on enslaved men, it served the church's interest to be led by free men. The church also confronted the complicated issue of marriage among enslaved people. While Virginia did not recognize marriages among enslaved people, the First African Baptist Church legitimized them by performing wedding ceremonies, thus honoring these unions. It also took up the matter of divorce, which was particularly thorny when enslavers sold someone's spouse out of the area. While deacons recognized the complexity and pain of the situation, they still required proof that the marriage had failed before granting a church-sanctioned divorce.

The church's affairs showcase the ways in which free and enslaved Black Richmonders created systems of community governance and accountability outside of state-sanctioned, white-controlled systems. Today, the original church building is used as part of Virginia Commonwealth University's medical campus. First African Baptist relocated its congregation to Northside at 2700 Hanes Avenue in 1955, where it still resides.

**TO LEARN MORE**

Takagi, Midori. *Rearing Wolves to Our Own Destruction: Slavery in Richmond, Virginia, 1782–1865.* Charlottesville: University of Virginia Press, 1999.

## 1.7 The Egyptian Building

1223 E. Marshall Street

The Egyptian Building on the campus of VCU Health.

Built in 1845, the Egyptian Building housed the first permanent space of what would become the Medical College of Virginia (MCV). In 1968, MCV merged with the Richmond Professional Institute to become Virginia Commonwealth University. In 1994, during construction of the Kontos Medical Sciences Building directly adjacent to the Egyptian Building, workers found bones representing over fifty bodies in a well. Grave robbers likely brought these bodies to the school between 1848 and 1860. While illegal, graverobbing was commonplace and generally ignored, especially if robbers targeted Black gravesites. Faculty and students used these bodies without consent for medical experimentation. Despite the discovery of these human remains in 1994, no formal memorialization attempts took place until the 2010s.

A descendent community group formed in 2016 to advocate for the study and memorialization of those who had been exploited by the medical facility. Joseph Jones, chair of the Family Representative Council for the East Marshall Street Well Project, asked:

"How are people's experiences with the health care system contextualized in light of this discovery? There tends to be a lot of distrust among African Americans and other communities, in part because of this history." Jones's statement makes the critical link between medical institutions' past racist practices and the deep distrust some African American community members still harbor toward them as a result, which has far-reaching implications in accessing healthcare today.

In 2021, VCU installed a series of panels acknowledging this history of harm in the Kontos Building. Carmen Foster, speaking on behalf of the Family Representative Council at the event, called the action "an important step toward reclaiming the full humanity of our ancestors . . . The bodies of these children, women and men were taken, not given, for the development of medical knowledge. From this day forward, every person who enters the Kontos Building will know that this is sacred ground."

**TO LEARN MORE**

Williams, Michael Paul. "MCV Robbed Black Graves for Medical Training. In Addressing This, VCU Must Move beyond Commemoration." *Richmond Times-Dispatch,* December 13, 2018.

Utsey, Shawn, dir. *Until the Well Runs Dry: Medicine and the Exploitation of Black Bodies.* Virginia Commonwealth University and Burn Baby Burn Productions, 2011.

VCU News. "This Is Sacred Ground," September 24, 2021. https://news.vcu.edu/article/2021/09/vcu-panels-commemorate-19th-century-human -remains-found-in-an-mcv-campus-well

## 1.8 Old City Hall

1001 E. Broad Street

Old City Hall, ca. 1970s. It functioned as the city government's center of business until the present-day City Hall opened in the mid-1970s.

This Gothic Revival building served as Richmond's City Hall from 1894 to 1971 and was the target of multiple protests, including an important welfare rights struggle in the late 1960s. In summer 1969, seventy welfare rights activists marched into its welfare department to protest rising food prices. Some mothers noted that they had nothing to feed their children. Receiving no response, fifty activists marched again on City Hall two days later. Mayor Philip Bagley argued that the city already spent $16 million per year on welfare and that he had received assurances that no one was actually starving. He said that people must go through "orderly channels" in order to meet with him, and he refused to answer questions as to whether he could live on a welfare budget for a week.

In October 1969, Easter Neroo, chair of the Fulton Committee of the Richmond Welfare Rights Organization (RWRO), led 200 activists to the mayor's office to protest cutbacks of clothing grants for welfare recipients. Augustine Brooks, mother of five, noted: "My three girls haven't been to school in over a week because they haven't any shoes to wear." The mayor refused to speak to them, and was accused of hiding in the bathroom to avoid them. The group left the office chanting: "I may be raggedy, I may be poor, but I am somebody." They then went to Thalhimers, a department store, where they selected a range of clothing and shoes and told the cashiers to charge the mayor's office. Security guards escorted them out of the building. Despite their actions, city officials did not raise the welfare budget.

This site represents attempts by Richmond's poorest citizens to access city leaders in order to hold them accountable for providing basic necessities to them and their children. It highlights the difficulty and indignity they often faced in doing so. Today, Old City Hall functions as an office building.

## 1.9  Governor's Mansion

Capitol Square, bounded by Broad St. (north), Bank St. (south), N. 9th St. (west), and Governor St. (east)

As a result of treaties signed in 1646 and 1677, the colony of Virginia pushed the Mattaponi and the Pamunkey onto reservations. Since that time, the tribes have presented tribute to the governor of Virginia. This ceremony takes place annually on the Wednesday before Thanksgiving in front of the Governor's Mansion. Tribal members dress in regalia and present the governor with game; many Virginia Indian tribes attend the event.

The Treaty of 1646 concluded decades-long warring between the English and the Powhatan, propelled by English policies of encroachment, removal, and extermination against the Powhatan. The treaty created peace while dismantling the powerful Powhatan chiefdom, confining the Pamunkey and the Mattaponi to reservations. Although the tribes selected sites that they hoped would preserve their way of living, the treaty greatly circumscribed their movement—they could no longer hunt and fish in traditional ways. Even then, in defiance of the treaty, white colonizers continued to encroach on their lands.

While the Pamunkey then lived in peace with the colonial government, Nathaniel Bacon and his men, in rebellion against the English crown, attacked and killed fifty Pamunkey men in 1676. By that time, Pamunkey leader Cockacoeske had spent twenty years leading the tribe, skillfully negotiating English

Governor Baliles presents photographs to Chief William Miles of the Pamunkey and Chief Webster Custalow of the Mattaponi at a Thanksgiving ceremony outside of the Governor's Mansion, 1988.

political and legal systems. She helped to both create and negotiate the 1677 Treaty of Middle Plantation. While Virginia Indians had limited negotiating power, Cockacoeske helped establish the legal framework that continues to guide the contemporary relationship between the Pamunkey, the Mattaponi, and the state.

Contemporary Virginia Indians express mixed feelings about the tribute ceremony. Some appreciate the recognition it confers. As a prominent public event covered by various media outlets, it brings visibility to Virginia Indians, who often convey that their top concern is the fact that people do not know they still exist. Others dismiss it as patronizing; Virginia Indians have been treated so poorly by the state, they argue, that tribes should not participate in any kind of tribute, not even a symbolic one. Although the ceremony remains disputed, this annual ceremony symbolizes the continued survival of Virginia Indians despite hundreds of years of state policies and practices aimed at their exclusion and eradication.

Raleigh Hotel ca. 1910 under a prior name.

**TO VISIT NEARBY**

While at Capitol Square, visit **MANTLE: A STATE TRIBUTE TO VIRGINIA INDIANS**, a labyrinth-style monument also found on the grounds.

## 1.10  Hotel Raleigh

901 Bank Street

In the 1970s, this hotel, located at the edge of Capitol Square, served as the headquarters for Virginia ERA Central, the statewide organization that lobbied for the passage of the Equal Rights Amendment (ERA). The National Women's Party first proposed the ERA to guarantee legal equality based on sex in 1923. Feminists renewed calls for the ERA in the 1970s, but the amendment ultimately failed.

In Virginia, a thousand women attended legislative sessions in 1973 to respond to the ERA. As a result, women's groups across the state became better organized to promote the amendment. Its proponents in Virginia stressed inequities as they related to the state's property and divorce laws, which favored men in property and custody battles. Virginia NOW (National Organization for Women) announced the state's ratification of the amendment as its top priority, and activists organized Virginia ERA Central to coordinate strategy and action across the state.

Women rally for the ERA at Capitol Square, 1984.

Given Virginia's conservative political climate, Virginia ERA Central established ground rules for its activists, stressing the need to act with "good" manners and behavior. They stressed their stance as a moderate one, claiming: "We're responsible citizens of Virginia, not New York radical feminists." They also downplayed some organizations' commitments to lesbian and gay rights. Virginia NOW published a handbook to help supporters speak and debate the topic with authority after delegate Jim Thomson circulated a thirteen-page secret memo to legislators alleging that the ERA would require Virginia to integrate all institutions and bathrooms, regardless of sex, during the 1974 legislative session. However, NOW's instructions included the advice to avoid discussing politically volatile issues like divorce and abortion laws. Yet Virginia Central ERA still did not generate enough support for the state to pass the ERA before the 1982 deadline expired. This highlights the challenges within movements to recognize and practice inclusive movement-building while also

working to garner broad support. In the late 2010s, a diverse group of activists pressured Virginia legislators to symbolically pass the ERA, which it did in January 2020. A hotel still operates at this site.

**TO LEARN MORE**

Shockley, Megan. *Creating a Progressive Commonwealth: Women Activists, Feminism, and the Politics of Social Change in Virginia, 1970s–2000s.* Baton Rouge: Louisiana State University Press, 2018.

## 1.11 John Marshall Courts Building

400 N. 9th Street

On July 1, 2020, crowds gathered at the intersection of Monument Avenue and Arthur Ashe Boulevard to view the dismantling of the monument honoring confederate general "Stonewall" Jackson, which the city had erected more than a hundred years ago, in 1919. As crews dismantled this white supremacist symbol, hundreds of protestors

John Marshall Courts Building following citizen demonstrations to protest eviction hearings during the COVID-19 pandemic in 2020.

gathered downtown at the John Marshall Courts Building to demand a moratorium on city evictions, with the structural and systemic causes of racial inequity in the city persisting as usual.

Two days earlier, a court-ordered moratorium issued in response to staggering job loss caused by COVID-19 had expired. As peaceful protestors assembled, police arrested a group trying to enter the building to conduct a sit-in. They then used tear gas to disperse the crowd outside. As a result of the disruptions, the courts did not meet that day, giving tenants longer to organize against their evictors. On July 9, the Richmond Tenants Union (RTU) protested outside the building to specifically target Zacharia's Brothers, a leasing company that owns property throughout Richmond. The company had more than a hundred eviction proceedings scheduled that day. When the RTU visited the homes of those facing eviction in the days leading up to the proceedings, they learned that most tenants were unaware of the impending court proceedings. If tenants do not attend the initial hearings, landlords automatically win the right to begin the process of eviction. Thanks to the organizing efforts of RTU, the problem began to shift. RTU volunteer Bee, a pseudonym, noted that Zacharia's Brothers "had one day where they were filing cases against 90 people and all but like a handful of them showed up. [Those evictions] either got dismissed or continued because so many tenants showed up."

In 2018, Princeton University Eviction Lab data revealed that from 2000 to 2016, Richmond had the nation's second-highest eviction rate. High eviction rates disproportionately affect African American and Latino communities. In Virginia, renters can be evicted within six weeks, a rent control system does not exist, and tenants have no guarantee of legal representation. Amidst protests for racial justice and economic relief, this site centers the struggle for low-income city residents to maintain secure housing. Amidst a pandemic in the city with the second-highest eviction rate in the country, these simultaneous actions, one dismantling a prominent symbol of white supremacy and another in response to hidden, insidious attempts to evict a hundred tenants, reinforce the need to acknowledge the complexities of collective vigilance in claiming space and asserting humanity.

**TO LEARN MORE**

McCoy, Terrence. "Eviction Isn't Just about Poverty. It's Also about Race—and Virginia Proves It." *Washington Post,* November 10, 2019.

Teresa, Benjamin. "The Geography of Eviction in Richmond: Beyond Poverty." *RVA Eviction Lab,* Virginia Commonwealth University.

## 1.12 Federal Building

400 N. 8th Street

Federal Building.

Congress created a selective service system in 1917 to draft men into the military, establishing state and local boards to manage this process. Virginia's state headquarters for managing the draft were housed in Richmond's Federal Building, which still operates as a state building. The site's history as a draft board demonstrates the complicated politics of race among Virginia's Indigenous communities.

Virginia Indians challenged the military's system of segregated service in World Wars I and II. During World War I, the government drafted members of the Pamunkey and Mattaponi tribes. The tribes protested that as non-U. S. citizens who lived on reservations, they could not be drafted for military service. Virginia's attorney general agreed, and the state exempted them from the draft. During World War II, all Indigenous people were subjected to the draft, since the U. S. government extended citizenship to them in 1924. However, the two-tiered racial classification system that distinguished only between white and "colored" soldiers, which generally meant Black, did

not address the existence of Indigenous soldiers.

At that time, the Selective Service had no standard for designating racial classifications. In 1940, the head of King William County's local draft board wrote to Virginia's Selective Service director for clarity on how to racially classify registrants who identified as Virginia Indian. When the local board ultimately classified them as "colored," Chickahominy leaders denounced the board's actions to the governor, reminding officials that during World War I, their members had served with white regiments. Meanwhile, the Pamunkey, who had a strong legal claim to their identity as they lived on a long-established reservation, appealed to their congressman, who assured them that they could serve alongside white soldiers.

Since the mid-1800s, Virginia officials had tried to deny the existence and sovereignty of Virginia Indians by claiming they had mixed with African American communities and, therefore, could no longer claim legitimate Indigenous heritage. As a result, Virginia Indians repeatedly had to advocate for their existence within a binary racial system that operated as if they did not exist. Within this system, perhaps not surprisingly, many Virginia Indians sought to align themselves with the privileges of whiteness, although they rarely gained them. The Pamunkey and Mattaponi, who had lived on reservations for centuries, won the right to serve alongside white soldiers. For Virginia Indians without reservation lands, results varied. Several Chickahominy men, classified as "colored," refused to leave their barracks until their leaders and influential allies secured their reclassification, allowing them to serve alongside whites. Three Rappahannock men refused induction when denied reclassification as white; initially imprisoned, they eventually worked in a program for conscientious objectors.

In 1944, officials agreed that an individual's racial classification had to follow what the registrant claimed. While no more than 300 men nationwide disputed the racial classification assigned to them during World War II, their actions highlighted the illogical levels of bureaucratic wrangling necessary to maintain racial segregation, as well as the ways in which systems of segregation and white supremacy incentivized Indigenous and non-Black communities of color to seek affiliation with whiteness.

Kanawha Plaza situated amidst downtown office buildings.

**TO LEARN MORE**

Hardin, Peter. "Documentary Genocide." *Richmond Times-Dispatch*, March 5, 2000.
Murray, Paul. "Who Is an Indian? Who Is a Negro? Virginia Indians in the World War II Draft." *Virginia Magazine of History and Biography* 95, no. 2 (1987): 215–31.

## 1.13 Kanawha Plaza

S. 9th Street between Canal and Byrd Streets

Situated across the street from the Federal Reserve Bank of Richmond amid state government buildings, the Kanawha Plaza filled with protesters for two weeks as part of a localized outgrowth of the Occupy Wall Street movement. Three hundred Occupiers first gathered in Monroe Park on October 11, 2011, and eventually set up camp in the plaza. The Occupy Movement formed to protest the amount of wealth held by the country's wealthiest 1 percent. As of 2019, this top 1 percent of Americans held 40 percent of the country's wealth, the largest gap ever recorded and one that continues to grow. Households in the wealthiest fifth of city residents receive more than half of the city's aggregate income while households in the bottom fifth receive only 2.4 percent. As a result, 1 in 4 adult Richmond residents live in poverty, a rate two and a half times higher than the state average. Sixty percent of Richmonders who live in poverty are Black.

Members of Occupy Richmond vocalized support for diverse issues ranging from economic equality to clean energy to mitigating corporate power in government. Participant Kimmy Certa noted: "We're exhausted. We're hard workers trying to raise our family." She stated that despite living modestly, her family often cannot afford essentials. "We didn't get our bailouts," she said, referencing the $700 billion bank bailout passed in the wake of the 2007–8 financial crisis.

By late October, the site at Kanawha bloomed into a tent city. Citing the city's prohibition against camping in public parks, police evicted protestors on October 31, 2011. In response, Raymond Boone, whose next-door neighbor was Richmond mayor Dwight C. Jones, offered space on his lawn to continue the movement. Protestors camped there through mid-December. Boone had established the independent newspaper *Richmond Free Press* in 1992 to serve the city's African American community, and he served as its editor and publisher until his death in 2014. With the move to Boone's less visible property and the coming winter, the encampment ceased.

Kanawha Plaza, located amidst heavily trafficked roads and expressway ramps, is isolated and underutilized by downtown residents. The name Kanawha refers to an Indigenous community once located in present-day Delaware and Maryland; white settlers later used it to name a river in what is now West Virginia. Thus, the plaza's naming is rooted in Indigenous appropriation. Some Indigenous people criticized the Occupy Movement itself, as the movement sought to "occupy" sites of state power and corporate wealth with little acknowledgment of the legacies of settler colonialism tied to those same sites. However, the movement broadcast a searing critique of capitalist wealth accumulation, and the language it created of "the 1 percent" to identify the country's wealthiest citizens remains a common way to highlight extreme wealth disparities.

**TO LEARN MORE**

Cushing, Nathan. "Occupy Richmond Group Convenes at Kanawha Plaza." *RVANews,* October 17, 2011.

## 1.14 Sing Residence (former)

*2 S. 7th Street*

Woo Sing and his wife, Sue, moved to Richmond around 1894 and resided at this address. Woo worked as a launderer at one of the few Chinese-run hand laundries operating in Richmond at the time. On November 16, 1895, Sue gave birth to a son, Charles. He is thought to be the first child of Chinese ancestry born in Richmond. Woo had emigrated from China in 1875; Sue was a U. S. citizen of Chinese descent born in San Francisco.

The Sings knew that their son's U. S. citizenship might later be questioned due to a series of laws targeting Chinese people who lived in the U. S. The Geary Act of 1892 extended the Chinese Exclusion Act of 1882, the first American law to significantly curtail immigration. The Geary Act placed new onerous restrictions on Chinese people living in the U. S. It required Chinese people to carry a resident permit at all times or face deportation, and it prohibited them from testifying in court. Given these restrictions and the fact that Virginia did not begin to systematically record births until 1912, the Sings had a series of affidavits recorded in Richmond's local chancery court to confirm the birth of their son in the city. Caroline Claton, an African American midwife, swore in an affidavit that she attended to Sue

Citizens protest racial segregation at Thalhimers, February 1960.

during Charles's birth. The owner of the property the Sings leased also swore an affidavit, as did others who used Woo's services as a laundryman. These records proved vital. In 1908, when returning from China, officials at the port of Norfolk barred Charles's reentry into the U. S. until they located these records. Congress eventually repealed all of the exclusion acts in 1943, when China was an ally of the U. S. in World War II. However, the number of Chinese immigrants permitted to enter the United States lawfully remained extremely low until 1965, and Chinese immigrants did not become eligible for naturalized citizenship until 1952.

This site highlights the ways in which both Chinese immigrants and U. S. citizens of Chinese descent had to methodically plan and carefully negotiate their transnational movements, despite having U. S. citizenship. This building no longer exists; today, commercial buildings line this area.

**TO LEARN MORE**

Ito, Emma. "Finding Asian Pacific Islander Desi Americans in Virginia Newspapers." *The Uncommonwealth*, May 22, 2020.

1.15 **Thalhimers Department Store (former)**

E. Broad Street at 7th Street

In 1842, German-Jewish immigrant William Thalhimer opened a dry goods store in Richmond, which his grandson transformed into the city's first department store. The company opened a six-story flagship store that covered an entire city block at this location in 1939. While the store was a civic institution for white Richmonders, Thalhimers became the site of multiple desegregation protests during the civil rights era.

On February 20, 1960, more than 200 students from Virginia Union University, a historically Black university, marched from their Northside campus to the downtown department store and staged a sit-in at the store's four whites-only restaurants. Two days later, management had those protestors who returned for additional sit-ins arrested for trespassing. These protestors became known as the Richmond 34 and represented the city's first major arrests of movement activists. Participant Elizabeth Rice recounted to Connor Rhiel: "I left home that morning planning to go to school. We got on campus and realized students were not in class. I looked down and I saw picket lines. I don't know where I put my books but we picked up signs. We're marching around the store and at some point, they said, 'We're going in.' I call it the lucky draw, I happened to be near the door and we got in. We were the Richmond 34."

Hamilton Glass and Matt Lively's mural, *In Conversation*, which is part of the Mending Walls RVA Project.

Thousands gathered that night at Fifth Street Baptist Church to show their support, agreeing to boycott and picket segregated stores and restaurants. The next morning, the Campaign for Human Dignity began, with Black women leading the picket lines. Their actions led to a year-long boycott of downtown segregated businesses before the businesses, fearing additional damage to both their finances and public reputation, decided to desegregate in August 1961. Thalhimers closed in 1992, and the city destroyed the building in 2004.

**TO LEARN MORE**

Matthews, Kimberly, and Raymond Pierre Hylton. *The Richmond 34 and the Civil Rights Movement*. Mt. Pleasant, SC: Arcadia, 2020.

Rheil, Connor. "The Richmond 34's Impact Still Looms." *13NewsNow*, February 21, 2021.

## 1.16 *In Conversation* Mural / Mending Walls RVA

4 W. Broad Street

In 2020, artist Hamilton Glass began collaborating with local artists to create a public mural project named Mending Walls RVA. The project adds colorful, impactful art around the city while inspiring conversations about racial justice and social equity, as noted by the project's tagline: "we need to talk." As the project makes clear, public art is one of the city's biggest assets; Richmond has one of the largest public mural collections in the country.

In 2020, pairs of artists completed sixteen murals around the city as activists took to the streets to demand an end to white supremacy embedded in the city's landscape and policies. Each mural was painted by two artists from different backgrounds in order to highlight the challenges and opportunities that arise when people who have different lived experiences come together to make art.

Podcasts featured each artistic pair so that listeners could learn more about the conversations and process that shaped the creation of the art, and the project also hosted community conversations. According to Glass, "We all are questioning what it is to live in America, and we all need to be talking."

This mural, entitled *In Conversation*, was the project's first. African American artist Hamilton Glass and white artist Matt Lively created it. As children growing up in the 1980s, the mural captures their different experiences and responses to popular culture. Glass, who grew up in an urban Philadelphia neighborhood, depicts water spewing from a fire hydrant alongside characters from the children's show *Fat Albert*. Also set in Philadelphia, the animated show featured numerous Black characters. Lively spent his childhood in the predominantly white suburbs of Richmond. He illustrates a lawn sprinkler and characters from the cartoon show *The Jetsons*, which imagined a white family living in a fifties-esque pseudo-utopian future where leisure and machine-based labor reigns.

The initial sixteen murals of Mending Walls RVA created by local artists speak directly to local impacts of national social justice issues. They stand in juxtaposition to institutional- and corporate-driven initiatives bolstered by tourism and economic development. Local artists and cultural workers like Glass, Lively, and others diligently work to create inclusive dialogue and speak to issues that impact city residents and communities.

PERSONAL REFLECTION

## HAMILTON GLASS
### Artist and Founder, Mending Walls Project

Mending Walls is an extension of my work, and the result of how I was feeling in reaction to George Floyd's murder. I had a conversation with a collaborator of a different race and culture. I was painting a mural in a school and having a bad day. I was upset someone was murdered, but I was upset that people were just waking up to that. We had a conversation. He told me why it was different for him. So, that made me lean hard into empathy, and talking with this artist, I thought: "What if we did this public mural that explored our conversations?" Then I thought, "Well, what if everyone did that? What if I could find a lot of artists that could go do that. Beyond the art, this is supposed to get people talking. I asked, "what if we could host civic talks around this?" It just kept growing.

One of the things I set out to do was be that example of a living, breathing, Black artist. I went into architecture because I didn't have that example, so the minute I started doing work with corporations and in public schools, it just hit me like a light bulb. I can't just walk in here and do a mural and leave. I've got to go talk to the art classes. That was my purpose, and I fell into my purpose. My work has always been about progressing and helping. That's why it stems so heavily in collaboration. Collaborate with a nonprofit, with an organization that's doing work. Use art for what it's good for, which is speaking beyond words, a tool that can be used to heal. That's how I respond to anything. What do we need in this moment? How can I help?

TO LEARN MORE

Visit the project's website at https://mendingwall
srva.com/ to access artist podcasts as well as a
map of the murals.

View *Mending Walls: The Documentary,* a project
of VPM, at https://vpm.org/mending-walls.
Glass, a co-producer, won a 2021 National
Capital Chesapeake Bay Region Emmy Award
for this production.

## 1.17 Spottswood W. Robinson III and Robert R. Merhige, Jr. U.S. Courthouse

701 E. Broad Street

On May 7, 2008, Immigration and Customs
Enforcement (ICE) conducted the city's first
large immigration raid at the U.S. Courthouse, which was then under construction.
ICE agents arrested thirty-three people who
had been working to construct the building. All were undocumented, and the raid
intentionally took place when the building
was nearing completion, so as not to delay
the courthouse's opening. A long history of
raids occurring near the end of such projects
exists, often when employers themselves call
in ICE in a deliberate move to not pay workers. The workers, whose countries of origin
included Mexico, Honduras, Guatemala, El
Salvador, Nicaragua, and Peru, were charged
with a host of immigration violations. During
the raid, and immediately after, workers were
held in the very cells they themselves built.

The year 2008 saw a sharp increase in
ICE activity in Virginia. The raid happened
amid intense public debate over the proposal
by Immigration Centers of America (ICA)
to build a for-profit ICE detention center in

Farmville, seventy miles southwest of Richmond. ICA opened this facility in 2010, the
largest of its kind in the mid-Atlantic region.
Both the courthouse raid and the Farmville facility illustrate the ongoing exploitation and dehumanization faced by undocumented immigrants.

Two days after the raid, dozens of community leaders and supporters of the Virginia Immigrant People's Coalition, a federation of grassroots organizations that
advocates for immigrant rights, rallied at
the construction site to protest the raid. ICE
still deported the workers. The courthouse
opened for business a few months later
in October, built in large part by undocumented laborers, who were later deported,
having cost in excess of $100 million.

## 1.18 Virginia Electric and Power Company

600 E. Canal Street

In March 1946, workers at the Virginia Electric and Power Company, the precursor to
today's power monopoly Dominion Energy,
proposed a walkout due to the prolonged
failure of the company and the International
Brotherhood of Electrical Workers, an affiliate of the American Federation of Labor
(AFL), to reach contract agreements.

When the union announced the strike,
which could lead to statewide power outages, Governor William Tuck declared: "I'll
be damned if they're going to cut the lights
out in Virginia." He issued a state of emergency and activated 2,500 members of the
Virginia State Guard. Using an obscure law,
he issued draft notices that ordered 1,600

company employees who fit certain criteria, which included being male and an "essential" employee, to report to work as members of the state's "unorganized militia." The notice stated that workers had been "drafted into the service of the Commonwealth to execute the law which requires the Virginia Electric and Power Company to provide electric service to the people of Virginia." If the union called a strike of its members, the order declared that those workers would no longer be company employees but instead "on active duty as a member of the State militia to assist in the operation of said company's plants and facilities which will be taken over by the Commonwealth of Virginia." It reminded workers that they were now subject to military law and would be court-martialed if they disobeyed.

While AFL president William Green called the move "involuntary servitude," union officials canceled the strike and reached a contract agreement ensuring better wages and working conditions two weeks later. However, any victory felt by the workers was short-lived. Virginia's next legislative assembly passed laws preventing public utilities' workers from striking alongside "right to work" legislation that allowed workers to reject mandatory union membership. Harry Byrd, a U.S. senator from Virginia, helped ensure the federal passage of the Taft-Hartley Act of 1947. The act devastated labor organizing by severely limiting the power of unions to successfully organize workers and declare strikes. It also laid the groundwork for aggressive union-busting

in the decades to come. This site illustrates the power that state officials and employers wielded against workers and the heinous methods that they employed to prevent workers from advocating for themselves. Today, this is the site of a new twenty-story Dominion Energy office tower.

**TO LEARN MORE**

"Virginia Governor Drafts Power Workers, Bars Strike." *New York Times,* March 29, 1946.

## 1.19  Tredegar Iron Works
470 Tredegar Street

The remnants of Tredegar today house the American Civil War Museum.

Tredegar Iron Works began operation here in 1837. It grew rapidly under the management of Joseph Anderson, who secured federal military contracts to produce munitions. Tredegar employed highly skilled laborers, initially relying on English, Welsh, and Irish immigrants familiar with the industry in their home countries. Most settled in

Tredegar Iron Works at the end of the Civil War, 1865.

Oregon Hill, a white enclave up the hill from Tredegar. In 1842, however, Anderson began cutting labor costs by increasing the number of enslaved laborers. He hired out many enslaved laborers from their enslavers, and bought others. In 1845, Emmanuel Quivers was hired out to work at Tredegar. Quivers negotiated with Anderson to purchase him and allow him to work toward buying his family's freedom. Anderson agreed, and the Quivers earned their freedom in 1853. At times, industrial enslavement offered enslaved people greater power and flexibility to negotiate unconventional arrangements like this one.

Anderson planned to have enslaved laborers shadow white workers to learn their skills. When white workers balked at this strategy, both as a threat to their own labor and due to their racism, Anderson offered them better working terms, including five-year contracts, which temporarily pacified them. In May 1847, as the number of enslaved laborers grew and the end of white workers' five-year contract approached, white workers went on strike, demanding the removal of Black workers from skilled labor jobs and a pay raise. Strikers received little support in the city, as influential whites saw the strike as an attack against the power of elite industrialists and enslaved labor.

As the strike continued, workers dropped their wage demand, exposing the underlying issues: the fear of competition from Black laborers, a legitimate fear given the widespread system of hiring out enslaved laborers by city industrialists, and racial prejudice. Anderson eventually fired the striking workers. Employment of enslaved people at Tredegar nearly doubled the following year, illustrating the ways in which employers often pitted white and Black workers, enslaved and free, against each other, as it made economic sense to do so.

By the start of the Civil War, Tredegar Iron Works was the largest producer of iron in the South, with a five-acre complex employing eight hundred laborers, Black and white, free and enslaved. It was the only iron works in the confederacy capable of producing heavy military weapons and supplies. Tredegar survived the war, and became critical to rebuilding southern industries afterwards. Today, what remains of the complex houses the American Civil War Museum.

## TO LEARN MORE

Schechter, Patricia. "Free and Slave Labor in the Old South: The Tredegar Ironworkers' Strike of 1847." *Labor History* 35, no. 3 (1994): 165–86.

Oast, Jennifer. *Institutional Slavery: Slaveholding Churches, Schools, Colleges, and Businesses in Virginia, 1680–1860.* Cambridge: Cambridge University Press, 2016.

GRAND REAPING.

SOUTHERN WOMEN FEELING THE EFFECTS OF REBELLION, AND CREATING BREAD RIOTS.

Depiction of Richmond "Bread Riots" published in Frank Leslie's *Illustrated Newspapers,* 1863.

## 1.20   Belvidere Hill Baptist Church (former)

Rowe Street at S. Belvidere Street

On April 1, 1863, two years into the nation's civil war, dozens of white women gathered at this church in the white working-class enclave of Oregon Hill. The women, struggling to provide for their families, decided to demand food from the governor and if he failed to provide it, to take it from nearby merchants. Access to food in the confederacy's capital was dire. The city's wartime population had ballooned to nearly 100,000 residents, more than double its prewar size. Battles had been fought all around the city, disrupting the food supply. When food did make it into the city, commissary agents earmarked much of it for the military. Enor-

mous inflation meant that even when food was available, many could not afford it.

The next day, hundreds of women gathered in Capitol Square, but they stormed out when the governor refused to offer food relief. As they left, a crowd of men followed, swelling their ranks to over a thousand people. At select businesses, the women took bacon, ham, coffee, candles and shoes, loaded the goods into wagons, and drove away. Mayor Mayo arrived to literally read the women the Riot Act, and within two hours, the Public Guard had restored order. While officials arrested a few dozen people, they dropped most charges. One notable exception was Minerva Meredith, a leader of the gathering, who was convicted of robbing a hospital steward of a wagon of beef intended for patients. He was the only victim compensated by the city for his loss.

This incident became known as the "bread riot" and the "women's riot," although little rioting took place. Similar demands for food by women trying to provide for their starving families during wartime occurred across the South, including one "riot" in nearby Petersburg only a day earlier. In Richmond, officials placed cannons on the streets as a future deterrent, and they also opened the Richmond Free Market, which offered food and fuel at significant discounts, although they denied access to those known to have participated in the April 2 uprising. This event marked the largest civil uprising in the confederacy during the Civil War and was notably led by white women. This church no longer exists; the Virginia War Memorial is now located here.

**TO LEARN MORE**

Chesson, Michael. "Harlots or Heroines? A New Look at the Richmond Bread Riot." *Virginia Magazine of History and Biography* 92, no. 2 (1984): 131–75.

# 2

# East
# End
## Richmond

# Introduction

**THE EAST END RESTS BETWEEN DOWNTOWN**
and the city's eastern boundary. Its hills over-
look the James River, a critical resource to
life and industry, and the city's earliest industrial markets to the west, once known for
trade in both tobacco and enslaved people. It
encompasses Powhatan's Hill (also known as
Fulton Hill), considered the site where colonizer Christopher Newport met Parahunt,
paramount chief Powhatan's son, who he
initially mistook for Powhatan. It envelops
the city's earliest residential neighborhood,
Church Hill, named for St. John's Episcopal
Church, the city's oldest congregation. The
East End represents shifting geographies
of power that fundamentally shape community life, economics, and politics, including early sites of conflict at the beginning
of European contact and stretching to the
present day. It features the experiences of
early Indigenous communities as well as
contemporary conflicts over highly controversial economic development initiatives. It
also serves as a critical space for organizing
against gentrification, intentionally planned
destruction of Black neighborhoods, environmental degradation, and the deliberate
concentration of poverty, often in direct
response to geographical flows of wealth,
politics, and power.

Residential East End communities grew
out of two notable neighborhoods: Church
Hill and Fulton. Church Hill represents the
first residential development in the city in
the late eighteenth and early nineteenth cen-

East End resident Henry Miles sits on a bench in Fulton
overlooking the city skyline to the west, 1981.

turies, atop a hill adjacent to the factory district along the river in Shockoe Bottom and
extending northward in multiple directions.
Fulton's expansion from the valley farther
east was initiated by Jewish, Irish, and German immigrants due to its proximity to the
river, jobs, and industry in the early nineteenth century. A large freed people's community developed around Chimborazo Hill
during the Civil War, and emancipation led
free people to reclaim Fulton, a former site
of power for the Powhatan, and an early
plantation site where white enslavers generated wealth from exploited labor. By the

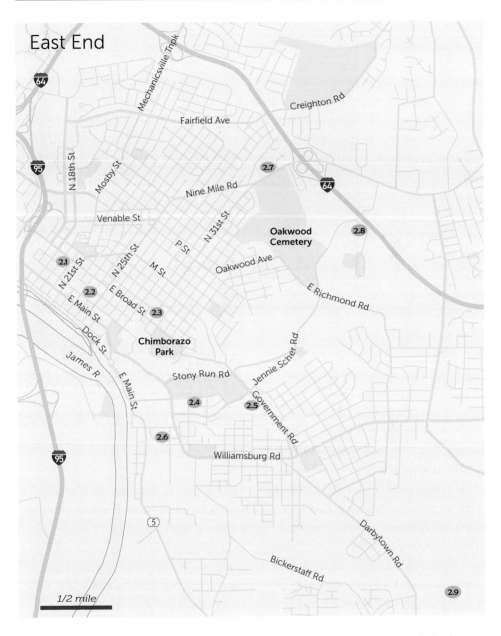

East End

Mechanicsville Tnpk

Creighton Rd

Fairfield Ave

N 18th St

Mosby St

Nine Mile Rd

2.7

Venable St

N 31st St

Oakwood
Cemetery

2.8

P St

N 25th St

M St

2.1

N 21st St

Oakwood Ave

2.2

E Broad St

E Main St

2.3

Dock St

E Richmond Rd

Chimborazo
Park

James R

E Main St

Stony Run Rd

Jennie Scher Rd

2.4

2.5

Government Rd

2.6

Williamsburg Rd

5

Darbytown Rd

Bickerstaff Rd

2.9

1/2 mile

late nineteenth century, free Black people built community in this valley by establishing close-knit intergenerational bonds that endure today.

Residents of the East End have stood against the ongoing impacts of state- and corporate-initiated changes to the built environment perpetuated by racism, classism, environmental injustice, and wealth accumulation. During the Great Depression, the Federal Home Owners Loan Corporation and the Federal Housing Authority initiated the practice of redlining. Redlining purportedly evaluated neighborhoods' level of risk in terms of extending federally backed mortgages to potential homeowners; it was in fact a deeply racialized practice, with most neighborhoods of color classified as too risky to insure, as denoted by the color red on accompanying maps. Private bank-

Neighbors working on the East End improvement campaign sponsored by the East End Ministers' Fellowship, 1967.

ing institutions later adopted the practice as well, until declared illegal by the Fair Housing Act of 1968. All East End neighborhoods, with two exceptions, received the worst rating of "hazardous," Church Hill and Fulton included. This classification initiated nearly a century of poverty concentration through segregated public housing development, community divestment, and urban removal as residents and businesses could rarely access money to develop or upkeep their properties. Similar to Northside, much of the East End's white population slowly moved out due to the combined post–World War II forces of suburbanization, school desegregation, highway construction, and housing covenants motivated by economic and racial animus, although they are returning today as gentrification expands.

In 1952, the city established Creighton Court, the first of four major public hous-

ing developments in the East End. City bureaucrats, alongside the Richmond Redevelopment and Housing Authority (RRHA), spatially isolated African American residents in neighborhoods within one mile of each other in efforts to concentrate poverty and enforce racial segregation. This coincided with Historic Richmond Foundation's (HRF) attempts in 1956 to redevelop Church Hill, an action motivated by fears that the increased presence of Black residents and businesses would make it less attractive to tourists and white residents. In one of their memos, the HRF explicitly stated, "In a neighborhood 99% colored the only way to reverse this trend is by concentrated buying and concentrated reversion to white occupancy." Triggered by elite, white, private investment and philanthropy, the HRF pursued an organized campaign to establish a wealthy, white presence in Church Hill while removing Black residents and businesses. RRHA imitated similar patterns. Its planned destruction of Fulton, beginning in 1966, culminated in the razing of more than 1,300 churches, businesses, and homes, affecting thousands of the neighborhood's mostly African American residents.

While many white residents left Church Hill in the mid-twentieth century, public and private partnerships continue to shape the area's spatial landscape as white residents have returned in the twenty-first century. Since 2000, tax credits, grant programs, public-private partnerships, and other incentives intended to induce business growth have heightened economic development in the neighborhood. Similar initiatives have catered to middle-class home buyers and their interests while rising tax rates and rents displace lower-income Black families, many of whom have lived in Church Hill for generations. As of this writing, the area features some of the city's trendiest and most quickly gentrifying neighborhoods along-

side others with high poverty and unemployment rates. By 2020, new single-family homes on M Street sold for more than half a million dollars; median home values that same year in the city as a whole were nearly half that amount. The blocks surrounding St. John's Church remain nearly all-white, while in a short walk to North Church Hill, Woodville, and Fairmount, the demographics sharply shift to nearly all-Black. These demographics contrast with the encroaching gentrification threat in neighborhoods farther east that include Fulton, Fulton Hill, and Montrose Heights. Even with publicly driven economic incentives, new business development, numerous nonprofit initiatives, and attempts to redevelop public housing communities, the East End still includes census tracts with the highest concentration of poverty in Richmond.

Despite immense inequities, the East End is a site of significant community mobilization and direct action to resist oppression. From Indigenous peoples' resistance to

Encroaching gentrification on M Street in Church Hill, 2020.

white occupation and encroachment, to the site of the first Freedman's Bureau in Richmond, to interracial labor strikes in the early twentieth century, communities continue to collectively organize against detrimental private development projects as well as in public housing communities like Creighton Court, which is under demolition as of this writing. Whether it is building power to resist urban renewal in Fulton in the late 1960s and 1970s, mobilizing to push the East End Landfill company to remove coal ash from its landfill in 2012, or the current work of Arthur Burton and others to establish the Food Justice Corridor in a city with the nation's largest food desert, the East End exemplifies resilience in resistance to coercive power.

# East End Richmond Sites

## 2.1 Belle Bryan Day Nursery (former)

201 N. 19th Street

In 1898, the Belle Bryan Day Nursery opened at this location after its founding eight years earlier. The day nursery opened at 6:30 a.m. every weekday, and it accepted children as young as one month old. Upon arrival, the children were bathed by attendants and placed in clean clothing. They received regular medical checkups as well as meals, naps, and playtimes. Their mothers, who worked in nearby factories, paid fifteen cents per week, about five dollars in today's

value, for this care. The nursery maintained a strict segregation line. Reflective of the racially divisive norms of the time, it only accepted white children.

In 1887, Isobel "Belle" Lamont Stewart Bryan, the daughter of a wealthy tobacco merchant, helped to found the Richmond Woman's Christian Association (RWCA), which became the South's first chapter of the Young Women's Christian Association (YWCA) in 1906. Bryan and a group of wealthy white women first focused on creating safe, clean, affordable housing for single white women working in the city's factories. The association opened its first boarding house in 1888. In addition to housing, boarders could take sewing classes, undertake religious training, access a library, and receive medical care. During her tenure as RWCA president, Bryan founded a free kindergarten alongside this day nursery for the children of married white women working in factories. Bryan's work reflected the tenets of late nineteenth-century social reform, which emphasized "uplifting" those less fortunate as an act of Christian charity, a philosophy and practice that reinforced notions of the "worthy" and "unworthy" poor.

This nursery location sat just east of downtown Richmond's nineteenth-century industrial core. To keep the cost low to mothers, Bryan worked as a major fundraiser, applying for city grants but also hosting extravagant fundraising events for the city's wealthy. This method of charity and philanthropy became the primary response to addressing social problems brought about by the industrial revolution. It laid the foun-

(Left) Children and childcare workers outside of the Belle Bryan Day Nursery, 1919.

(Below) Early twentieth-century white female tobacco workers, like the women pictured here, utilized the daycare's services.

contradictory progressive values. It offered highly subsidized childcare to the city's white industrial women laborers, but it maintained racial segregation. Black women working in industrial factories, who made less money than white women, could not access it.

The day nursery operated in this space for forty-eight years. In the 1950s, it relocated downtown, and in 1961, the nursery built its own space at 601 N. 9th Street. At the same time, its racial segregation and the remaking of downtown through urban renewal projects meant that those who most needed subsidized childcare no longer lived nearby. In 1971, the Medical College of Virginia converted it into a daycare for its employees.

dation for how private philanthropy operates into the present day, with the white wealthy elite determining which issues to prioritize and address and how.

Before child labor laws, children labored alongside their mothers, were cared for by other women within kin networks, or were left unattended. Textile mills and tobacco factories relied heavily on women-majority workforces. The day nursery reflected

### TO LEARN MORE

Brinson, Betsy. "Isobel Lamont Stewart Bryan (1847–1910)." *Dictionary of Virginia Biography*, 2001.

Van Lew Mansion, ca. 1900.

## 2.2 Van Lew Mansion (former)

2301 E. Grace Street

Born in Richmond in 1818 and educated at a Quaker school in Pennsylvania, Elizabeth Van Lew was a known abolitionist. Van Lew worked as a spy for the Union army during the Civil War. Mary Richards was born into enslavement around 1840 and labored for the Van Lew family. They sent Mary to Philadelphia to be educated and later to Liberia as a missionary. She returned to Richmond in 1860, and while free in practice, it is likely that the Van Lews did not legally emancipate her, since Virginia law required that free people leave the state within one year of their emancipation.

During the war, Van Lew persuaded Varina Davis, wife of confederate president Jefferson Davis, to hire Mary as a household servant in the White House of the Confederacy. There, Mary conveyed sensitive information back to Van Lew and, ultimately, the Union. Mary gathered much of her intelligence by eavesdropping on confederate meetings. Mary was integral to Van Lew's spy network; this network funneled messages into and out of prisons holding Union soldiers and provided safe houses, disguises, forged passes, and important contacts to Union soldiers and Unionist civilians hoping to escape north. Van Lew used her mansion as a safe house and as a site to recruit others to the cause.

After the war, Mary organized schooling for freed people, but because she received no compensation for the espionage work she conducted during the war, she struggled to support herself. As historian Lois Leveen documents, much of Mary's history has been obscured due to inaccuracies concerning her name. While most know her as Mary Bowser, since Mary married Wilson Bowser at St. John's Episcopal Church in 1861, the marriage did not last long, and there is no evidence that Mary herself used the name Bowser. She was known most often as Mary Jane Richards.

Van Lew faced ostracization for being a traitor in Reconstruction-era Richmond and lived in increased destitution as she had used most of her family's wealth for espionage during the war; her attempts to receive repayment from the federal government failed. The city acquired and then destroyed her home in 1911, building Bellevue Elementary School on the site.

## TO LEARN MORE

Leveen, Lois. "She Was Born into Slavery . . . But We're Missing the Point of the 'Mary Bowser' Story." *Time Magazine,* June 19, 2019.

Leveen, Lois. "The Vanishing Black Woman Spy Reappears." *Los Angeles Review of Books,* June 19, 2019.

Varon, Elizabeth. *Southern Lady, Yankee Spy: The True Story of Elizabeth Van Lew, a Union Agent in the Heart of the Confederacy.* Oxford: Oxford University Press, 2005.

## TO VISIT NEARBY

**ST. JOHN'S EPISCOPAL CHURCH** at 2401 E. Broad Street. Van Lew attended this church, and Mary was both baptized and married here, which was unusual given that the church served white elites. It dates to 1741, and its restoration by the Historic Richmond Foundation in the 1950s fueled the removal of nearby Black businesses and residents.

## 2.3 Site of Battle of Bloody Run

E. Marshall Street and N. 31th Street

In 1656, the Battle of Bloody Run took place at this location. Two years earlier, an Indigenous tribe migrating from the Lake Erie area, the Westo, briefly settled here before establishing a more permanent community several hundred miles south along the Savannah River. Growing unease among both whites and local Indigenous communities prompted Virginia's colonial government to grant Col. Edward Hill permission to drive out the Westo, preferably without military action.

Hill led a group of rangers with support from a hundred Pamunkey warriors, as a 1646 treaty required certain Indigenous trib-utary communities to provide military assistance when the English deemed it necessary. Defying orders, Hill attacked the Westo almost immediately. During the battle, Hill and his men retreated, leaving their Pamunkey allies to be slaughtered. The Pamunkey chief Totopotomoy died in battle; Cockacoeske, who the colonists later called Queen of the Pamunkey, assumed leadership of the tribe. The Westo remained.

During this time before the large-scale establishment of African enslavement in this region, Indigenous enslavement grew. Immediately after this battle, the colony of Virginia lifted certain restrictions on trade in enslaved labor and goods. The Westo subsequently crafted agreements with the English whereby they provided enslaved Indigenous people from western lands to the English in exchange for guns. In addition to obtaining enslaved Indigenous people, colonizers also concocted coercive means to insist that their Indigenous tributaries send children to them for education and training, a ruse that often meant enslavement.

This site illustrates the ways in which English colonization exacerbated conflict among existing Indigenous communities. The colonizers' desire for cheap labor sources directly accounted for the rise in the trade of human captives, as did Indigenous communities' desire for guns, as they sought to protect themselves against European war and encroachment.

## TO LEARN MORE

Rountree, Helen. *Pocahontas's People: The Powhatan Indians of Virginia through Four*

*Centuries.* Norman: University of Oklahoma Press, 1990.

Shefveland, Kristalyn. "Cockacoeske and Sarah Harris Stegge Grendon: Bacon's Rebellion and the Roles of Women." In *Virginia Women: Their Lives and Times*, ed. Cynthia Kierner and Sandra Treadway. Athens: University of Georgia, 2015.

## 2.4 Spencer E. Jones III Residence (former)

*702 Old Denny Street*

In the far east end of Richmond sits a development of suburban-style family homes adjacent to a brewery, an industrial park, and factory infrastructure recently redeveloped into luxury housing. The African American community of Fulton once flourished here, but since the 1970s it has experienced waves of urban removal and development as a result of partnerships between private developers and the Richmond Redevelopment and Housing Authority (RRHA).

Hailed by the *Richmond Times-Dispatch* as "the Birthplace of Richmond," Fulton was a seat of power for paramount chief Powhatan prior to English colonization. It was one of the first communities that African Americans established after emancipation; it contained grocery stores, barber shops, churches, and community centers. Samuel Gravely, the U.S. Navy's first Black admiral, lived here. Residents built deep intergenerational relationships as they established a self-sustaining community.

In the 1930s, as a result of redlining, many African American communities, including Fulton, could not access private or public funds for infrastructure improve-ments and homeownership programs. In 1967, RRHA conducted a survey of the neighborhood, calling Fulton "a slum, the worst in Richmond," priming it for urban "renewal" efforts. Residents led by William Henderson developed an alternate plan to demolition, creating the Fulton Ad-Hoc Committee. RRHA espoused a commitment to work alongside residents, but in 1972, local policy makers accelerated their efforts after the neighborhood flooded.

Rising Mt. Zion Baptist Church, a prominent African American congregation, rested among the neighborhood's 850 homes and 2,900 residents. After conducting their final service at their 800 Denby Street location in October 1977, they formed a hundreds-car-long motorcade to their new church in nearby Henrico County. Concerned about the well-being of the church, the leadership hired Spencer E. Jones III to watch over it. A committed community activist and Fulton resident, Jones noted: "Where you grew up, whether it was Wisconsin [Street], Norfolk [Street], Maine [Street], you had houses all around you. Visualize . . . sitting on the porch and just watching the community disappear in front of your very eyes." After a protracted legal battle, the city destroyed Mr. Jones's residence, home to at least three generations of his family, the last in the neighborhood to be razed. While rendering his decision, Judge D. Dortch Warriner blasted RRHA's action: "[Fulton residents] were afraid you were going to destroy [Fulton] and they were right . . . There was a community. There isn't one anymore."

(Above) View looking west from Powhatan / Fulton Hill in 2020.

(Left) Fulton Gas Works flooded in 1972, along with much of the Fulton neighborhood.

Fulton continues to celebrate a rich tradition of organizing. The Greater Fulton Civic Association thrives, and in recent years, residents have implemented initiatives to establish a community center, complete an oral history project, and create a memorial park. Freda Johnson, a former Fulton resident, coordinated the Fulton Oral History Project to help preserve the neighborhood's history. She recalls: "As a child, I watched my grandmother and neighbors in Historic Fulton fight and protest injustices in the late '60s and '70s. In 2012, I joined meetings held in the community . . . It was truly rewarding learning of our community and its people, from its people. We put together a prominent piece of history for generations to come. It was done in truth. It was a joy.

Newspapers, books, and magazines claim Fulton was a horrible place to live. The interviews proved otherwise."

## TO LEARN MORE

Historic Fulton Oral History Project: https://digital.library.vcu.edu/islandora/object/vcu%3Aful

Campbell, Benjamin. *Richmond's Unhealed History*. Richmond: Brandylane, 2012.

Richardson, Selden. *Built by Blacks: African American Architecture and Neighborhoods in Richmond*. Mt. Pleasant, SC: History Press, 2008.

Komp, Catherine. "Indelible Roots: Historic Fulton and Urban Renewal." *VPM News*, July 21, 2016.

## 2.5  Willie Mallory Residence (former)

*1208 Denny Street*

On September 27, 1916, police invaded the Fulton home of Willie Mallory, a white woman, where she lived with her husband, George, and their eight children. Targeted because of their poverty, their number of children, and the fact that George was frequently away from home for work, the police arrested Willie and two of her teen-aged girls under the guise of prostitution. Rather than charge them, they took them to the Virginia State Colony for Epileptics and the Feebleminded in Lynchburg, which opened in 1911. Within six months of their arrival, the colony, under the direction of superintendent Albert Priddy, sterilized Willie and her fifteen-year-old daughter Jessie. Thirteen-year-old Nannie was spared only because her family sued the state.

In 1918, Willie's husband George initiated legal proceedings against the state. He petitioned for the release of Willie and his two daughters, monetary compensation for Willie and Jessie's forced sterilizations, and the return of their younger children who had been placed in foster care after Willie's arrest. The petition argued that Willie and their daughters were not being held for health reasons but for unpaid labor, calling their confinement "an actual state of involuntary servitude." While the eugenics movement, which focused on "better breeding," exalted the superiority of white people, eugenicists were equally interested in controlling the labor of poor people, especially women, regardless of race.

George won the release of Willie, Jessie, and Nannie as well as the return of their younger children from foster care. However, they received no compensation for Willie and Jessie's forced sterilization. This legal challenge to sterilization, pursued by a poor white family, galvanized state support for a sterilization statute that would prevent this kind of lawsuit in the future. It led to the passage of a state sterilization law in 1924, touted by eugenicists and lawmakers as a way to reduce the state's economic burden to care for poor people. The law allowed anyone in the state's five mental health institutions to be sterilized without consent. The Lynchburg Colony alone sterilized over 2,700 people, and by the time the program ended in the 1970s, the state had forcibly sterilized over 8,000 people. The Mallory home was destroyed as part of the city's destruction of the Fulton neighborhood in the 1970s. Today, it is an empty lot.

**TO LEARN MORE**

Catte, Elizabeth. *Pure America: Eugenics and the Making of Modern Virginia.* Cleveland: Belt, 2021.

Lombardo, Paul. *Three Generations, No Imbeciles: Eugenics, the Supreme Court, and* Buck v. Bell. Baltimore: Johns Hopkins University Press, 2010.

### 2.6 CSX Fulton Yard

*500 Goddin Street*

A railyard has existed in this location since the late nineteenth century. On June 17, 1903, 667 members of the local Amalgamated Association of Street Railway Employees went on strike against the Virginia Passenger and Power Company for sixty-eight days. Their demands included higher wages, a nine-hour workday, union recognition, and arbitration power in employee-employer disputes. That day, 200 streetcars sat idle. Many strikers lived on Lester Street in Fulton near this railyard, and it became a key site for the disruption of streetcar service.

The company immediately hired strikebreakers. Initially, the strikers successfully persuaded these strikebreakers to return home or seek other employment. The union strategically placed men at city railway stations around the clock. On June 18, when sixty-seven strikebreakers arrived via train, all but seven turned back. As a result, the company soon relied on professional strikebreakers undeterred by strikers.

Union members, including Black unionists, sent monetary support to the white strikers. The strikers had immense community support, as evidenced by sustained resistance against the streetcar company. On the second day of the strike, thousands gathered to pelt the cars with potatoes, mud, eggs, and stones. They threw projectiles into the

City workers spread asphalt over the city's last trolley tracks on Orleans Street in Fulton, 1967.

car sheds where strikebreakers slept. They attempted to burn down bridges that carried the cars and cut down poles containing the cars' electric wires. Nightly, protestors stacked the tracks with obstructions. At this railyard, they tore up car tracks overnight and hauled them away.

The governor called in state troops to impose unofficial martial law on June 23 as daily protests continued. Residents stood on street corners and reported minor streetcar violations, like speeding. Protestors blew up cars with dynamite, and violence escalated. A soldier shot sixteen-year-old Lester Wilcox; another soldier killed Luther Taylor when he resisted arrest for supporting strikers. Company guards fired into a hundreds-strong crowd on June 24 at Lombardy and Main Streets. Streetcars often returned to their barns under the cover of Gatling guns for protection.

Sustained citizen action did not convince the company to meet the workers' demands. The presence of the state militia and strikebreakers allowed the company to run their routes normally by late July. With none of their demands met, union members officially ended the strike on August 24, and the union dissolved. While unsuccessful in meeting its goals, the strike was the largest and longest sustained labor strike in early twentieth-century Richmond. It is notable for the large number of Richmonders who engaged in civil disobedience to support local laborers. Today, this area has been redeveloped into high-end apartment housing but a railyard, now owned by CSX, still operates here.

"Draw In" for East End youth at Creighton Court, 1968.

## TO LEARN MORE

Meier, August, and Elliott Rudwick. "Negro Boycotts of Segregated Streetcars in Virginia, 1904–1907." *Virginia Magazine of History and Biography* 81, no. 4 (1973): 479–80.

## 2.7  Creighton Court

Nine Mile Road at Creighton Road

Creighton Court sits on the border between Richmond and Henrico County alongside Interstate 64. Its construction initiated a repeated pattern of establishing public housing communities in neighborhoods redlined during the 1930s. Built in 1952, it was the first of five public housing communities in the East End, four of which lie within a one-mile radius. The Richmond Redevelopment and Housing Authority (RRHA) intentionally concentrated poverty along racial lines by geographically isolating public housing in the East End. This action led businesses and industries to locate in more affluent, majority-white neighborhoods, leaving few nearby work options available for public housing residents.

Creighton residents have a long history of organizing for tenant rights. As a result of a work-related injury, Curtis Holt and his family moved into Creighton Court in the 1950s, where he protested a number of repressive policies, and he organized fellow tenants to do the same. At the time, RRHA forbade tenant organizations as well as tenants from conducting meetings on RRHA property, which Holt learned about when he attempted to organize the Creighton Court Civic Association. He was nearly evicted for organizing the group. When he sued RRHA, a federal judge found that RRHA had unlawfully tried to evict him due to his activism. The judge ordered a permanent injunction to prevent RRHA from any future attempts to evict him. Housing authorities in cities across the country implemented similar restrictions, including prohibitions against female single heads of household living in public housing. These restrictions activated tenants nationwide to mobilize collectively with other Black-led organizing efforts.

Activism at Creighton continues. In 2019, RRHA developed plans to turn administrative control of the city's public housing over to private entities to remake them into mixed-use, mixed-income developments. This national trend, initiated by the U. S. Department of Housing and Urban Development, means public authorities retain little control over how private developers prioritize low-income residents. Most critically, residents point out that there has been no promise of one-to-one replacement, or guaranteed right of return to ensure that current public housing residents are not displaced. As activist and former Creighton resident Esco Bowden states: "We [still] have RRHA trying to knock down historically Black neighborhoods and then presenting no plan on what they're going to do in return."

With a waiting list of nearly 4,000 residents, RRHA has not renewed expired leases at Creighton for years. Half of Creighton units were boarded up by summer 2021, causing rodent infestations and exacerbating public health problems in what Richmond community organizer Omari Al-Quadaffi has called "de facto demolition," whereby authorities neglect properties to coerce residents to seek out alternatives. Over 9,000 people live in Richmond's public housing communities, and RRHA hopes to replicate this private, mixed-income development model in all of its communities. As of this writing, demolition work has begun at the site but is expected to be a years-long process.

## TO LEARN MORE

Meagher, Richard. "Privatizing Creighton." *Style Weekly*, May 25, 2021.

Randolph, Lewis A., and Gale T. Tate. *Rights for a Season: Politics of Race, Class, and Gender in Richmond, Virginia.* Knoxville: University of Tennessee Press, 2003.

East End Cemetery in 2020.

## 2.8 East End Cemetery

*50 Evergreen Road*

The East End Memorial Burial Association, a group of prominent African Americans, founded East End Cemetery in 1897. The cemetery contains burial sites for doctors and lawyers as well as laborers, teachers, and ministers, representing many generations and broad cross-sections of the area's African American community. The sixteen-acre site likely contains over 15,000 graves.

Most cemeteries in Virginia were segregated until the 1960s, and until 2017, historic Black cemeteries received no state funding for upkeep, unlike many of their white counterparts. Founded during Jim Crow, East End was left fallow as the twentieth century wore on. State neglect of East End, and many other historic Black cemeteries, is emblematic of the long-lasting effect of political and economic disenfranchisement faced by Black Virginians under

legal segregation and, later, intentional divestment from African American communities. As Thomas Taylor, a family descendant of those buried here, points out in his oral history: "I knew we owned the plot. I never knew who owned the roads. But I knew that somebody in the white cemeteries were taking care of them, because their roads were paved—never knowing that the General Assembly allocated funds for that. I think that needs to be done for the East End and for Evergreen and wherever else Black people are being buried, so it can't be forgotten. There's just as much history there as there is in the white cemeteries."

A volunteer effort led by the Friends of East End began in 2013 to reclaim the cemetery. Dense vegetation had obscured parts of the site, and it served as an illegal de facto dumping ground for household trash, tires, and other detritus. During weekly workdays, volunteers, some of whom were descendants of those buried here, cleared tons of brush and garbage, and uncovered thousands of gravesites, diligently restoring a space long overgrown and neglected. The enormous effort made to restore this sacred space and to research those buried there galvanized thousands of volunteers between 2013 and 2020. Taylor notes: "It's good that this is being pursued. To look at history, to see that these cemeteries are being taken care of. What's being done here is a great opportunity to maintain and have history preserved."

In 2019, Enrichmond Foundation took possession of the cemetery, raising concerns over illegitimate power, displacement, and inadequate preservation efforts. In March 2021, forty descendants and other Black community members wrote an open letter to the governor to document intermittent, haphazard maintenance by the owner and to request that they be integrated into decision-making related to sacred sites where their ancestors lie. Once again, descendants were forced to negotiate a complex political terrain of city politics and private philanthropy that threatened prior progress in carefully preserving this sacred space. Enrichmond Foundation abruptly dissolved in 2022. What that means for East End Cemetery, as well as for many other local groups who collectively entrusted the organization with $3 million, is unclear as of this writing.

**TO VISIT NEARBY**

**EVERGREEN CEMETERY** at 50 Evergreen Road. Evergreen is also a historic African American cemetery adjacent to East End Cemetery. Established in 1891, it contains the gravesites of prominent Black Richmonders Maggie Walker and John Mitchell Jr., who are featured elsewhere in this guide.

**TO LEARN MORE**

Visit the East End Cemetery website, a vital resource in the effort to restore the cemetery: https://eastendcemeteryrva.com/

View oral histories at the Friends of East End Cemetery's website: https://friendsofeastend.com/

Palmer, Brian. "For the Forgotten African-American Dead." *New York Times*, January 7, 2017.

## 2.9 The East End Landfill

1820 Darbytown Road

Four large landfills exist within a two-mile radius near the border between Richmond and Henrico County. The East End Landfill (TEEL), which holds construction and demolition debris, consistently sparks ongoing controversy and tensions with adjacent communities. From 2007 until 2011, TEEL illegally stored over 150,000 tons of coal ash and later deposited it onto its site as structural fill. Coal ash, also known as coal combustion byproduct, is a toxic carcinogen. It contains hazardous chemicals, including arsenic, lead, and mercury, which cause reproductive problems, neurological damage, developmental disorders, and heart and lung disease. Coal ash is also widely known to kill fish and wildlife.

In 2010, after coal ash was discovered on the site during an inspection initiated by neighborhood resident complaints, Henrico County found TEEL in violation of its conditional use permit. TEEL responded

PERSONAL REFLECTION

**CATHY WOODSON**
Community Organizer, Virginia Organizing

The work that I did before organizing was all in direct service. We were putting band aids on a bigger problem. We were not addressing the root cause.

I had been introduced to a different way of organizing. It was amazing to sit and listen to concerns from individuals from around the state. I really got hooked learning how to organize grassroots folks, lift their voices, not my voice, helping build leadership within the community. Saying to people, "You are the expert of your experience. Let's lift that up and help other people do the same and build this crescendo of leadership and action to make change in your community."

Good organizing helps people understand the systemic issues. Getting everyday people to understand the systems impacting their lives, and how those systems can be changed. Charity is not going to do that. People directly affected by issues, telling their stories to decision makers have greater impact. We saw that with the East End Landfill. It wasn't me telling their stories. It was them telling what it was like daily to look at the smoke and to smell the smells and the trucks and all that.

Organizing is relational. It really makes a difference when you have a relationship with people on an equal footing and there is dignity and respect. We can accomplish something great in that way of being together. We expand the circle, and that's the reward of organizing for me.

by appealing to the Henrico Board of Zoning Appeals (BZA). Community activists and concerned residents, alongside members of the Greater Fulton Hill Civic Association and Virginia Organizing, mobilized in a few days to attend the hearing and provide public comment. At that hearing, in December 2010, the board denied the landfill's appeal and found TEEL in violation of its permit.

TEEL refused to remove coal ash from the site, escalating a contentious dispute among the county, state regulators, community residents, and local leaders. From December 2010 to April 2011 alone, TEEL made two million dollars in revenue from illegally taking coal ash onto its site. In another public comment session with Virginia's Department of Environmental Quality (DEQ) in October 2011, Greater Fulton Civic Association community leader Rebecca Fralin reported: "The waste is seen being carried right down Darbytown Road destined for my community and others. Toxic waste is in their landfill, period. It is escaping into residential areas, period. It is illegal to have hazardous materials in this landfill, period. When they use up four years of coal ash, where has it gone? Into the atmosphere? Washed away into our water? Absorbed into our lungs? Settled into our garden soil? At present we live within spitting distance of a landfill whose illegal stores of toxic waste are literally contaminating our backyards."

After a protracted two-year battle, the Henrico Board of Zoning Appeals eventually renewed TEEL's permit after it agreed to remove coal ash from the site. In 2012, TEEL transported the last truck full of coal

The East End Landfill.

ash from its site to the Shoesmith landfill in Chesterfield County. This action demonstrates the many gaps in local environmental protections that allow toxic waste to be removed from one location and deposited into another without citizen input or institutional accountability. Due to another permit violation involving toxic waste, the Board of Zoning Appeals ordered TEEL closed in 2018. As of this writing, litigation to reopen the site continues.

**TO LEARN MORE**

Sinclair, Melissa Scott. "Dust in the Wind: What Should We Do with the Big Heap of Coal Ash in Henrico County?" *Style Weekly,* May 24, 2011.

Berti, Daniel. "The East End Landfill Is the Environmental Disaster No One Is Talking About." *RVA Magazine,* July 5, 2018.

Anderson-Ellis, Nicole. "Poison's Peak." *Style Weekly,* April 26, 2011.

# 3

# North-side
# Richmond

# Introduction

**AS THE CITY EXPANDED IN THE NINETEENTH** century, white immigrants and Black Richmonders settled north of Broad Street on land that previously had been divided into large estates and farms. After the Civil War, the city created Jackson Ward here, a gerrymandered ward meant to limit the impact of Black voting by concentrating most African Americans into one political district. Despite the racist, anti-democratic reason for its creation, Jackson Ward became a vibrant Black community, a site of significant African American economic, political, and cultural production with people of all class levels living there as a result of increasingly strict segregation in the early twentieth century. It became nationally known as a cultural destination, the Harlem of the South, and as a community driven by economic self-determination. As home to the offices of the city's activist Black newspaper, the *Richmond Planet* (1882–1938), and innumerable Black mutual aid, philanthropic, and religious organizations, the neighborhood functioned as the city's center for Black resistance to, and survival amidst, white supremacy.

Development of a trolley system that Richmond debuted in 1888 extended city development farther north. Wealthy, white Richmonders built "country homes" along

Brook Road, and the trolley line triggered development of white neighborhoods north of Jackson Ward. Lewis Ginter, founder of the American Tobacco Company, and later his niece, Grace Arents, concentrated development here, which included the creation of the Ginter Park neighborhood and Union Theological Seminary. This area also became home to Virginia Union University (VUU), a Historically Black university, whose beginnings are rooted in the founding of the Richmond Theological School for Freedmen in 1865. It moved to its present-day location in 1899, establishing a thriving center for Black intellectual life in the city's Northside.

In the 1940s, the city built its first public housing community, Gilpin Court, adjacent to Jackson Ward. In the 1950s, the building of what would become Interstate 95 cut

Constructing Interstate 95 through Jackson Ward, the city's largest African American community, in 1957.

# Northside

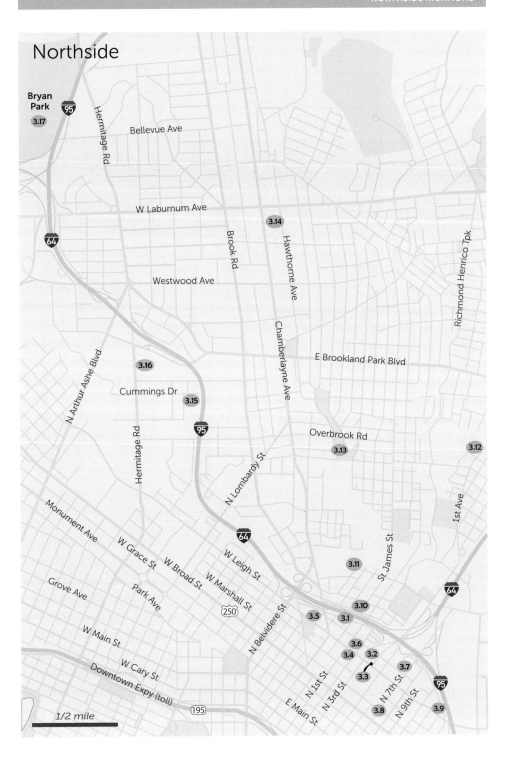

Bryan Park
3.17

Bellevue Ave

Hermitage Rd

W Laburnum Ave

3.14

Brook Rd

Hawthorne Ave

Westwood Ave

Chamberlayne Ave

Richmond Henrico Tpk

3.16

Cummings Dr

3.15

N Arthur Ashe Blvd

E Brookland Park Blvd

Hermitage Rd

95

Overbrook Rd

3.13

3.12

N Lombardy St

1st Ave

Monument Ave

64

W Grace St

W Broad St

W Leigh St

W Marshall St

3.11

St James St

Grove Ave

Park Ave

250

N Belvidere St

3.5

3.1

3.10

64

W Main St

3.6

3.4

3.2

3.7

W Cary St

3.3

Downtown Expy (toll)

N 1st St

N 3rd St

N 7th St

N 9th St

95

1/2 mile

195

E Main St

3.8

3.9

Students at Virginia Union University, Richmond's first Historically Black College, enjoy a day on campus in 1974. The university moved to its present-day Northside location on N. Lombardy in 1899.

through Jackson Ward, displacing 10 percent of the city's African American population. The highway brought noise, air pollution, and displacement; it also cut off Gilpin Court from the city center, a harbinger for future public housing communities.

After World War II, white residents left Northside in favor of homes in the suburban counties. New highways fueled this white flight to escape desegregating schools. African Americans moved into these neighborhoods, as their communities closer to downtown faced destruction in the name of urban renewal. In the 1950s and 1960s, the city destroyed Navy Hill, another African American neighborhood, displacing an additional thousand families. In its place, developers built the now-defunct Richmond Coliseum and other entities like the convention center, a behemoth of a building that occupies sev-

eral city blocks and continues to isolate Jackson Ward from downtown. Not one single building from the former Navy Hill neighborhood remains.

Today, Jackson Ward is a lively center for arts, culture, and business. Street art adorns many of its buildings, and it is a major player in the city's artistic and cultural scene. Black churches founded more than a century ago still cultivate large congregations who undertake significant community work. While still a diverse neighborhood of community businesses and residences, its proximity adjacent to the ever-expanding campus of Virginia Commonwealth University and the city's downtown corridor threatens to encourage further gentrification and cause the displacement of longtime African American residents.

Gentrification threatens several other historically African American, working-class neighborhoods in Northside. Highland Park, Barton Heights, and Brookland Parkway are all sites of uneven but expanding gentrification. The expansion of LGBTQ communities into Northside also has led to sites of LGBTQ resistance to anti-LGBTQ policies as well as LGBTQ community making, as evidenced by LGBTQ community and service organizations now located here.

Like similarly situated spots in the East End, some neighborhoods contain immense poverty concentrations due to systemic racism. Residents at Gilpin Court, mentioned above, have a life expectancy rate ten years lower than city residents as a whole. Its residents need better educational opportunities, transportation, and food options, issues being addressed by a range of activist and community work, including Gilpin Farm and the Food Justice Corridor. The relationship between racism, poverty, and the city's rising housing costs particularly impacts the city's Northside and East End communities as gentrification grows.

This chapter features pivotal sites that illustrate histories of the intentionally planned concentration of poverty as a result of urban development. It also emphasizes historic and contemporary community-driven responses to gentrification, food insecurity, and public health issues. Community work to combat poverty linked to white supremacy and colonization is accompanied by the cultivation of community; this grassroots work crosses identities of gender, sexuality, race, and class to affirm humanity and dignity while centering community wisdom and culture.

# Northside Richmond Sites

### 3.1 Sixth Mount Zion Baptist Church

14 W. Duval Street

In 1867, famed preacher John Jasper founded the Sixth Mount Zion Baptist Church in Richmond. Originally located on Brown's Island in an abandoned confederate horse stable, the church moved to its present-day

Sixth Mount Zion Baptist Church.

Example of Jackson Ward housing as photographed by Dorothea Lange in 1938.

The construction of this six-lane highway running north–south between Richmond and Petersburg cut a swath through Jackson Ward, the city's largest African American neighborhood. Jackson Ward had been a thriving center of Black life for decades, with its **Hippodrome** (see page 76) regularly visited by celebrities like Ella Fitzgerald and Duke Ellington. By the 1920s, its vibrancy was captured in its nickname, "the Harlem of the South." This highway building project demolished over 700 homes in Jackson Ward, which displaced 10 percent of the city's African American population. The displacement of so many people sparked neighborhood decline and opened Jackson Ward to further destruction under later urban renewal plans.

While highway construction destroyed many homes, the church was preserved. Rev. A. W. Brown rallied powerful supporters to the cause of preserving the church, and members who worked at City Hall kept the congregation apprised of officials' plans. While unable to save the neighborhood, members of Sixth Mount Zion Baptist Church protected the church by working to ensure that the road swung around the church in order to leave it standing in its original position. Today, visitors can see the church situated above the sharp curve in Interstate 95 in the heart of the city. Church tours, including a visit to the John Jasper Memorial Room and Museum, can be arranged with advance notice. The church celebrates John Jasper Day annually in February. It also maintains its long tradition of community support and advocacy, both in Jackson Ward and the larger city.

site in 1869. It was the first Black church established by a Black minister in Richmond.

Sixth Mount Zion Baptist Church has been a critical site for building social and political power in African American communities. In the 1950s, church members fought heartily to protect both the Jackson Ward neighborhood and the church during the building of what would become Interstate 95. African American and working-class white residents affected by the proposed highway project organized to rebuff the proposal, successfully defeating two highway-building referendums in the early 1950s. Undeterred, city leaders asked the state legislature to create an "authority" to build the road, which allowed the city to bypass the democratic process. The new turnpike opened in July 1958.

PERSONAL REFLECTION

**BENJAMIN ROSS**
Church Historian,
Sixth Mount Zion Baptist Church

*On John Jasper, founder of Sixth Mount Zion Baptist Church:* His career began as a slave funeral preacher, and he traveled around the state to preach many funerals. He worked as a tobacco stemmer in Richmond, and if he was requested to go out of town to preach a slave funeral, you had to pay his owner one dollar for every day he was away from work. In 1867, after the Civil War was over he organized the Sixth Mount Zion Baptist Church, initially in an abandoned confederate horse stable on Brown's Island.

Although he didn't have a formal education, he eventually learned to read and write. With a vivid imagination, a good set of lungs, and a penchant for drama, he became famous throughout the state of Virginia. The drama, and the preaching, caught the attention of the media and thousands of people. His sincere belief in the Bible, which he believed very literally, led him to his most popular sermon, called *De Sun Do Move, and De Earth Am Square,* which he perfected in the late 1870s. People loved it; some people questioned it because it didn't make scientific sense: the sun doesn't move, and the earth is not square. But Jasper found pages in the Bible that alluded to these things. He would say don't get mad at me if you don't like the sermon; go to the Lord. Thousands of people came to hear it. White people in particular loved it; they packed out the church every time he preached it.

TO VISIT NEARBY

**MAMA J'S** at 415 N. First Street. A popular local soul food restaurant run by Velma Johnson.

TO LEARN MORE

Ross, Benjamin. "The Challenges, Responsibilities, and Rewards of Preserving the John Jasper Legacy." *Baptist History and Heritage Society* 42, no. 3 (2007).

Silver, Christopher. *Twentieth-Century Richmond: Planning, Politics, and Race.* Knoxville: University of Tennessee Press, 1984.

Sinclair, Melissa Scott. "Beacon on a Hill." *Style Weekly,* February 14, 2012.

## 3.2 Law Offices of Oliver Hill (former)

*623 N. 3rd Street*

Civil rights attorney Oliver Hill Sr. practiced law with various partners for most of his nearly sixty-year career (1939–98) at this office. After earning a law degree from Howard University, he eventually returned to his birthplace of Richmond, where he became one of the attorneys leading the fight against legal segregation in Virginia. Hill and his colleagues legally challenged more statutes related to race-based discrimination than anyone in the South, placing them at the forefront of dismantling the South's racist system of Jim Crow.

When Hill returned to Richmond in 1939, he worked closely with the State Conference of the NAACP (National Association for the Advancement of Colored People), initially representing Black teachers in Norfolk to secure equal pay for equal work. One

(Right) Former law offices of Oliver Hill and his partners.

(Below Right) Oliver Hill and his law partner Spottswood Robinson III are memorialized in the Virginia Civil Rights Monument on Capitol Square in downtown Richmond.

of those teachers was Aline Black, a chemistry teacher at Norfolk's Booker T. Washington High School. She earned $1,045 annually, while her white counterparts with the same credentials and experience earned $2,100.

That salary equalization case, which the teachers won on appeal, was Hill's first federal court case. He then became the lead NAACP lawyer in Virginia, and Black teachers in fourteen other Virginia localities challenged race-based pay discrimination. Hill expanded his law firm to include civil rights lawyers Spottswood Robinson III and Martin E. Martin, who continued the work when Hill was drafted in 1943. They represented Irene Morgan in a landmark case that desegregated interstate transportation.

In 1951, students at Robert Russa Moton High School in Prince Edward County, seventy miles southwest of Richmond, went on strike to protest poor conditions at their Black high school in comparison to the county's new white high school. Hill took their case, and it became one of five cases, and the only student-instigated one, that the U. S. Supreme Court reviewed in *Brown v. Board of Education of Topeka, Kansas,* which declared segregated schools unconstitutional in 1954.

The site of this law firm represents decades of work to dismantle white supremacy embedded in the legal system. Some of the most significant civil rights lawsuits in the nation were argued, and won, by Hill and his partners. While new development surrounds this modest building, its locally known significance has helped to preserve it.

**TO LEARN MORE**

Edds, Margaret. *We Face the Dawn: Oliver Hill, Spottswood Robinson, and the Legal Team That Dismantled Jim Crow.* Charlottesville: University of Virginia Press, 2018.

Fergeson, Larissa. "Hill, Oliver W. (1907–2007)." *Encyclopedia Virginia.* Virginia Humanities, February 12, 2012.

*Richmond Planet* newsroom, ca. 1900.

**TO VISIT NEARBY**

**THE VIRGINIA CIVIL RIGHTS MEMORIAL ON CAPITOL SQUARE** (1000 Bank Street) honors the legacy of Hill, his fellow lawyers, and his clients.

## 3.3 *Richmond Planet* Offices

311 N. 4th Street

The *Richmond Planet,* the city's first Black newspaper, began publishing in 1882 at 814 E. Broad Street. Thirteen formerly enslaved people established the paper, which became a vital outlet for Black news and advocacy. In 1889, it moved to this location, where it operated until it ceased independent publishing in 1938.

John Mitchell Jr. edited the *Planet* from 1884 until his death in 1929. He shunned more moderate opinions, instead crafting a newspaper that unapologetically centered the fight for Black liberation, earning him the nickname "the Fighting Editor." The paper's masthead, which featured a flexed bicep and clenched first, emblematized this image. A fellow Black newspaper publisher wrote that Mitchell hurled "thunderbolts of truth into the ranks of the wicked."

Mitchell and his staff routinely reported on lynching and other acts of white violence, endangering themselves. A Charlotte County mob threatened to lynch Mitchell while he investigated the lynching of Richard Walker in May 1886. A mob of fifty white men took Walker, who had been accused of attempting to rape a white woman, from the local jail and hanged him. Accusations of attempted rape were a common means that whites used to justify the lynching of Black men. Reporting by Mitchell and other African American investigators revealed that these accusations were rarely accurate. Despite receiving numerous death threats, Mitchell remained undeterred. He published the threats in the *Planet* and continued his investigation, urging that the police, judges, and jury be allowed to do their jobs. Mitchell also advocated for self-defense. He wrote: "The best remedy for a lyncher or a cursed midnight rider is a 16 shot Winchester rifle in the hands of a dead shot Negro who has nerve enough to pull the trigger." Mitchell himself often wore a set of twin revolvers on his hips while investigating lynchings.

Many Black newspapers struggled for a number of reasons. Black communities often had low literacy rates, since learning to read and write was legally prohibited under enslavement, and afterwards localities allocated few resources for the education of Black children. Black citizens also were more likely to be unable to afford newspaper subscription prices. The white establishment also wielded substantial economic and political power against Black newspapers. In fact, before Mitchell joined the *Planet,* the Richmond School Board fired him. The board had been incensed by the *Planet*'s publication of their plans to fire the city's three Black school principals. As retribution, the board also fired a number of Black male teachers, including Mitchell. But Mitchell's uncompromising writings and investigations to challenge white supremacy earned his newspaper a national following.

Mitchell was deeply embedded in the city's civic life. He served as a city alderman in the late nineteenth century. In 1902, he opened Mechanics Savings Bank, the city's

third Black-owned bank, which operated for twenty years. He helped to organize a streetcar boycott in 1904 to protest segregated seating on the cars, and in 1921, he ran for governor to protest the all-white Republican ticket. Mitchell died in 1929, but the *Planet* operated until its merger with the Baltimore-based *Afro-American* in 1938. Its local focus ended with this merger, although it published until 1996. In 1992, Raymond H. Boone founded the weekly *Richmond Free Press,* again giving the city a Black-owned, independent media outlet that centers African American communities.

**TO LEARN MORE**

Alexander, Ann. *Race Man: The Rise and Fall of the "Fighting Editor," John Mitchell Jr.* Charlottesville: University of Virginia Press, 2002.

Meier, August, and Elliott Rudwick. "Negro Boycotts of Segregated Streetcars in Virginia, 1904–1907." *Virginia Magazine of History and Biography* 81, no. 4 (1973): 479–80.

Read the *Richmond Free Press* online at https://richmondfreepress.com/.

**TO VISIT NEARBY**

**THE BUILDING THAT HOUSED MECHANICS SAVINGS BANK** still stands at 212 E. Clay Street.

**MITCHELL** is buried at Evergreen Cemetery, 50 Evergreen Road, Richmond.

## 3.4  The Hippodrome

528 N. 2nd Street

The Hippodrome, a performance venue, opened in 1914 with seating for more than a thousand people. It represented the heart of Jackson Ward's cultural and artistic scene

A crowd gathers outside the Hippodrome, 1959.

the Chitlin' Circuit mostly catered to lesser-known performers who had no access to white venues. According to scholar Preston Lauterbach, Chitlin' Circuit venues featured "brash performers in raucous nightspots" and contributed to the creation of new musical genres within traditions of blues, jazz, and the birth of rock'n'roll.

and was one of the prime reasons the neighborhood became known as the "Harlem of the South." It was built on Second Street, known as The Deuce, the center of Black nightlife in Richmond during the early twentieth century.

The Hippodrome's stage attracted the most well-known African American performers of its day, including Richmonder Bill "Bojangles" Robinson as well as Ella Fitzgerald, Billie Holiday, Ray Charles, Duke Ellington, and James Brown, among others. It also was active on the Chitlin' Circuit, a network of performance venues that showcased African American performers and musicians in the South during the Jim Crow era. The Black entrepreneurs who ran the circuit provided work to Black artists, musicians, and performers who otherwise struggled to find performance venues that welcomed Black entertainers. While popular Black entertainers often performed to white audiences out of economic necessity,

The Hippodrome caught fire in 1945. It was gutted, redesigned in an Art Deco style, and reopened in 1946 as a movie theater, which closed in 1967. It remained largely vacant until a meticulous restoration in 2010. It now functions as a private event venue.

### TO LEARN MORE

Brown, Elsa Barkley, and Gregg Kimball. "Mapping the Terrain of Black Richmond." *Journal of Urban History* 21, no. 3 (1995): 296–346.

### TO VISIT NEARBY

**BILL "BOJANGLES" ROBINSON STATUE** at the intersection of W. Leigh Street and Chamberlayne Avenue. Robinson was a popular Black entertainer in the early twentieth century who also worked on projects promoting equal rights for African Americans. He was born and raised in Jackson Ward.

**THE BLACK HISTORY MUSEUM AND CULTURAL CENTER OF VIRGINIA** at 122 W. Leigh Street celebrates the cultures and histories of African Americans in Virginia.

## 3.5 Ebenezer Baptist Church

216 W. Leigh Street

Ebenezer Baptist Church, formed in 1857 as an outgrowth of the First African Baptist congregation, has provided space for community growth and support since its inception. After the Civil War, it housed the city's first school for African American children as well as Hartshorn Memorial College, established to educate Black women. Rev. William Stokes became pastor of the church and married Ora Brown (Stokes) in 1902. That year, Virginia ratified a new constitution that severely restricted voting access for Black men and poor white men. It disenfranchised 90 percent of Black voters and half of white ones, all men, since women were not allowed to vote.

In 1909, white women suffragists formed the Equal Suffrage League of Virginia (ESL). Anti-suffragists played up racial fears, arguing that allowing Black women to vote would endanger white supremacy, ignoring the fact that Virginia had severely limited the ability of Black men to vote and those same barriers would affect Black women. Virginia's white suffragists refused to work with Black suffragists. Not all white women agreed with this strategy. In 1913, Richmond author Mary Johnston wrote to the ESL that "as women we should be most prayerfully careful lest, in the future, women—whether coloured women or white women who are merely poor—should be able to say that we had betrayed them for freedom."

Given their exclusion from the ESL, Stokes, Maggie Walker, and other Black women formed their own organizations to promote Black women's suffrage. Upon the 19th Amendment's ratification in 1920, they organized so many Black women for voter registration that they had to petition the city for additional registrars. Segregated in city hall's basement, Black women were often turned away from registering after standing in line all day. Stokes organized a phone system to alert women when their turn came to register. Stokes also unsuccessfully petitioned the city to employ Black deputies to oversee elections in Black neighborhoods, in contrast to white deputies known to intimidate Black voters. This voter registration effort, which mobilized mass educational meetings on how to circumvent voting barriers, enabled over 2,400 African American women in Richmond to vote in the 1920 election. By comparison, 10,645 white women voted.

Black voters could not vote unimpeded until the Voting Rights Act of 1965 outlawed the discriminatory practices that Virginia used to suppress the state's Black voters. Churches like Ebenezer were and are incubators for political and social action, especially because they function as spaces removed from white surveillance, and Black members economically sustain them.

### TO LEARN MORE

McDaid, Jennifer. "Woman Suffrage in Virginia." *Encyclopedia Virginia*. Virginia Humanities, February 2021.

Bonis, Ray. "Ora E. Brown Stokes (1882–1957)." *Dictionary of Virginia Biography*. Library of Virginia (2019).

## 3.6 True Reformers Hall (former)

604–608 N. 2nd Street

Built in the early 1890s, this hall became the largest building in Richmond constructed and owned by African Americans. William Washington Browne, leader of the fraternal organization known as the Grand Fountain United Order of True Reformers, envisioned it as a monument to Black self-reliance. On April 19, 1904, over 600 African Americans attended a rally here organized by John Mitchell Jr. and Maggie Walker to publicize the boycott of Richmond's segregated streetcars. New state legislation allowed for, but did not require, segregated streetcar seating, which *Richmond Planet* editor John Mitchell Jr. called "optional discrimination." The Virginia Passenger and Power Company of Richmond chose to segregate its cars, the only transit company at the time to do so. Most transit companies opposed segregation attempts because they saw the provision as being difficult to enforce, expensive due to the need for separate carriages, and a deterrent to African American ridership, which they depended on for their economic viability.

A particularly pernicious part of the new segregation law granted police authority to transit workers for the first time. It gave conductors the power to carry guns and enforce segregation statutes in cars. A group of Black Baptist ministers immediately orchestrated a meeting with the company to discuss this problematic expansion of policing power in a space that Black streetcar riders would have to contend with daily, as streetcars were everyday spaces people used to navigate from their homes to work and social events.

The *Richmond Planet* estimated that 80–90 percent of Black residents boycotted the streetcars in 1904. The boycott required sustained daily practice, commitment,

True Reformers Hall, ca. 1900.

and strategizing about alternative ways to move around the city at a time of expansive growth. Black carriage owners loaned them out. Black undertakers used their wagons as buses. People hitched rides on delivery wagons. As editor of the city's Black newspaper, Mitchell continually implored people to just buy more shoes.

In the first six weeks of the boycott, only one person was arrested for refusing segregated seating, a Black woman visiting from New York who told the conductor "to hell with the Jim Crow car." Many more citations were issued to white passengers, who bristled at being told they had to sit in a specific area. By the year's end, the Virginia Passenger and Power Company declared bankruptcy, weakened both by the boycott and a violent months-long labor strike in 1903. Subsequently, Virginia passed legislation in 1906 requiring segregation on all streetcars. The Supreme Court declared segregation on public transportation illegal in the 1960 *Boydton v. Virginia* ruling. The hall was demolished in 1955.

Navy Hill Barber Shop, 404 E. Duval Street, 1950.

**TO LEARN MORE**

"Seeds of Resistance: The Richmond Streetcar Boycotts." *The Uncommonwealth,* May 23, 2017.
Watkinson, James. "William Washington Browne and the True Reformers of Richmond, Virginia." *Virginia Magazine of History and Biography* 97, no. 3 (1989): 375–98.

**TO VISIT NEARBY**

Visit the privately owned **HOME OF W.W. BROWNE** at 105 W. Jackson Street.

## 3.7  Navy Hill School (former)

E. Duval Street at Navy Hill Drive

In the early nineteenth century, private developers created the Navy Hill neighborhood north of downtown, naming it after a proposed War of 1812 memorial that never materialized. Originally settled by German immigrants, the neighborhood was almost exclusively populated by African Americans by the twentieth century. It became a center of mutual aid, education, and empowerment, which included one of the most prestigious early schools for Black children.

Navy Hill School opened in 1866 and operated under the protection of local Black militias, as local whites had set fire to Fifth Street Baptist Church, just around the corner, a few months earlier out of resentment over the community's growth. Future prominent Black citizens, like businesswoman and civil rights leader Maggie Walker and *Richmond Planet* editor John Mitchell Jr., attended this school as children. Because of its proximity to downtown and its occupancy by Black citizens, the area faced continual threats of destruction due to various urban renewal schemes.

In the 1950s and 1960s, the building of Interstate 95 and other development completely destroyed Navy Hill, displacing over a thousand people. Navy Hill School closed suddenly in 1965, and that location became an interstate on-ramp. The Richmond Coliseum, a 13,000-person arena that operated between 1971 and 2019, and the Virginia Biotechnology Research Park, which opened in 1995, occupy much of the former neighborhood.

In the late 2010s, the city proposed the controversial Navy Hill Development Project, a $1.5 billion project that included the

Children leaving Navy Hill School days before its destruction, 1965.

Richmond's underfunded school system. It initially garnered support from city bureaucrats, the mayor, developers, and city council. The project failed to meet the city's own guidelines for inclusion of affordable housing units for development projects on city property. A groundswell of grassroots activism killed the proposal in early 2020.

### TO LEARN MORE

Kollatz Jr., Harry. "The Original Navy Hill." *Richmond Magazine,* December 29, 2019.

Lazarus, Jeremy. "Navy Hill Ship Sinking?" *Richmond Free Press,* October 31, 2019.

Richardson, Selden. *Built by Blacks: African American Neighborhoods and Architecture in Richmond.* Mt. Pleasant, SC: History Press, 2008.

building of a much larger arena to replace the now defunct Coliseum. Promotional material for the project heavily connected it to the history of Navy Hill, claiming the project would bring back a "shattered" neighborhood "on the verge of being forgotten." Promoters utilized false nostalgia to ignore the fact that the project did not center working-class African American citizens, who had made up the core of the neighborhood when their homes and community spaces were obliterated by city building projects in the mid-twentieth century. It also spoke of neighborhood revitalization when there was no neighborhood to revitalize, as it was completely destroyed decades ago.

The proposed project involved building a controversial arena and required hundreds of millions in tax dollars, which activists argued should be earmarked instead for

## 3.8 Virginia First Regiment Armory (former)

7th and Marshall Streets

The Knights of Labor, the most powerful labor organization in the late nineteenth century, held their annual convention here, at the former site of the Virginia First Regiment Armory in October 1886. In stark contrast to similar organizations at the time, the Knights welcomed people of all races, men and women, skilled and unskilled laborers. By 1886, 20 percent of U.S. workers were affiliated with the organization. The Knights supported a number of labor initiatives, including an eight-hour workday.

With the convention in Richmond, the Knights hoped to better organize southern laborers, which presented a particular problem given the South's racial segregation and the Knight's commitment to "make no distinction based on nationality, sex, creed or color." While the Knights professed racial solidarity, this intention often did not succeed in practice. In Richmond, for example, white Knights successfully prevented Black laborers from gaining employment on municipal building projects.

Richmond's Jim Crow customs marked the convention from the beginning. Prior to it, a white hotelier notified the powerful Assembly District 49 from New York City that he would not provide lodging to their Black delegate, Frank Ferrell. Assembly 49 rebooked their party at a Black-owned hotel. Ferrell also was scheduled to introduce Virginia's governor Fitzhugh Lee, nephew of confederate general Robert E. Lee, at the convention. State leaders found the arrangement of a Black man introducing a white man unacceptable; in the end, Ferrell introduced Terence Powderly, a white leader of the Knights of Labor, who then introduced Lee. Even so, Assembly 49 found other ways to openly flout Richmond's customary segregation while in town. They went as an interracial group to see *Hamlet* at the Richmond Academy of Music. While they were left alone that evening, hundreds of angry white Richmonders gathered the following night to prevent a repeat, but Assembly 49 did not make an appearance.

Although a growing number of Black laborers joined the Knights of Labor after the convention, the Knights' success steadily deteriorated. Six months before the Richmond convention, a bomb had exploded amidst labor protests in Chicago's Haymar-

ket Square. As the country's largest and most successful labor union, the Knights were blamed for the incident, even though no evidence linked them to it. As well, entrenched racism proved to be a nearly insurmountable barrier to interracial organizing in the South. By 1891, most Black workers had left the Knights, beginning the organization's permanent decline. Built in 1881, the original armory was located here until it was destroyed and rebuilt in the 1910s. The city later razed that building for downtown expansion.

**TO LEARN MORE**

Minor, Claudia. "The 1886 Convention of the Knights of Labor." *Phylon* 44, no. 2 (1983): 147–59.

Rachleff, Peter J. *Black Labor in Richmond, 1865–1890*. Urbana: University of Illinois Press, 1989.

### 3.9 Richmond Colored Normal School (former)

*12th and Leigh Streets*

The Richmond Colored Normal School opened in 1873 as Richmond's first public secondary school for the city's Black students. It both trained teachers and served as a high school. Initially funded by the Freedmen's Bureau, Black mechanics and laborers donated their services to help construct the building. It became part of Richmond's public school system in 1876. In 1909, the school's location moved and the city renamed it Armstrong High after Samuel Armstrong, a white commander of U. S. Colored Troops (USCT) during the Civil War.

Richmond Colored Normal School, ca. 1900.

Virginia Randolph studied at the school before beginning her extensive career in educational leadership. In 1894, she began teaching at the one-room Mountain Road School, part of neighboring Henrico County's school system. She focused on traditional academic subjects as well as vocational training, including cooking, sewing, and woodworking. In 1908, she became the county-wide "Jeanes Supervising Industrial Teacher" as part of a program to advance education for Black children in the rural South. She created the county's first in-service program for Black teachers, and tailored each individual school's curriculum according to the needs of the local community. Her educational approaches, known as the Henrico Plan, were widely disseminated as she traveled across the South mentoring other Black teachers. To honor her contributions, in 1915, Henrico County opened the Virginia

E. Randolph Training School at the original Mountain Road School site in Henrico. Deeply involved in her local community throughout her career, she housed and cared for dozens of children who needed support. By the time she retired in 1949 as supervisor of Black schools in Henrico, she had worked to improve access to and the quality of schooling for Black students and teachers for nearly sixty years. Her start as a student at Richmond Colored Normal School served as the catalyst for this work, carried out during the height of the Jim Crow era.

The city destroyed the school's original building due to highway construction in 1955. The present-day Armstrong High is located in Richmond's East End at 2300 Cool Lane. While the school formally desegregated in 1971, its student body today remains over 95 percent Black, and its present location sits adjacent to four predominantly African American public housing communities.

**TO LEARN MORE**

Belsches, Elvatrice Parker. "Virginia Estelle Randolph (1870–1958)." *Encyclopedia Virginia* (2019).
Kollatz Jr., Harry. "Miss Randolph." *Richmond Magazine,* March 23, 2018.

## 3.10 St. Luke Penny Savings Bank

900 St. James Street

Founded by Maggie Lena Walker, the St. Luke Penny Savings Bank opened on November 3, 1903. It stood as a prime example of Black mutual aid, education, and social uplift. Walker was the daughter of enslaved

St. Luke Building being converting into apartment housing, 2020.

Independent Order of St. Luke's Children Group, 1925.

Crowds gather for the unveiling of the Maggie Walker statue at the corner of N. Adams and Broad Streets, 2017.

people and became a leader in the Independent Order of St. Luke, a benevolent society that served African American elders and children. She used her voice as a writer for the order's newspaper to educate readers about Black empowerment, and she became the first female bank owner in the United States.

Walker's plans to address the needs of Black citizens by consolidating and building economic power included the creation of St. Luke Penny Savings Bank as well as forming a newspaper, a factory, and an empo-

rium that became the only department store in the city to employ Black women as sales clerks in the early twentieth century. She advocated: "Let us put our money out at usury among ourselves and reap the benefit ourselves. Let us have a bank that will take the nickels and turn them into dollars." This economic self-determination was especially transformative in the segregated South where white-owned banks refused banking services to African Americans.

Branches of the St. Luke Penny Savings Bank spread, and at its height boasted more than 50,000 cooperative members. One of many Black-owned banks in Richmond, it thrived during the Great Depression when many others collapsed. Merging with other Black-owned banks in 1931, it continues to operate in the same community in which it was founded. Now known as Premier Bank, it is the oldest Black-owned bank in the country, currently located at 320 N. 1st Street. Its original building reopened in 2020 after sitting vacant for decades. The bottom floor houses a social service agency and the upper floors feature residential apartments.

**TO LEARN MORE**

Brown, Elsa Barkley. "Womanist Consciousness: Maggie Lena Walker and the Independent Order of St. Luke." *Signs* 14, no. 3 (1989): 610–33.
Lazarus, Jeremy. "St. Luke Building Ready for Tenants." *Richmond Free Press,* February 28, 2020.
Marlowe, Gertrude Woodruff. *A Right Worthy Grand Mission: Maggie Lena Walker and the Quest for Black Economic Empowerment.* Washington, DC: Howard University Press, 2003.

**TO VISIT NEARBY**

**TOUR WALKER'S HOME,** a National Historic Site, at 600 N. 2nd Street.

Visit **MAGGIE LENA WALKER MEMORIAL PLAZA** at W. Broad and N. Adams Streets.

Visit her **GRAVESITE** at Evergreen Cemetery, 50 Evergreen Road.

## 3.11 Charles S. Gilpin Community Farm

St. Peter Street at W. Hill Street

Built in 1942, Gilpin Court is Richmond's oldest and largest public housing community. The city first developed this area in the early nineteenth century, just north of what would become Jackson Ward. The community was originally called Apostle Town, as the streets surrounding its trapezoidal blocks were named after saints. The neighborhood contained both residences and businesses, including a number of Black-led mutual aid organizations. During World War II, the city cleared much of the land in this African American neighborhood to establish its first public housing community, named after Charles Sydney Gilpin, a popular African American actor who grew up in Jackson Ward.

In 2018, veteran community organizer and Gilpin Court resident Lillie Estes unveiled Gilpin Court residents' vision for a community garden. Under her leadership, the Gilpin Court Tenant Council partnered with the city and nonprofits to organize community-led planning, fundraising, and workdays. Estes envisioned the space as an incubator not only for health and wellness but also as a community building tool to strengthen relationships while reducing crime. According to Estes, "We have an opportunity to build a garden in the community to honor who it was named after to educate the young people and the not so young . . . and use it as an opportunity to grow." What once was a vacant, overgrown space that had a reputation as a crime hot

(Top) Clearing for new interstate highway adjacent to Gilpin Court residences, 1957.

(Above) Vegetable beds with Gilpin Court housing in the background.

(Left) Gilpin Community Farm.

spot is now a place where residents gather regularly to maintain an orchard and vegetable garden.

Estes was a tireless advocate for Gilpin Court, a public housing community with one of the state's highest poverty rates. She co-founded RePHRAME (Residents of Public Housing in Richmond Against Mass Eviction) in 2008, which brought together community members to advocate for public housing. As Estes noted: "The problem with affordable housing right now is that it's not affordable. By the city's estimates, [more than 50,000] people live in poverty, and we have a set number of units in public housing citywide, which is 4,100. That's over 45,000 people for which we do not have an affordable housing plan."

Today, nearly 3,000 residents live in Gilpin, making it the largest public housing community in the state. Over 95 percent of the residents are Black. Gilpin is surrounded by asphalt and concrete, which absorb and radiate heat. On hot days, Gilpin can be fifteen degrees hotter than vegetation-dense areas of the city, an increasingly significant health problem. In 2020, the city announced a plan to identify unoccupied parcels of city land that could be used to develop green space to ensure that all Richmonders live within a ten-minute walk of a park. Residents fear that development could incite gentrification and result in displacement.

This garden remains one of Estes's most memorable achievements; it was one of her final contributions to a community and city she spent decades improving. In 2019, she died unexpectedly. She nurtured multiple generations of community organizers in her thirty years of community work, many of whose words and work are featured in this guide. The garden endures as a symbol of her efforts, while her legacies run much deeper.

**TO LEARN MORE**

Howard, Amy, and Thad Williamson. "Reframing Public Housing in Richmond: Segregation, Resident Resistance, and the Future of Development." *Cities* 57 (2016): 33–39.

Plumer, Brad, and Nadja Popovich. "How Decades of Racist Housing Policy Left Neighborhoods Sweltering." *New York Times,* August 24, 2020.

Williams, Michael Paul. "Lillie Estes, 'Exemplar' of Community Organizing, Left Her Mark on Gilpin Court and Well Beyond." *Richmond Times Dispatch,* January 31, 2019.

## 3.12 Overby-Sheppard Elementary School

*2300 1st Avenue*

Opened in 1976, this elementary school is named after Ethel Overby, a Black Richmond educator, and Eleanor Sheppard, the city's first white female mayor. The school serves the Highland Park neighborhood, which European immigrants developed as a streetcar suburb at the end of the nineteenth century. The neighborhood became majority African American after post–World War II white flight.

Ethel Thompson Overby led crucial mid-century racial justice struggles in labor, education, and voting rights. In 1933, she

Overby-Sheppard students protest school budget cuts, 1989.

became the first female African American principal of a Black school in Richmond, the Elba School. There, she supervised fourteen teachers and advocated for civic engagement and participatory democratic practice. Overby publicly questioned why Black teachers and administrators made much less money for the same work as their white counterparts. Then, in the mid-1950s, after Virginia responded to federally mandated school desegregation with a plan of "massive resistance," she educated Black parents about Virginia's Pupil Placement Board. Created in 1956, Virginia's Pupil Placement Board claimed to indiscriminately place students at schools based on student welfare and efficient school management. In reality, it maintained school segregation under the guise of neutrality. Thus, Overby encouraged parents not to sign the forms. When the new school year began in 1957, 150 African American students arrived without their forms. Alice Calloway, representing a group of African American parents, challenged the constitutionality of the board in federal court; civil rights attorney Oliver Hill represented her. While legal challenges like this one weakened the impact of the board, it remained active until 1966 given its outwardly inconspicuous mission, which did not explicitly mention race.

Overby also was a founding member of the Richmond Crusade for Voters (RCV), created in 1956. Scholar Julian Hayter notes that "no civic organization did more to democratize local politics in twentieth-century Richmond." RCV registered thousands of Black voters, paid their poll taxes, and laid the groundwork for federal voting rights legislation. Virginia's "massive resistance" to school desegregation led to the initial founding of the RCV, and some of its first meetings took place in Overby's home. When Richmond elected its first majority-Black city council in 1977, all of its Black members were active RCV members.

**TO LEARN MORE**

Eskridge, Sara. "Virginia Pupil Placement Board and the Practical Applications of Massive Resistance." *Virginia Magazine of History and Biography* 118, no. 3 (2010): 246–76.
Hayter, Julian. *The Dream Is Lost: Voting Rights and the Politics of Race in Richmond, Virginia.* Lexington: University Press of Kentucky, 2017.
Pratt, Robert. *The Color of Their Skin: Education and Race in Richmond, Virginia, 1954–1989.* Charlottesville: University of Virginia Press, 1992.

## 3.13  Battery Park

Intersection of Hawthorne Avenue and Overbrook Road

In 1946, Richmond began using a ravine in Battery Park as a city dump, creating the Fells Street Landfill. The landfill generated controversy even before it opened, as residents of the newly opened Brookfield Gardens neighborhood, one of the first housing developments in the city created for professional Black residents, expressed concerns that their homes stood adjacent to it. Environmental concerns related to the landfill continued with the construction of A. V. Norrell Elementary in 1964, built on top of the landfill's northern section. From the outset, school officials reported prob-

Battery Park with basketball courts in the background. Tennis star Arthur Ashe trained on the park's tennis courts as a child in the 1950s and early 1960s, as the city denied him access to other city courts due to racial segregation.

lems related to gas from the landfill leaking into the school. In 1975, the school's population relocated for two years due to the presence of methane gas. As well, methane gas emanating from the landfill caused an explosion at a nearby apartment building, where fortunately no one was injured. The school reopened in 1977, and the city continued to use the dumpsite until 1979, when it placed a shallow cap over the site and deemed the landfill closed.

In summer 2006, severe flooding took place due to a tropical depression. The storm severely damaged the neighborhood's sewer lines when a sinkhole collapsed and caused wastewater to flow into the park and community. At its worst, floodwaters reached thirty feet deep and covered eighty acres of land. The city condemned over seventy homes and evacuated over 240 dwellings, including Norrell Elementary. For months, even small amounts of rain caused sewer water to flood into the park and neighborhood. The city received $21 million from FEMA to fix the problem, the largest grant given to a locality after Hurricane Katrina devastated the Gulf Coast in 2005.

Exposure to toxins can linger for decades as long-term environmental harm is difficult to fully contain or eradicate. In September 2012, after approval from the Richmond School Board, a Head Start preschool program moved into Norrell amid opposition from community members over whether methane gas, formaldehyde, and other toxins were present at the site. Parents and environmental justice activists organized to protest the board's lack of transparency and seeming lack of concern for the health and welfare of children. At a protest on September 4, 2012, activists handed out fliers and held picket signs that read, "Should gas masks be on our back to school list?" and "This is what environmental racism looks like." The movement quickly drew in prominent local civil rights activists, like Roxie Raines Allison, former president of the Richmond Crusade for Voters (RCV) and member of **Ebenezer Baptist Church** (page 78). At a 2013 protest, she told the local press: "It's on a dump, and we all know what that means if it's on a dump. Why did they pick children from our projects to come here? They didn't pick children from affluent families, who wouldn't stand for this. Not one second." Sustained pressure pushed for permanent closure, which succeeded in 2017.

**TO LEARN MORE**

Holmberg, Mark. "Would Wealthier Citizens Let Their Children Attend a 'Toxic' School?" *WTVR 6News Richmond*, January 21, 2013.

Williams, Michael Paul. "City Students Deserve Better Than Norrell." *Richmond Times-Dispatch*, September 7, 2012.

## 3.14  Walter Plecker Residence (former)

3610 Hawthorne Avenue

In 1912, Virginia lawmakers established the Bureau of Vital Statistics, which issued standardized birth, death, and marriage certificates to Virginians. Walter Plecker headed the bureau from 1912 to 1946, and he resided at this home in Ginter Park. Ginter Park was developed as a suburb for affluent white Richmonders at the turn of the twentieth century by industrialist Lewis Ginter. A streetcar line linked it to the city center.

Plecker, who served as a leader of the Anglo-Saxon Clubs of America, a Richmond-based white supremacist organization, also drafted the Racial Integrity Act. Passed by the state legislature in 1924, the Racial Integrity Act forbade interracial marriage and codified racial classifications. It also declared that someone could be classified as white only if they had "no trace whatsoever of any blood other than Caucasian," which became known as the "one drop rule." It also required birth certificates to denote racial designations, and birth certificates issued by the state were then required for enrolling children in school, further reinforcing racial segregation.

Plecker's position and clout afforded him enormous power over racial categorization. From 1924 onward, birth certificates for Indigenous people would no longer indicate "Indian" but "colored." Virginia Indians sought to be recognized as Indians in order to protect their sovereignty and survival as Indigenous people. While the act provided a small exception for people with marginal Indigenous ancestry, Plecker contended that Virginia contained no "true" Indians, arguing that all Indigenous communities had mixed with Black Virginians, making them "colored" as well.

Plecker's work tightened the boundaries surrounding who could gain the privileges of whiteness; it also caused what Pamunkey tribal chief William Miles later called "statistical genocide." By purging the classification of "Indian" from official state records, Virginia Indians, in pursuit of state and federal recognition, as well as other critical services related to housing, health care, and education, have faced enormous difficulty in proving their existence due to this intentional erasure of their Indigenous identification by the state. This work impacted both Black and Indigenous communities, but in different ways, as it tried to render Virginia Indians nonexistent while relegating Black Virginians to a legally inferior position in relation to white citizens.

**TO LEARN MORE**

Catte, Elizabeth. *Pure America: Eugenics and the Making of Modern Virginia*. Cleveland: Belt, 2021.

Fiske, Walter. "The Black and White World of Walter Ashby Plecker." *The Virginian-Pilot*, August 18, 2004.

Smith, J. Douglas. *Managing White Supremacy: Race, Politics, and Citizenship in Jim Crow Virginia*. Chapel Hill: University of North Carolina Press, 2002.

## 3.15 A. H. Robins Company (former)

*1407 Cummings Drive*

A family business with roots dating back to A. H. Robins Apothecary in 1866, the A. H. Robins Company opened its first manufacturing plant in 1953, moving its headquarters to this building in an industrial park. Perhaps best known for the products Robitussin and Chapstick, the company focused on creating medicines at low prices for common illnesses, then sold them worldwide to soaring profits.

In 1971, the company began selling the Dalkon Shield, a crab-shaped intrauterine contraceptive device (IUD). The company distributed 4.5 million devices in eighty countries before halting sales in 1975. The shield seriously injured tens of thousands of women and caused the deaths of at least twenty wearers in the U. S. alone. The device also caused premature birth, which led to severe birth defects in some cases. In addition to being deadly, it functioned poorly as a method of birth control. While the company insisted the Shield had a 1.1 percent pregnancy rate, accurate studies showed a 5–10 percent pregnancy rate, far higher than any other IUD on the market at the time. The Agency for International Development purchased nearly 700,000 for use in low-income countries. Deadly side effects were higher in areas that already had inadequate healthcare access.

Problems with the device mounted quickly. In 1972, physician Thad Earl of Ohio sent a letter to the company stating that in the women in which he had implanted the device, five had suffered life-threatening spontaneous septic abortions, an incredibly high number for one physician to observe. It was a particularly ominous sign since Earl was one of the first to promote the device as a well-paid consultant for the Robins Company. The Food and Drug Administration

New construction at the A.H. Robins Company, ca. 1960.

(FDA) asked the company to halt distribution in May 1974. The company declined, stating in company memos that such action would be a confession of liability. The company suspended U. S. sales later in 1974, but it continued to sell internationally for several more months. The company distributed 4.5 million devices in eighty countries before halting sales in 1975. Even so, the company was not forced to recall the device until 1985, a full decade after sales had been suspended. By the company's own conservative estimate, 4 percent of all Shield users had been injured by that time, and more than 200,000 U. S. women eventually testified to being harmed by the device. The company filed for bankruptcy in 1985 amidst protests. As part of its court-ordered settlement, the company established the Dalkon Shield Claimants Trust, a settlement fund in excess of $2 billion to compensate those injured by the devices. Today, this building houses a large plumbing company.

## TO LEARN MORE

Grant, Nicole. *The Selling of Contraception: The Dalkon Shield Case, Sexuality, and Women's Autonomy.* Columbus: Ohio State University Press, 1992.

Mintz, Morton. *At Any Cost: Corporate Greed, Women, and the Dalkon Shield.* New York: Pantheon, 1985.

## 3.16 Virginia Department of Alcoholic Beverage Control (ABC) Headquarters (former location)

*2901 Hermitage Road*

Established in 1934, the Virginia ABC (Alcoholic Beverage Control) agency regulates and enforces the state's alcohol laws. This agency often functioned as a leading state adversary against LGBTQ communities as it sought to close alcohol-serving establishments catering to LGBTQ folks. In the 1940s, ABC crafted a number of regulations to eliminate gay and lesbian communities' access to businesses that served alcohol. Statutes noted that a bar's license could be suspended or revoked if it became a meeting place for "homosexuals" as well as "users of narcotics, drunks, prostitutes, pimps, panderers, and gamblers." It also forbade owners of alcohol-serving establishments from hiring anyone with a "general reputation" of being homosexual.

Enforcement of ABC laws became more rigorous after World War II as the visibility of LGBTQ community members increased. In March 1969, ABC agents closed two popular LGBTQ-friendly bars in Richmond: Renee's and Rathskellers. Agents sus-

Virginia Alcoholic Beverage Control Headquarters from 1971–2021.

pended Renee's license after ABC agents reported seeing men wearing makeup and kissing inside, and they closed Rathskellers on claims that it served homosexuals. From the 1930s to the 1980s, many LGBTQ gathering spaces faced a similar fate. These closures sparked some of the first public actions against LGBTQ discrimination, with Hunter Patch Adams, a student at the Medical College of Virginia, protesting the closures in a letter published in the local newspaper. He wrote: "I find myself too humble to be presumptuous enough to think I'm more deserving a beer than a homosexual is. I'm afraid that in the atomic powered age, I feel no safer drinking with heterosexuals."

Virginians for Justice organized in 1989 to fight for LGBTQ equality in the state. In 1991, their efforts to organize citizens and legislators alike led to a court ruling that declared the ABC agency's anti-LGBTQ regulations unconstitutional. Shirley Lesser, the organization's chair, called the court order a "victory that will help invigorate our movement and the fight for equal justice. The

Commonwealth of Virginia can no longer assume that gays and lesbians are unable to organize to protect themselves from bad laws whether they are on the books or under consideration." Virginians for Justice continues its mission today as Equality Virginia. This site served as Virginia ABC headquarters until 2021, when it relocated to a larger site in Hanover County.

**TO LEARN MORE**

Marschak, Beth, and Alex Lorch. *Lesbian and Gay Richmond*. Charleston: Arcadia, 2008.

### 3.17  Bryan Park

4308 Hermitage Road

Formally opened as a park in 1910, enslaved and free Black people prior to the Civil War often gathered in this isolated space five miles from downtown Richmond on Sundays. Many enslaved people who lived and worked in Richmond were hired out from surrounding plantations. This arrangement meant they spent much of their time away from their enslavers. They made money not

Bryan Park.

only for their enslavers but also for themselves. Freedom of movement provided more opportunity to turn their labor into profit, as they could hire out their services. While still enslaved, they often faced less scrutiny and were allowed more freedom of movement than those living on plantations. Custom dictated that most hired-out enslaved people did not work on Sundays. They used that time to gather at places like today's Bryan Park.

It is here that Gabriel, enslaved to Thomas Prosser, and others planned a rebellion against slavery in 1800. As a skilled blacksmith hired out by Prosser, Gabriel traveled widely for work and knew the city well. The conspirators planned to start a fire in downtown Richmond to draw residents out of their homes and create disorder. Meanwhile, others prepared to overwhelm

Tribute to Gabriel at Devil's Half Acre, 2020.

guards at key sites where state arms and ammunition were stored. In the chaos, they hoped to seize the governor and demand an end to enslavement. To prepare, the group transformed tools into weapons, made musket balls, and gathered gunpowder, using their places of work to create and gather supplies. The group intended to attack on the evening of August 30, but that morning, officials learned of the plot. At the same time, the conspirators delayed the attack due to a bad storm, and patrols began jailing suspected conspirators. Gabriel boarded a ship to Norfolk and initially evaded capture, but a crew member turned him in on September 23. Virginia publicly executed Gabriel and twenty-five co-conspirators.

In response to the narrowly thwarted threat of armed rebellion among enslaved people, Virginia tightened legal restrictions around enslavement. Teaching enslaved people to read again became illegal as did some forms of hiring out, although this system, which continued to benefit white enslavers, did not slow in Richmond. In Black communities, the fame of Gabriel grew, and he became known as "General Gabriel" to recognize his extraordinary contributions to liberation. In 2002, the city of Richmond passed a resolution honoring Gabriel, and in 2007, Virginia governor Tim Kaine issued a pardon, praising Gabriel's aim of securing equality for all people. Public historian and activist Ana Edwards notes that Gabriel's story "remains the underground good story," signaling how the memory of the rebellion has endured and spread in Black communities and beyond despite a lack of public memorialization in the landscape and historical texts. A road in Bryan Park bears Gabriel's name, but no other memorialization exists here.

## TO LEARN MORE

Egerton, Douglas. *Gabriel's Rebellion: The Virginia Slave Conspiracies of 1800 and 1802.* Chapel Hill: University of North Carolina Press, 1993.

Sidbury, James. *Ploughshares into Swords: Race, Rebellion, and Identity in Gabriel's Virginia, 1730–1810.* Cambridge: Cambridge University Press, 1997.

4

The
Fan
and
West
End

# Introduction

**LARGELY UNDEVELOPED PRIOR TO THE CIVIL** War, the city planned this area to incentivize white residency west of downtown in the late nineteenth century. To aid in this effort, officials erected a statue of confederate general Robert E. Lee on Monument Avenue in 1890. The monument glorified the Lost Cause, a white supremacist understanding of the Civil War that interpreted it as a just, heroic battle over states' rights rather than a war fought over the enslavement of African Americans. Monument Avenue became a well-manicured, tree-lined street that eventually included five confederate statues. These statues, erected in the early twentieth century alongside laws and practices aimed at residential segregation, spatially marked this area of the city as white.

Richmonders contested and reshaped placemaking along Monument Avenue in response to these monuments. From the avenue's inception, Black activists and community leaders consistently spoke out against lionizing white racist leaders in the city landscape, and in 1996, the city placed a statue in recognition of African American tennis star, humanitarian, and Richmonder Arthur Ashe at its western edge. In 2019, the city changed the name of the boulevard, a north–south artery that intersects with Monument Avenue, to Arthur Ashe Boulevard. That same year, African American artist Kehinde Wiley installed his *Rumors of War* statue three blocks south of Monument Avenue at the Virginia Museum of

Fine Arts, deliberately challenging the dominance of the city's confederate memorialization at the time.

Monument Avenue became the center of anti-racist activism during the summer of 2020. Amidst a global pandemic, Black activists and their allies led daily demonstrations to demand policy changes to end systemic racism in the aftermath of George Floyd's murder by Minneapolis police. Confederate monuments loomed large as symbols of white supremacy, and by the end of 2020, only the Lee statue remained on the avenue. Community members renamed the circle surrounding Lee the Marcus-David Peters Circle and reclaimed it as an inclusive community space. The state removed this monument in 2021.

Monument Avenue's history illustrates the contentious legacies and geographies of white supremacy and affluence in this area. The Fan and West End include the city's most affluent census tract, Windsor Farms, but it also contains hidden neighborhoods. Ziontown and Westwood, for example, developed here following the Civil War, as African Americans who worked for nearby white families and businesses, as well as those who created their own businesses, moved nearby.

In the 1970s, the building of the Downtown Expressway bit into the working-class white neighborhood of Oregon Hill as well as African American neighborhoods. Today, much of Oregon Hill is occupied by Virginia

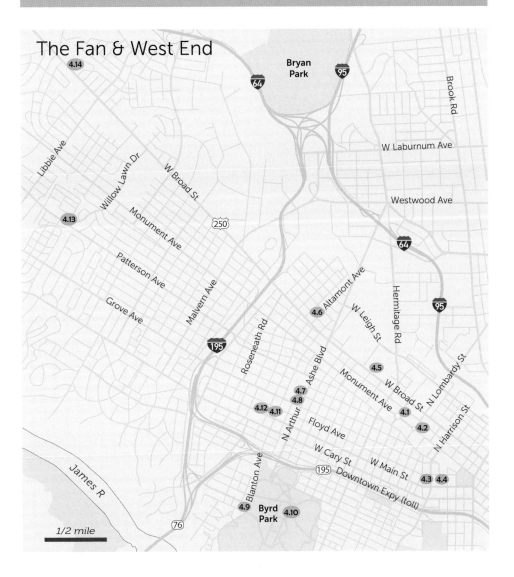

## The Fan & West End

4.14

Bryan Park

Brook Rd

W Laburnum Ave

Westwood Ave

Libbie Ave

Willow Lawn Dr

W Broad St

Monument Ave

4.13

Patterson Ave

Grove Ave

Malvern Ave

Roseneath Rd

Altamont Ave

4.6

W Leigh St

Hermitage Rd

N Lombardy St

4.5

Ashe Blvd

W Broad St

Monument Ave

4.1

N Harrison St

4.7

4.8

4.12 4.11

N Arthur

Floyd Ave

4.2

W Cary St

W Main St

4.3 4.4

Blanton Ave

Downtown Expy (toll)

4.9 Byrd 4.10
Park

James R

1/2 mile

Commonwealth University (VCU) students as the university has steadily encroached into this neighborhood over the last fifty years. The state founded VCU in 1968 when it merged the Medical College of Virginia with the Richmond Professional Institute. Its growth into a large urban institution has reshaped many adjacent neighborhoods. Much of the lower Fan became a

racially diverse space occupied by students, artists, and LGBTQ folks. Due to continual expansion in student population and real estate development, VCU generates tension among city residents, who are concerned over heightened policing in the name of student safety and escalating real estate prices as a result of the ways in which the university's expansive development has pushed out

The *Say Their Names* mural features the image of Richmond rapper Radio Blitz situated among the names of people of color murdered by police. Silly Genius and Nils Westergard created it as part of the 2020 Mending Walls RVA project.

longtime residents of neighborhoods like Jackson Ward, Oregon Hill, and Carver.

In the 1960s and 1970s, significant rehabilitation projects began in the Fan. Scholar Matthew Lassiter described the neighborhood at that time as an "island suburb," a cluster of affluent white residences within the city limits that resisted racial integration through a range of exclusionary residential and zoning policies. While always majority white, the Fan became a center for LGBTQ organizing and gathering as the growth of its student and artist populations in the 1970s made it a more welcoming, progressive neighborhood.

Likewise, Carytown, a shopping district occupied primarily by independent businesses, has historically been an LGBTQ-friendly space, cultivating LGBTQ-owned and -friendly businesses as well as sites of LGBTQ activism, like pride parades. Carytown once housed an African American neighborhood immediately to its south, displaced by the Downtown Expressway and, later, by economically mobile whites looking to move closer to this popular area. Today, local, independent businesses organize to fend off infringement by corporate chains with varying levels of success.

The Fan and West End are also artistic and cultural centers, due to VCU's flourishing art school as well as its proximity to the downtown and Jackson Ward art scenes. The Virginia Museum of Fine Arts (VMFA) and the VCU Institute for Contemporary Art (ICA), two artistic centers of power, are located here. The VMFA, as a white-led, exclusive, traditional art space, often exists in tension with the city's grassroots artists, cultural producers, and community makers. This area also houses smaller, edgy spaces of artistic production, like Richmond Triangle Players' Robert B. Moss Theatre, which produces LGBTQ-centered productions, and Firehouse Theatre, which brings community-engaged work to a former firehouse just steps from VCU's campus.

Scott's Addition, a newly developed enclave fueled largely by the city's exten-

## VINNIE GONZALEZ
**Interdisciplinary Artist, Actor, Theatre Director, and Theatre Designer**

My father and his brother were adopted by my grandparents in Colorado. My grandfather immigrated from Mexico. Both my parents grew up in Colorado. I never paid attention to race. I never focused on it until I started doing theatre because there were no roles for me. I told another actor, "You can play a John Smith. They look at me, they see a Juan Smith." That was the issue here in Richmond. Diversity is often a black/white issue, not a multicultural issue. It's starting to change, but for the longest time, in practice, it wasn't.

This is how we read people. Until you get to know me, you might think of me as just another Hispanic. I do not think of myself in that way. I don't even speak Spanish.

I have always loved the arts. Everything about the arts: painting, sculpture, design, building, and entertaining. It is an addiction. Theatre is an addiction; arts is an addiction. It's all addictive to me.

You don't see many Hispanic people doing theatre in Richmond, because they are not producing work for Hispanics. Do something against the norm, make it diverse. That's how my idea for directing *Oedipus* at Firehouse Theater with an all-Black cast set in the South came about. It's my favorite piece I've ever directed. I was there every night of the show. Not because I had to be there. I wanted to be there because I loved it. I love theatre.

sive craft brewery and food scene, is the city's hippest neighborhood at the start of the 2020s. Drawn to this longtime industrial and commercial district, Richmond Triangle Players pioneered a move into a former radiator shop here in 2010. Since then, developers have transformed the area's former warehouses and garages into luxury lofts, restaurants, breweries, and cideries, attracting a young, affluent crowd of residents and patrons.

To the west, Willow Lawn opened as the city's first suburban shopping center in 1956; today, residential and commercial development continues to extend farther west. Along with white residents, Asian communities, particularly immigrants from India, Vietnam, and Cambodia, make their home

in the West End. The locations of Indian restaurants off of Broad Street and Vietnamese restaurants along Staples Mill and Horsepen Roads, as well as numerous Asian grocers and markets, point to these growing communities. The University of Richmond sits on the city's western edge, and in the early 2020s, was a site of contestation over buildings bearing the names of once-prominent university figures who were enslavers and segregationists.

While the neighborhoods of the Fan and West End grow in affluency, their public spaces continue to be reshaped and renegotiated. Key themes of exclusive, often racist, and classist economic and community development policies resonate throughout this chapter alongside the origins and remnants of Lost Cause mythologies, Black resistance, and ongoing community organizing. Themes of artistic and cultural work and LGBTQ community-building also are prominent.

# The Fan and West End Sites

## 4.1 Marcus-David Peters Circle (formerly Lee Circle)

1600 Monument Avenue

On May 29, 1890, to direct development west of downtown while also delineating white space, the city erected a sixty-foot statue of confederate general Robert E. Lee here. John Mitchell Jr., editor of the African American newspaper the *Richmond Planet,* presciently noted that the labor of Black men helped to transport and erect the monument and "should the time come, will be there to take it down."

One hundred thirty years later, on June 1, 2020, police used tear gas to disperse a crowd of peaceful protestors gathered at the site. Protests across the country, including Richmond, began five days earlier in the wake of Minneapolis police officer Derek Chauvin killing George Floyd by kneeling on his neck for almost nine minutes. As activist Kalia Harris noted for the *Race Capitol* podcast, "Here, in the fallen capital of the confederacy, when we ask what makes us feel truly safe and what we need to protect ourselves from harm and to heal from harm when it's done to us, it is clear that we

don't need more police and punishment but material resources, reparations, and a move away from a carceral system that doesn't prevent or end so-called crime . . . We know that the safest communities are not the ones with more police; they are the ones with more resources and equitable access for all to those resources."

After police action here, this space transformed into a site of protest, celebration, and community reclamation. Community members renamed it Marcus-David Peters Circle and erected a sign declaring "Welcome to Beautiful Marcus-David Peters Circle, Liberated by the People MMXX." The site commemorated the life of Peters, a twenty-four-year-old African American man who Richmond police killed as he suffered a mental health crisis in May 2018. Demands for a Marcus Alert system that would send mental health professionals to respond first in a mental health crisis, instead of police, gained national attention in the aftermath of his death.

The circle became a vibrant community gathering space. People sold hot dogs and water, played basketball on makeshift courts, and dancers and musicians performed regularly. People covered the statue's base with slogans and signs in support of racial justice and police abolition. They created makeshift memorials for those killed by police. Local artists projected images of Black liberators onto the statue after dark. The circle also became more accessible. Richmonders spray-painted a crosswalk onto the street and created ramps for wheelchair users, making it both more pedestrian friendly and

(Above) Marcus-David Peters Circle, 2020.

(Left) Musicians playing at Marcus-David Peters Circle, 2020.

accessible for people who use chairs for the first time in its history. At times, police and others destroyed some of this material, but almost always, destroyed or stolen material reappeared, often in larger and improved forms. In October 2020, the *New York Times* named the circle the number-one site of protest art in the U.S. since World War II. It remains a contested space of negotiation between community members and local officials.

**TO LEARN MORE**

Gordon, Wyatt. "A New Kind of Placemaking Has Transformed Richmond's Monument Avenue." *Greater Greater Washington,* August 24, 2020.

La Force, Thessaly. "The 25 Most Influential Works of American Protest Art since World War II." *New York Times Style Magazine,* October 15, 2020.

Listen to the award-winning local podcast *Race Capitol,* founded by Chelsea Higgs Wise and co-hosted by Wise, Naomi Isaac, and Kalia Harris at https://www.racecapitol.com/.

Pedestal of confederate general J.E.B. Stuart statue, removed in 2020.

## 4.2 Stuart Circle

*Monument Avenue at N. Lombardy Street*

The city named Stuart Circle for the monument to confederate general J. E. B Stuart, erected in 1907 and dismantled as a result of anti-racist protests in 2020. On August 13, 2016, more than 8,000 people marched in hundred-degree heat down this section of Monument Avenue to demand a federal minimum wage of $15 per hour. The marchers intentionally chose this highly trafficked part of the avenue for their action in direct contradiction to the symbols of white supremacy that lined it, as they linked economic and racial justice.

The Fight for $15 brought its third convention to Richmond that weekend. This national organization chose Richmond due to its history as the second-largest slave trading center in the U.S. and the former capital of the confederacy. Its organizers drew explicit connections between centuries of racial injustice and present-day poverty wages earned by low-wage workers, most of whom are workers of color. The Fight for $15 movement originated when fast-food workers in New York City walked off of

their minimum-wage jobs in 2012 to demand higher wages. The movement for a $15 hourly minimum wage expanded to include anyone earning poverty-level wages. Advocates emphasized the critical intersections between economic rights, workers' rights, and racial justice. This convention brought together low-wage workers from industries as wide ranging as airport workers, childcare workers, home health workers, security officers, restaurant workers, custodians, and adjunct professors. Lauralyn Clark, a home health worker from Caroline County who attended the convention, commented: "Home care workers like me have never been treated with the respect we deserve. For far too long, we've been left out of basic labor protections and denied the minimum wage and overtime pay. This has to stop, and that's what this convention is all about."

According to the Economic Policy Institute, raising the federal minimum hourly wage to $15 would lift the wages of over 28 million Americans, disproportionally raising the wages of women and people of color. Due to the work of Fight for $15 activists and others, dozens of municipalities around the nation have instituted a $15 minimum wage. Their work led to policy change in Virginia as well; legislators voted in 2020 to incrementally raise the minimum wage to $12 by 2023. Unfortunately, this raise did not meet the group's demand for $15 per hour. It also fell short of a living wage, which MIT's 2020 Living Wage Calculator set at $16 per hour in Richmond for one adult supporting no dependents.

**TO LEARN MORE**

Lazarus, Jeremy. "Fight for $15." *Richmond Free Press,* August 12, 2016.

Rupcich, Claudia. "Thousands March on Monument for $15 Minimum Wage." wtvr. com, August 13, 2016.

Hundreds of people march in Richmond's third annual AIDS vigil, sponsored by Fan Free Clinic, in 1988.

## 4.3  Fan Free Clinic (former)

1103 Floyd Avenue

In 1970, a group of medical professionals established the Fan Free Clinic, Virginia's first free health clinic. According to co-founder Robert Bulford: "In the summer of 1969, I was asked by Mary File, a nurse who lived in the Fan, to help start a free clinic, primarily to serve college students . . . File was determined that it would succeed and engaged the services of Drs. Robert Petres and William Fitzhugh. She asked me to give general help and do counseling. There was no other free clinic anywhere that we knew that could serve as a model. With nothing to emulate, we simply did it on our own." The clinic temporarily operated out of this small space before moving to the Unitarian Universalist church in October 1970; it moved frequently

in the beginning as it quickly outgrew space due to high patient volume. From its inception, the clinic provided care for low-income and uninsured community members. It was uniquely situated to serve high-risk populations, like those experiencing homelessness and living in extreme poverty.

Initially focused on providing women with access to oral contraceptives and preventing sexually transmitted diseases, the clinic responded with both medical and personal support when HIV/AIDS arrived in the city in the 1980s. It established the state's first community-based HIV/AIDS outreach program. Community care teams went into neighborhood communities to provide services to those living and dying with HIV/AIDS, which included outreach to many individuals who had been abandoned by their friends and families. Early in the twenty-first century, the clinic began providing medical services to transgender people and changed its name. Its legacy continues today as Health Brigade, located a couple of miles away at 1010 N. Thompson Street. This building is now a private residence.

**TO LEARN MORE**

Bluford, Robert. "Fan Free Clinic: A Glow in the Midst of the Shadows." *Richmond Times-Dispatch,* March 7, 2010.

## 4.4 University Student Commons, Virginia Commonwealth University

907 Floyd Avenue

The University Student Commons and the surrounding public space is a central site for student organizing at Virginia Commonwealth University (VCU). Starting in 2018, the student group UndocuRams used it to mobilize students, staff, and faculty to improve life on campus for undocumented students. In 2014, Virginia allowed state DACA (Deferred Action for Childhood Arrivals) recipients to establish residency in Virginia. President Barack Obama created this federal program in 2012 via executive memorandum to allow some undocumented people brought into the country as children to receive renewable, temporary protections against deportation and work permits. This meant that undocumented young people born outside of the U. S. brought to the country as children could qualify for in-state tuition at Virginia's public universities.

Activists continue to push for both higher-education access and in-state tuition for all undocumented Virginians, regardless of DACA status. To raise awareness and exert pressure at their university, Yanet Limon-Amado and other students formed UndocuRams at VCU in 2018. (The name references the university's mascot.) VCU is a large, public university that sits adjacent to downtown Richmond. UndocuRams advocates for the specific needs of undocumented college students, both on campus and at the state legislature. Members share stories that illustrate the difficulties of navigating a complicated system that often fails to recognize undocumented students. As of this writing, VCU, like most of Virginia's public institutions of higher education, admits undocumented students but does not enroll them without some form of legal documentation. This establishes a system whereby students spend time and money applying for admission, but because they are unaware of, or cannot attain, the required documentation, they are ultimately unable to enroll. UndocuRams regularly held marches and press conferences to bring attention to this issue in this heavily trafficked campus space outside of the Student Commons.

In early 2020, Virginia passed in-state tuition for all undocumented Virginians, regardless of DACA status, which represents a significant financial savings, as most state institutions charge more than double for out-of-state tuition. However, for this change to be effective in increasing higher-education access for undocumented Virginians, institu-

PERSONAL REFLECTION

**YANET LIMON-AMADO**
Immigrant Rights Organizer and Activist

My work started in 2013 when I graduated from high school in Henrico County. Back then, there weren't any support systems for undocumented students. Even the words undocumented or illegal seemed forbidden; we were not allowed to talk about it. We were scared to talk about it. I told myself that I was going to college and I did go to college. I first went to a local community college and paid out-of-state tuition. Even with DACA (Deferred Action for Childhood Arrivals), it was confusing and it took me a year to obtain DACA status. So my college application was initially denied because of my status. I knew they couldn't do that but I didn't know how to advocate for myself. That's where all of my advocacy started. I knew how lonely I felt and I knew that's not what I wanted my sister or any other undocumented student to go through. I've always followed my intuition when things did not feel good to me. My foundation for advocacy came from thinking that if we were going to fight for something, we were going to fight for all undocumented students, not just those with DACA.

tions will need to change their current policies that require documentation for matriculation. Activists organized through groups like UndocuRams have been fundamental in pressuring the state to make these changes, and college students have taken the lead in the fight for in-state tuition alongside equitable treatment of undocumented students in campus admission processes.

**TO LEARN MORE**

Limon-Amado, Yanet. "Losing DACA Would, On Top of Everything Else, Double My College Tuition." *Washington Post,* November 12, 2019.

Halloran, Sybil. "Fear, Funding, and Ambiguity: The Policy Dilemmas of Undocumented Students in Virginia Institutions of Higher Education." Virginia Commonwealth University thesis, 2015.

## 4.5 Department of Motor Vehicles

2300 W. Broad Street

On September 22, 2010, activists led a protest outside of Richmond's Department of Motor Vehicles (DMV) to protest Governor Bob McDonnell's decision to further restrict who could acquire a state-issued driver's license. Protestors chanted: "Hey McDonnell, shame on you, immigrants are people too" and "Land of the free? Not for me!" One month earlier, Carlos Montano was involved in a traffic accident that killed Sister Denise Mosier, a Benedictine nun. Montano, an undocumented immigrant, held a Virginia-issued license that he had legally acquired using a federal employment authorization document. At the time of the accident, Montano was intoxicated and awaiting deportation due to prior charges of driving while intoxicated. In 1996, Congress passed the Illegal Immigration Reform and Immigrant Responsibility Act, which expanded deportation for undocumented people who committed crimes like this one within the U.S.

McDonnell ordered the DMV to stop accepting federal employment authorization documents as proof of residency in the U. S. Montano possessed this document even though his deportation was pending. McDonnell seized conservative momentum to argue that the federal government could not be trusted to properly issue or rescind these documents, ordering the DMV to stop using them as proof of residency. This policy created a significant change since establishing residency is required for a license and this form was the primary one used for that purpose. It made it nearly impossible for undocumented immigrants, including refugees, to obtain licenses that they needed to commute to work in order to provide for their families.

Prior to 2004, Virginia required no proof of authorization to live in the U. S. to acquire a license. However, the state came under national scrutiny in the aftermath of 9/11, as seven of the nineteen people who hijacked planes that day had legally obtained identification cards from a Virginia DMV. After 9/11, how states issued driver's licenses became heavily influenced by federal national security standards. As a result, Virginia's 2003 General Assembly passed laws mandating that those applying for a driver's license must show proof of authorization to be in the United States. McDonnell's restrictions in 2010 worked to further restrict these categories.

The protest called out the governor's attempt to use one tragic incident to make life harder for all undocumented immigrants. In 2020, with a Democratic majority and years of pressure from immigrant rights groups, the General Assembly passed the "licenses for all" act, allowing undocu-

mented residents to apply for a driver privilege card, which is similar to a license except it cannot be used as proof of identity for voting. Sendy Portillo, who immigrated to Richmond from El Salvador in 2008, worked alongside Virginia Organizing to advocate for this legislation. As she comments, undocumented immigrants "know that they don't have documents but they're trying to do things right. They just want to work and take care of their families."

**TO LEARN MORE**

Nguyen, Tram. "A Win for Undocumented Immigrants Is a Win for All." *Virginia Mercury,* March 27, 2020.

## 4.6  Richmond Triangle Players' Robert B. Moss Theatre

1300 Altamont Avenue

This present-day location of Richmond Triangle Players opened in a former radiator shop in 2010.

In November 1992, at the height of the AIDS epidemic, a group of local theatre artists and business owners gathered to discuss how they could bring attention and voice to the experiences of people in their community.

Playbill for Richmond Triangle Players' 1997 production of *Deranged Durang: An Evening of Dementia* written by Christopher Durang and directed by Steve J. Earle.

PERSONAL REFLECTION

**STEVE EARLE**
**Co-Founder, Richmond Triangle Players and Chair, Theatre Department at the Governor's School of the Arts**

It was hard to find plays about gay people that were positive back then. We were just longing for community that was positive. I was having beers with friends. I was complaining. They didn't want to do this play, and we were talking about the raging AIDS epidemic. It was a scary time in our community in the late '80s and early '90s. Michael Gooding, who became the Managing Director and the driving force, said, "Steve, if I find you a space, do you want to do your play?" We were not trying to form a theatre company. We were trying to do something for our community. Everywhere I went, I would run into people saying, "We saw you in that play. You have to do another one!" That's when we realized the community was just aching for this. We called it a basement theatre in an attic room. We were putting together money to build sets ourselves. We built a stage. We tore the door out of a bifold closet, and took plexiglass using the pane from my front door to create the light booth. We built our own lightboard. The stage was so small we could reach up and focus lights standing in a chair. It wasn't until it started to explode that I even realized what it was. I found a home, an amazing community of like-minded people with love in their hearts, and did they give back! I'm just grateful to have been part of it.

They presented a three-night sold-out benefit to raise money for local AIDS organizations. Actors performed a series of one-act plays called *Safe Sex* at Fielden's, an after-hours, members-only club formerly located one mile away at 2033 W. Broad Street that catered to the LGBTQ community.

The success of the benefit galvanized the community and demonstrated the need to produce socially significant theatre directly related to the experiences of the LGBTQ community. As a result of support from the LGBTQ community, Michael Gooding, Steve J. Earle, Jackie Singleton, and Marcus Miller founded the Richmond Triangle Players (RTP) at Fielden's in 1993. The theater drew seasoned and aspiring artists alike, volunteers, and community members to support productions portraying empowered stories of resilience, survival, and strength of the LGBTQ community.

After seventeen years of operating in donated space at the top floor of Fielden's,

RTP transformed a car repair shop formerly at this address on Altamont Avenue into a performing arts facility that opened in 2010. According to cofounder Steve Earle, "Michael Gooding, who started the campaign, was a genius. Through the generosity of so much of the LGBT community coming out to our shows and supporting us to do more, we were able to get people behind us to build a capital fund. People poured out their hearts and were incredibly generous." The theater is named after local realtor Robert B. Moss, whose naming gift helped make the move financially possible.

Since its founding, RTP moved from a fringe theater that produced works by, for, and with LGBTQ folks to a much broader audience base, while still maintaining its focus on showcasing diverse LGBTQ stories. Its move into Scott's Addition, known for its repair shops and warehouses, led the neighborhood's transition into what has become one of Richmond's most popular cultural centers. It began as, and remains, the only LGBTQ-focused theater in the state.

**TO LEARN MORE**

Timberline, David. "A Proud Quarter Century." *Style Weekly*, November 14, 2017.

Marschak, Beth, and Alex Lorch. *Lesbian and Gay Richmond*. Charleston: Arcadia, 2008.

Visit the Richmond Triangle Players website at https://rtriangle.org/.

Kehinde Wiley's *Rumors of War* statue on the grounds of the Virginia Museum of Fine Arts.

## 4.7 *Rumors of War* Statue at the Virginia Museum of Fine Arts

*200 N. Arthur Ashe Boulevard*

On December 10, 2019, the Virginia Museum of Fine Arts (VMFA) unveiled Kehinde Wiley's *Rumors of War* statue to a crowd of thousands. The twenty-seven-foot-tall, thirty-ton bronze statue atop a limestone pedestal sits just three blocks south of Monument Avenue along Arthur Ashe Boulevard, which had been renamed for the African American tennis star six months before the unveiling. Wiley is known for creating works utilizing classic European art traditions that center Black individuals in contemporary settings. His work addresses the historic absence of Black people from artwork considered canonical.

*Rumors of War* deliberately referenced the statue of confederate general J. E. B. Stuart

On January 26, 2021, community member and Richmond Public School music teacher Beth Almore wrote An Open Letter to the Virginia Museum of Fine Arts after the state gave the institution oversight to reimagine Monument Avenue. Concerned about the lack of community inclusion in the process, this excerpt speaks to what must remain at Marcus-David Peters Circle. Read the letter in its entirety at https://monumentalmemorials.blogspot.com/2021/01/open-letter-to-director-of-virginia.html.

We have brilliant artists right here in Richmond, and we expect their work, their voices, their vision to be centered. Spontaneous music and dance performances should continue. We do not want the Commonwealth to require permitting that will quash spontaneous expressions of joy and freedom.

We know that wealthy white residents don't "like" the basketball hoops. That is why they must stay. We know that wealthy white residents don't "like" being forced to look at Black bodies wearing culturally symbolic clothing whilst expressing their opinions, enjoying sunshine, and relaxing, when they are ordinarily confined to "Black" neighborhoods. That is why they, the protestors, must stay.

In short, we do not want this space sanitized for the comfort of the wealthy and those who prefer the status quo.

We are curious to hear how a museum can operate in this space. Your goals are preservation, while our goals are progress. Can these two modalities overlap? You will want artifacts to remain unchanged so that they can be cataloged and have monetary value assigned to them. We celebrate change. We love how the plinth changes almost daily. We love that we cannot predict what artists or musicians will appear and spontaneously make music or install 2-D artworks.

that stood on Monument Avenue from 1907 until its removal in 2020. Instead of a white general on horseback, Wiley's version features a young Black man with dreadlocks wearing a hoodie, ripped jeans, and high-top Nikes astride a horse. Its counterpoint, formerly located on Monument Avenue, no longer exists. While no protestors or confederate flags were present at the unveiling, VMFA's next-door neighbor, the United Daughters of the Confederacy, refused to let spectators gather on its lawn to watch the ceremony. At the event, Richmond mayor Levar Stoney noted that for the first time, many Richmonders had a monument of a rider on a horse that looked like them.

Within two years of *Rumors of War*'s installation, all of the confederate monuments lining Monument Avenue had been removed.

Spatial contestations of power and leadership endure. In 2021, Virginia awarded the VMFA several million dollars to spearhead the work to reenvision Monument Avenue. Community activists and artists quickly organized to express their concern at the power afforded a white-led, elite art institution to control what had begun and been sustained as a Black-led and Black-centered community effort. In April 2022, the state conveyed all of the property in question to the city and severed project ties to the VMFA, noting that the city now owned all of the property, thus removing the state from the process. The work to reenvision Monument Avenue remains in limbo.

## TO LEARN MORE

Almore, Beth. "Open Letter to the Director of the Virginia Museum of Fine Arts." January 26, 2021.

Capps, Kriston. "Kehinde Wiley's Anti-confederate Memorial." *New Yorker,* December 24, 2019.

Smith, Ryan K. *"Rumors of War* Arrives in the South: Changes to Richmond's Monumental Landscape." *Perspectives on History,* May 18, 2020.

## 4.8 The Virginia Flaggers

Corner of Arthur Ashe Boulevard at Grove Avenue in front of the Virginia Museum of Fine Arts

In 2010, when the Sons of Confederate Veterans (SCV) renewed their lease on the Confederate War Memorial Chapel, also known as the Pelham Chapel, on the grounds of the Virginia Museum of Fine Arts (VMFA), the museum required the group to remove the two confederate battle flags being flown at the site. The location where the VMFA currently resides is the former site of Robert E. Lee Camp No. 1, a soldiers' home for ailing confederate veterans founded in 1884, to which the chapel was connected. The site reverted to the state when the last veteran died in 1941. Research done by the VMFA showed that confederate flags had not historically been flown at the chapel. Instead, the flag-flying began in the 1990s when the SCV began leasing it.

In response to the removal of the flags, Susan Hathaway founded the Virginia Flag-

gers in September 2011. This group began twice-weekly protests featuring a highly visible display of confederate flags stationed in front of the museum. The group extended its work across the state, attending local government meetings to advocate for the preservation of confederate statues and flags. Due to the group's lack of success in derailing the momentum to remove confederate sites and symbols, the flaggers began buying small plots of land alongside interstates in order to erect enormous confederate flags in highly trafficked locations. The group raised its first flag just south of Richmond adjacent to Interstate 95 in 2013. In 2015, the VMFA did not renew the SCV's lease on the chapel, instead negotiating a use agreement that gave the VMFA control over the interpretation of the chapel to visitors. The flaggers still protest at this site, although with much less frequency as the movement in the city has clearly shifted to eradicating symbols of white supremacy.

## TO LEARN MORE

Levin, Kevin. "For Virginia Flaggers, It's Hate, Not Heritage." *Daily Beast,* April 13, 2017.

Maurantonio, Nicole. *Confederate Exceptionalism: Civil War Myth and Memory in the Twenty-First Century.* Lawrence: University Press of Kansas, 2019.

## 4.9 First Unitarian Universalist Church of Richmond

1000 Blanton Avenue

Abbie Arevalo-Herrera and her family moved into this church on June 18, 2018, to seek sanctuary from deportation. Five years earlier, Arevalo-Herrera and her daughter fled an abusive relationship in Honduras, seeking asylum in the United States. Processed by the U. S. Border Patrol in Texas, Arevalo-Herrera was issued a "notice to appear" with no date attached to the notice; she then traveled to Richmond, where she had family and where Latino communities have experienced expansive growth since 2000. She was tried in absentia without notice of the court date in 2015; at that time, a judge ordered her to leave the country. She has been fighting the verdict since she received no notice of it, but she cannot apply for asylum since she missed her court date. Her case illustrates the bureaucratic tangle facing many asylum-seekers and refugees in the United States. With mass deportations on the rise, she and her family moved into this church, hoping to find sanctuary there, given the tacit agreement that immigration officials will not enter certain spaces like religious institutions. Arevalo-Herrera joined several dozen undocumented immigrant families nationwide seeking sanctuary in churches, synagogues, and mosques as a result of increasingly draconian deportation actions undertaken by U. S. Immigration and Customs Enforcement (ICE).

In June 2019, ICE ordered Arevalo-Herrera to pay nearly $300,000 in fines as part of a nationwide move, utilizing a rarely used civil code that allows the government to impose fines on those evading deportation. On July 12, 2019, more than a thousand community members gathered at the Virginia Capitol as part of the nationwide Lights for Liberty vigil to protest federal immigration policy and the treatment of migrants at the border. Arevalo-Herrera spoke remotely at the event, since leaving the church would have made her susceptible to ICE detention. #HandsOffAbbie, a volunteer group and movement that formed to provide support for Arevalo-Herrera while she lived in sanctuary and to fight against inhumane immigration policies, galvanized widespread local backing for her. After living in the church's basement for nearly three years, Arevalo-Herrera left the church on February 25, 2021, to live with her family in nearby Henrico County, following the issuance of a one-year deportation stay of removal by ICE.

**TO LEARN MORE**

Eggers, Dave. "The Trump Administration Seeks to Deport an Abuse Victim Who Fears for Her Life." *New Yorker,* October 24, 2018.

4.10   Byrd Park

600 S. Arthur Ashe Boulevard

Richmond's first Lesbian and Gay Pride Day took place on June 23, 1979 in Byrd Park. Its theme was "death of denial, birth of pride." It began with a motorcade through the city, and after a day of speakers and concerts, it ended with a dance sponsored by the Richmond Lesbian Feminists. A series of Women's Festivals, alongside the creation of several gay and lesbian organizations like Gay Awareness in Perspective (1974), Richmond Lesbian Feminists (1975), and the Gay Rights Association (1977), helped cultivate the space that made the city's first pride event possible. In 1974, a series of women's organizations

Byrd Park has long served as a community gathering space.

Hundreds gather at the city's first Women's Festival in 1974. These earlier festivals built momentum toward Richmond's first pride event in 1979.

throughout Virginia had organized the first Richmond Women's Festival in Monroe Park, located at 620 W. Main Street adjacent to the campus of Virginia Commonwealth University (VCU). Speakers included Margaret Sloan and Florynce Kennedy, founders of the National Black Feminist Organization, and lesbian author Rita Mae Brown. While not specifically lesbian, it was the city's first public festival that cultivated a sense of lesbian and gay pride.

The Richmond Lesbian Feminists is the longest-existing LGBTQ group in Richmond. It grew out of the 1975 convention of the Virginia Women's Political Caucus, which sought to increase women's participation in government. Held at a Richmond middle school, Beth Marschak led a workshop at the convention entitled "Laws for Lesbian Legal Rights." She and the other participants recognized a glaring need for a feminist space that centered lesbians and organized for issues critical to their needs. One month later, the Richmond Lesbian Feminists held their first meeting at Pace Memorial United Methodist Church, then located at 700 W. Franklin Street, with thirty-five people from across the state attending. Over the decades, the group has hosted hundreds of social gatherings, partnered with numerous LGBTQ and human rights organizations, and done immeasurable work to advocate for LGBTQ Virginians.

Occupying public space through festivals spread visibility and awareness about Richmond's LGBTQ community at a time when many viewed LGBTQ folks as unworthy of basic human rights. Byrd Park was, and is, one of the city's most popular gath-

PERSONAL REFLECTION

**BETH MARSCHAK**

Co-founder of Richmond Lesbian-Feminists,
and Co-author, *Lesbian and Gay Richmond*

For me, feminism was a framework of analysis much bigger than just women were equal to men legally. It was about the patriarchy; it was about racism and sexism and classism. It was about looking at power and power dynamics. It was also about valuing the things that women were traditionally associated with, things like child care and social networking. At the Virginia Women's Political Caucus annual meeting, we had a workshop on lesbian issues and concerns. I hoped to start a Lesbian Caucus within that group, to mirror their national structure. But at the workshop, many lesbian women wanted a separate group. I am a community organizer, so we set up another meeting, and we were already talking about the group as lesbian-feminist. I felt that within the feminist movement, there was not the level of support for lesbians and for lesbian issues that I wanted to see. I certainly had not seen it within the gay organizations that I knew about or had participated in. They were not really thinking about what was important to women and to lesbians. There wasn't a group doing that work. The fact that many of those women did not belong to a group at all tells you something. And there was a real need for social activities so we did monthly potlucks, we organized dances, we helped promote women's music concerts; we did all kinds of things.

ering sites; hosting the city's first pride event here made it visible to a diverse group of Richmonders. Pride events continued to be hosted in the park throughout the 1980s and into the 1990s. These events educated the broader community, enabled a broad base of support for future organizing initiatives, and provided community space for out LGBTQ folks to gather while also signaling to closeted Richmonders that there was a welcoming community for them to join.

**TO LEARN MORE**

Marschak, Beth, and Alex Lorch. *Lesbian and Gay Richmond*. Charleston: Arcadia, 2008.
Bray, Cindy. "Rainbow Richmond: LGBTQ History of Richmond, VA." https://outhistory.org/exhibits/show/rainbow-richmond
Virginia Department of Historic Resources. "LGBTQ Heritage in Richmond." https://www.dhr.virginia.gov/survey-planning/lgbtq-heritage-in-virginia/

## 4.11  Phoenix Rising (former)

*19 N. Belmont Avenue*

Phoenix Rising opened in 1993 as an independent bookstore carrying LGBT-themed books, magazines, and media near Richmond's Carytown shopping corridor. It followed a rich tradition of Richmond bookstores that centered lesbian and gay community-building. The first, Labrys Books, opened at 8 N. Allen Avenue in 1978; it sold books by and for women. When it closed in 1981, Womensbooks opened as a cooperative bookstore, initially operating out of the YWCA on N. 5th Street. When it closed in 1993, Phoenix Rising continued the tradition of cultivating space for LGBTQ communities. As an LGBTQ community hub, it designated space for patrons to place

Former site of Phoenix Rising bookstore.

*v. Texas* (2003) declared laws that prohibited private sexual conduct between people of the same sex illegal throughout the country, preventing future cases like this one that hinged on sodomy laws.

At a time when few LGBTQ gathering spaces outside of nightlife venues existed in the city, Phoenix Rising provided a platform to raise awareness and galvanize action around gay and lesbian issues like unjust divorce and custody laws. Phoenix Rising closed in the mid-2010s, as online sales hammered many bookstores and retail rental costs soared. Patrons lost a vital community gathering space, although other LGBTQ spaces in the city continue to flourish.

information related to local LGBTQ activities and connections. One of those community connections was raising funds for the Sharon Bottoms and April Wade Defense Fund in the 1990s.

In 1993, Sharon Bottoms lost custody of her two-year-old son, Tyler, in a case that made national headlines. Kay Bottoms had sued her daughter, Sharon, for custody of Tyler because Sharon identified as lesbian. Judge Buford Parsons declared Sharon an unfit parent and granted custody to Kay Bottoms. Parsons called Sharon's conduct "immoral" and "illegal" based on Virginia's sodomy laws at the time. The judge allowed Sharon to visit her son two days each week, but they could not meet in Sharon's home and they could not meet in the presence of her partner, April Wade. The Virginia Supreme Court soon granted permanent custody to Tyler's grandmother, Kay. This case gained national attention because Bottoms insisted on using her real name in her fight to retain custody of her son, which was highly unusual at the time. A decade later, the U. S. Supreme Court decision in *Lawrence*

### TO VISIT NEARBY

**MULBERRY HOUSE**, 2701–2703 W. Grace Street. In the early 1970s, a group of lesbian and gay Richmonders lived communally here and cultivated close kinship ties at a time when many gay men and lesbians were closeted or shunned by their families. The house is now a private home.

**DIVERSITY THRIFT** at 1407 Sherwood Avenue. Founded in 1999, it is part of Diversity Richmond, an organization that has raised over one million dollars for local LGBTQ support organizations.

## 4.12  *Athena* Mural

8 N. Belmont Avenue

This mural, located in an alley behind a branch of the Richmond Public Library, playfully depicts Athena, goddess of wisdom. Mickeal Broth, also known as Night Owl, an artist who has painted dozens of murals in Richmond and hundreds more

Mickael Broth's *Athena* mural behind Richmond Public Library's Belmont Branch near the Carytown shopping district.

demand harsh sentencing for graffiti-based vandalism. As a result, the city aggressively prosecuted these cases, highlighting tensions between artistic license, policing, and protection of private property.

Since then, the work of Broth and many others have led to an artistic and cultural rebirth in the city. Broth and local artist Ed Trask created the city's first RVA Street Art Festival in 2012. Broth later founded the Welcoming Walls project to engage local artists in creating large-scale public art alongside prominent gateways around the city. These creative projects have deliberately cultivated relationships with city leadership, business owners, and residents alike to help legitimize street art among groups that once sought to regulate and eradicate it. In addition, gentrification and economic development incentivized by city policies has meant that the places once targeted by graffiti artists, such as abandoned industrial lots, have greatly diminished. Street art has entered the mainstream, and the city now readily promotes it in development and tourism campaigns.

globally, created it in 2015. In 2004, Broth was arrested and sentenced to ten months in jail in a high-profile case of vandalism after tagging a prominent train bridge that towered over four lanes of interstate traffic. Local courts prosecuted him both for this act and other previous acts of graffiti and street art. At the time of his arrest, twenty-one-year-old Broth was a Fine Arts student at Virginia Commonwealth University (VCU). He completed his degree while serving his jail time.

In the early 2000s, the city prosecuted dozens of graffiti cases; every defendant was a student at VCU. The 1990s fostered an underground street art scene in the city, which coincided with the rising national prominence of VCU's School of the Arts. Broth's case reflected the mounting hostility toward young people who were creating cutting-edge street art, breaking local graffiti laws, and studying to be artists in a time of increased gentrification within the city. That gentrification, particularly in areas adjacent to VCU, led home and business owners to

## TO LEARN MORE

Broth, Mickael, and Ed Trask. *Murals of Richmond*. Richmond: Chop Suey Books, 2018. This text includes 300 photographs of local murals and street art, as well as dozens of interviews with artists based both locally and globally who have created public art in Richmond.

Westwood neighborhood, 2020.

### 4.13 Public Water Hydrant in Westwood Neighborhood (former)

*Corner of Willow Lawn Drive and Patterson Avenue*

Former enslaved people established the small Black community known as Westwood soon after the Civil War. The neighborhood grew due to demand for Black labor in the surrounding white suburbs. In 1942, the city annexed Westwood and condemned several local water wells in the process. By 1945, Westwood's two hundred residents had to gather their water from this one public hydrant. At any outbreak of disease, nearby white residents pointed to the community as its source. Despite several attempts to detail the need for better sanitation in the neighborhood, which the Richmond Health Director supported, the city's Board of Aldermen repeatedly rejected the neighborhood's requests for city water and sewer service. The board forthrightly noted that extending those services to the neighborhood would likely encourage more Black families to move there, which they sought to discourage. In 1947, the city council finally passed a resolution to extend city water and sewer services to the neighborhood. Rev. Alfred Waller of Westwood Baptist Church, located at 915 Glenburnie Road, made it clear that any resident who could not afford connection costs could turn to the church for funding to ensure that all community homes received these services.

Northwest of this community, a white community appropriated the name Westwood when it formed in 1937. It is this Westwood neighborhood that most Richmonders know today. The Westwood sign for this neighborhood stands at the corner of Monument and Libbie Avenues.

**TO LEARN MORE**

Richardson, Selden. *Built by Blacks: African American Neighborhoods and Architecture in Richmond, VA.* Charleston: History Press, 2008.

**TO VISIT NEARBY**

**HOME AT 903 GLENBURNIE ROAD.** Famous tennis star and Richmonder Arthur Ashe's grandmother once owned this home. His parents, Maddie and Arthur, married in its living room in 1938.

### 4.14 Mekong Restaurant

*6004 W. Broad Street*

In 1986, twelve-year-old An Bui and his siblings spent one week in a homemade boat fleeing from Vietnam to Malaysia; they eventually made their way to Richmond via sponsorship from St. Bridget's Catholic Church. When his father, who had spent nine years as a political prisoner in Vietnam,

Mekong Restaurant has anchored this shopping center since its opening in 1995.

arrived in 1991, the family raised money to open a Vietnamese restaurant managed by Bui. They opened what would become the city's iconic Mekong in 1995. Mekong opened in a nondescript shopping strip in the city's West End, where most of the local Asian restaurants operate as it is closest to neighborhoods where Asian families reside. When the restaurant started serving Belgian-style beer, beer enthusiasts followed. In 2006, as the economy slowed, Bui switched to draft beer, initially buying a single tap kegerator. The popularity of Mekong's draft beer program skyrocketed.

The growth of Richmond's brewery scene, a staple of the local economy since the early 2010s, is largely attributed to the beer program that Mekong pioneered when Richmond had only one local brewery. At the time, state laws made it illegal for breweries to serve beer without a restaurant on site. Mekong's success led a team to open the large Hardywood Park Brewery in the city instead of other, larger cities that they had considered. That momentum led Virginia to change its laws in 2012 so that breweries could open taprooms without restaurants. The large inventory of unused warehouse space in the city then drew brewery entrepreneurs from around the country to town, and contributed to economic development in neighborhoods like Scott's Addition. The city boasts more than thirty craft breweries, and in 2018, Vinepair.com declared Richmond the world's top beer destination.

Mekong now serves fifty-five beers on tap and continually beats every other craft beer bar in the country in national rankings. In 2015, Bui opened The Answer, a brewpub, next door. According to Bui, "Fifteen years ago, I had this dream of trying to put Richmond on the beer map. But I never thought it would be the brewery scene. I thought it would be the beer bar scene." But breweries are "the complete product. You brew here. You create employees. You sell here. The money cycles within the city. So it's great."

## TO LEARN MORE

Gould, Kenny. "How a Vietnamese Strip Mall Restaurant Launched One of America's Coolest Craft Beer Scenes." *Vice,* August 31, 2017.

Bernstein, Joshua. "Characters: An Bui." *Imbibe Magazine,* November / December 2014.

# 5

# South-side
# Richmond

# Introduction

**SOUTHSIDE RICHMOND LIES JUST SOUTH OF** the James River. In 1910, Richmond annexed the city of Manchester. Located across the river within sight of Richmond's downtown, many of the same industries that flourished in Richmond did so in Manchester as well, including flour, tobacco, and the slave trade. Slave ships docked near present-day Ancarrow's Landing, unloading enslaved people who crossed Mayo's bridge, built in 1788, into the slave jails of downtown Richmond. Today, Manchester represents a mix of industrial, small business, and residential zoning, although increasingly, luxury lofts and art spaces transform areas formerly used for industry as those businesses relocate elsewhere. It is connected to the city by a number of bridges, including the pedestrian T. Tyler Potterfield Memorial Bridge that spans the James River to link public park space in the city's southside to the river's north bank. It is one of the first completed projects in the city's Richmond Riverfront Plan to cultivate and connect recreational space along both sides of the river.

Blackwell, Swansboro, and other historic African American neighborhoods line the northeastern section of Southside closest to the river. For decades, developers and city planners have targeted these communities for revitalization projects, resulting in uneven development. Between 2017 and 2018, property values in some areas of Blackwell rose as much as 30 percent, triggering fears of displacement and community organizing efforts from the neighborhood's African American residents in response to this clear indicator of gentrification.

The city of Richmond annexed much of the area south of the river that now lies within the city limits as part of a racist political scheme in 1970. The city annexed a portion of northeast Chesterfield County in order to preserve white leadership in the city by shrinking Black voting strength from a majority to a minority. Still, city residents elected a majority-Black city council,

African American men work in a Southside quarry, ca. 1900.

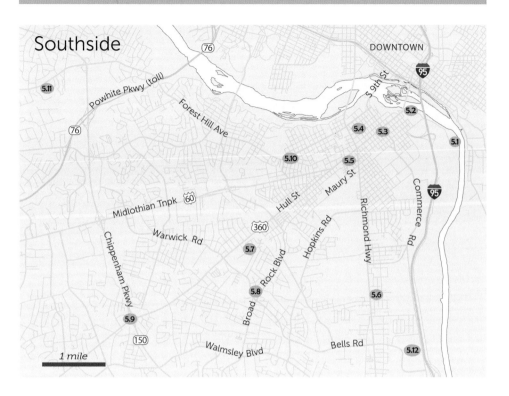

which in turn elected the city's first Black mayor, in 1977, after a prolonged court battle with the U.S. Department of Justice.

Residential and commercial growth in Southside has progressed alongside highway building projects, linking the area to other parts of the city and region. In 1927, Route 1 opened, providing an important north–south link into and out of the city. By 1940, a Work Projects Administration guide to Virginia described this thoroughfare as "lined with tourist cabins, garages, and lunchrooms swathed in neon lights that at night convert the road as far as Petersburg into a glittering midway." Other projects, which included the construction of Chippenham and Powhite Parkways in the 1960s and 1970s, displaced historic African American neighborhoods

like Granite, which included communities of both free and enslaved Black Richmonders that formed around Southside's nineteenth-century mining industries. Established in the early 1700s, these coal mines represented the start of commercial coal mining in the United States. During World War II, the federal government opened a large Defense Supply Center along Route 1 at the city's southernmost border. More industrial development followed, and in 1973, Philip Morris opened the world's largest manufacturing plant to produce the world's best-selling cigarette, Marlboro.

Rising industry also accompanied major health and environmental justice concerns. The James River has suffered repeated polluting due to toxic industrial dumping, leading

Jeff Davis Flea Market has become a popular gathering spot for the region's Latino communities.

to a need for environmental hazard remediation at multiple sites throughout the region. The Defense Supply Center, for example, is a Superfund site, a designation that recognizes it as one of the nation's most hazardous waste sites due to effects from dumping toxic pesticides. Additionally, Philip Morris has battled innumerable decades-long lawsuits related to the negative health effects of its tobacco products.

Southside also represents the area of the city most changed by growing Latino immigration. Today, as three major thoroughfares, Hull Street, Midlothian Turnpike, and Route 1, approach the city's southern border and enter Chesterfield county, neighborhoods and schools that were nearly all Black in the early twenty-first century now overwhelmingly serve Latino communities. Most of the city's Latino population lives in Southside, both within the city and in north Chesterfield County. Early Latino immigrant groups settled here in the 1970s,

and as they built Latino-serving businesses and forged strong community ties within area churches and schools, those who immigrated later moved to this area as well. This population is very diverse, with no majority country of origin but instead includes people whose home countries include Mexico, Guatemala, El Salvador, Honduras, Colombia, Puerto Rico, and more.

## Southside Richmond Sites

### 5.1 Ancarrow's Landing

1200 Brander Street

Ancarrow's Landing marks the start of the Richmond Slave Trail, a formally designated history trail established by the city in the 1990s. Ships carrying enslaved people anchored here at the Manchester Docks in the decades prior to the Civil War. Captors

(Left) Along the Richmond Slave Trail at Ancarrow's Landing.

(Below Left) Ancarrow's Landing.

Richmond's many unmarked sites of Black history. Over 500 people participated, and it sparked a series of public forums and dialogues where people advocated for better preservation of this history. Richmond's city council established the Slave Trail Commission in 1998 to formally memorialize the city's role in the slave trade. The commission helped to memorialize the trail, which included placing educational signs along it in 2011. However, many Richmonders want a more accessible space to be clearly designated as a memorial, one that would center the extensive history of the city's slave trade. The city has repeatedly failed to prioritize such a space.

often marched the enslaved under the cover of night north across the 14th Street bridge, also known as Mayo's Bridge, to the slave markets and jails housed on the north side of the river in Shockoe Bottom. The trail ends in Shockoe Bottom at **Devil's Half Acre** (see page 22) and the **African Burial Ground** (see page 23).

The Richmond Slave Trail is a product of community advocacy. In 1993, organizations that included Hope in the Cities, Richmond Hill ecumenical center, and Elegba Folklore Society sponsored a walk through

Ancarrow's Landing itself has languished as a relatively remote and obscure location. While a popular fishing spot, the area was contaminated for decades due to its use by a fertilizer plant. In 2014, the plant's legal successor,

Exxon Mobil, made improvements at the site upon pressure from the city. This work included removing large amounts of soil containing lead and arsenic, and also creating better access to the Slave Trail entrance. Ancarrow's remains difficult to locate for those unfamiliar with the site. Its entrance is tucked behind the city's wastewater treatment plant, and when driving, it does not look accessible to the public, but it is. Also, the trail is not a loop. Visitors either must walk or arrange private transportation back to Ancarrow's after the one-way, 2.8-mile walk.

**TO LEARN MORE**

Trammel, Jack. *The Richmond Slave Trade: The Economic Backbone of the Old Dominion.* Charleston: History Press, 2012.

**TO VISIT NEARBY**

**ELEGBA FOLKLORE SOCIETY**, 101 E. Broad Street. A cultural arts and educational organization, this society has hosted events to celebrate African and African American history and culture in Richmond since Janine Bell opened it in 1990. The society notes that *elegba*, from the Yoruba cosmology of West Africa, is an *Orisa* or intercessor who opens the roads, bringing clarity out of confusion. https://efsinc.org/

## 5.2 Perdue Farms Inc. (former)

4 Manchester Road

Until the late 2010s, Perdue Farms' Richmond port facility shipped grain from here to its meat processing plants located farther east. Perdue is a multibillion-dollar agribusiness firm that is the third-largest producer of chicken meat in the country. Several of

Virginia's 122 meat processing plants reside on Virginia's rural Eastern Shore. Both Perdue and Tyson Foods, the nation's largest chicken producer, operate plants there. Most workers in Virginia's meatpacking industry are Latino; on the Eastern Shore, many migrated from their homes in Mexico and Guatemala to work there.

From the start of the COVID-19 outbreak in March 2020, workers in the meatpacking industry faced a disproportionately high risk of contracting the virus. Local health officials worried about how quickly outbreaks could overwhelm local medical facilities. Officials noted that the majority of cases in this area could be traced to workers employed at meatpacking plants. Workers increasingly called in sick, as they feared working in close contact with others. They and other essential workers were critical in organizing to pass the state's COVID-19 workplace safety regulations, which included limited walkouts and contacting state agencies to demand that management better enforce safety protocols. However, in April 2020, President Trump invoked the Defense Production Act to keep these plants open, citing the need to maintain the food supply during the pandemic

On July 15, 2020, Virginia became the first state in the nation to implement temporary work-based COVID-19 protections. The guidelines required employers to implement a number of new safety protocols as well as a system to notify employees when coworkers tested positive for the virus. In the weeks prior to the new regulations, Latino Virginians made up nearly 50 percent of all new

South of the James River with the former site of Perdue Farms to the left.

cases, despite accounting for less than 10 percent of the state's population.

The meatpacking industry is known for its hazardous work and poor treatment of workers, and the COVID-19 pandemic only exacerbated those concerns. Two workers at Tyson plants in the Richmond metro area highlighted those problems in a *New York Times* video where they called for slowing the line of production in order to allow for appropriate social distancing between workers in meat processing plants. As worker Jerald Brooks noted, "We may be feeding America, but we are sacrificing ourselves." While the state initially required these plants to implement safer operating procedures, it eliminated these enhanced protocols in early 2022, shortly after the election of Republican governor Glenn Youngkin.

**TO LEARN MORE**

Brooks, Jerald, and Lakesha Bailey. "We're Feeding America, but We're Sacrificing Ourselves." *New York Times,* June 15, 2020.

Garcia-Navarro, Lulu, and Christianna Silva, "Virginia Poultry Workers See Victory in New COVID-19 Protection Rules." NPR, July, 19 2020.

### 5.3 New Life Deliverance Tabernacle

900 Decatur Street

The Blackwell neighborhood, a majority-Black neighborhood that experienced mid-twentieth-century divestment due to redlining, is named after James Heyward Blackwell, a Black principal after whom the city renamed the neighborhood school in 1951. In 2015, white developers Michael

Blackwell neighborhood, 2020.

that people who are not in the community find out what's going on before the people who live in the community? I would like to see us be able to coexist, but I don't want us to be forced into a predicament where we are being forced out." Working with the Richmond NAACP chapter,

and Laura Hild began buying numerous properties in Blackwell. The Hilds initiated a historic district expansion, which would have supplanted the name Blackwell and allowed them to qualify for tax credits to significantly lessen the costs of development. The developers did no community outreach, and while Virginia Department of Historic Resources (DHR) ostensibly sent letters to property owners, many never received them. Concerned citizens went door-to-door catalyzing the neighborhood once they learned of the impending action.

Residents expressed their opposition not to development but rather to not being included in the process. They collectively expressed concerns over the loss of neighborhood identity with a name change, as well as the impact of rising property taxes spurred by encroaching gentrification. The New Life Deliverance Tabernacle, pastored by Rev. Robert Winfree, became a center for community information. As Winfree lamented at an NAACP meeting: "How is it

parishioners organized home visits to educate residents about the issue. At the same time, DHR representatives attended several community meetings to aid in this effort. In October 2018, with community support, DHR voted both to extend the existing Manchester historic district and to make Blackwell its own historic district, thereby retaining the neighborhood's name.

In April 2021, the federal government found Michael Hild guilty of corporate fraud for orchestrating a scheme in which he illegally diverted more than $20 million into his personal financial accounts. In addition, the U. S. Securities and Exchange Commission charged him with five civil charges. As of this writing, Hild awaits a hearing to request a new trial. Meanwhile, the government has seized dozens of Hild's properties, including several in Blackwell. These properties will remain vacant and in limbo for years to come, with neighborhood residents unable to access them.

**TO LEARN MORE**

Francis, Lauren, and Kate Andrews. "Bad Manners and Broken Promises." *Richmond Magazine,* August 22, 2018.

Eshleman, Tina. "Preserving Blackwell." *Richmond Magazine,* September 29, 2018.

## 5.4 Sacred Heart Catholic Church / Iglesia del Sagrado Corazon

1400 Perry Street

Sacred Heart Catholic Church / Iglesia del Sagrado Corazón.

On July 29, 1999, Father Ricardo Seidel held the city's first official Spanish-language masses at Sacred Heart and St. Augustine's Catholic Churches. Although he died only weeks later, his work created an inclusive space where Latinos could gather in community to worship. Born in Peru, he came to Richmond because he felt led to serve here. Seidel advocated for the Latino community throughout Virginia and his commitment to Latino parishioners made a lasting impact. Today, 90 percent of Sacred Heart's members are Latino. Located in a historically African American neighborhood, the church welcomes a diverse group of worshippers and continues to expand at a time when most city churches are experiencing shrinking membership rolls.

Sacred Heart represents a larger trend within U. S. Catholic churches of growing Latino membership in the past decades. As a result of Latino activism in the 1960s and 1970s, the U. S. Catholic Church released a national strategic plan in 1988 calling for the full and equal integration of Latino Catholics into its churches. While Latinos represent 40 percent of Catholics in the U. S., that number is declining. Statistics show Latinos increasingly embrace both nonreligious affiliation and Pentecostalism in larger numbers.

Today, Sacred Heart serves over 1,200 families with six weekly masses, four in Spanish and two in English. It also hosts a number of quinceañeras each month, an important cultural tradition in many Latino communities. Additionally, it supports community engagement efforts and service to Latino immigrant communities through the neighboring Sacred Heart Center. Both the church and the center serve as critical spaces for Latino communities to gather and organize, which is especially important given the

PERSONAL REFLECTION

**TANYA GONZALEZ**
Community Worker and Executive Director,
Sacred Heart Center

I was born on the U.S./Mexico border. My formative years were spent between both countries, both cultures, both languages. I was experiencing issues I work with now on a daily basis. At age 14, we came to Richmond. In the early '90s, there were few Spanish-speaking people here. If I ran into someone who spoke Spanish, it was like meeting a long-lost cousin. I attended Brown University. For the first time since leaving Texas, I was surrounded with peers who spoke Spanish. I came back and taught English. One day, two gentlemen from Guatemala shared that they'd been on opposing sides in the [Guatemalan] civil war and seen horrific things. I point to that moment as a catalyst. Here they were in the U.S. sitting next to each other peacefully sharing their experiences. Richmond is not one Latin American identity. Eight or nine countries have large groups here. That speaks to diversity around language, background, education, socioeconomics, and reasons for arrival. We have people who have been here for decades, people who are coming from Latin America. We also have second and third generations coming from other parts of the country, so when we talk about the Latino community, it's really communities. We can look at needs around language access, education, legal systems, and all of these things. We also look at contributions like businesses, workforce, artistry, music, cultural activities, and food. I make efforts to stay connected. Accessibility and proximity is important. I see my boss as the community. That's my value system.

rapid growth of these communities in the Richmond area.

**TO LEARN MORE**

Biegelsen, Amy. "Sanctuary." *Style Weekly*, 2017.
Lizama, Juan. "Sacred Heart Catholic: A Church in Transition." *Richmond Times-Dispatch*, November 24, 2008.

**TO VISIT NEARBY**

SACRED HEART CENTER, across the street. Founded in 1990, the center serves as a Latino community hub with a wide range of bilingual programs and services for children and adults.

## 5.5 Carrington and Michaux Plant (former)

*2200 Decatur Street*

On the morning of Friday, April 16, 1937, fifteen African American machine operators at the Carrington and Michaux Plant, a tobacco factory, stopped work, but they soon resumed temporarily when white foremen threatened to fire them. Word spread to other employees, and when a lone female stemmer yelled "strike," laborers refused to return to work. After three hours, management decided to pay the workers for the week's work and send them home for the weekend. Responding to reports of a strike, general manager W. W. Michaux Jr. reported that there had been no strike; the employees had simply been fired.

Black tobacco workers were notoriously underpaid. Only the most hazardous and worst-paying jobs were open to them, and those earning the highest pay of nine dollars

The TSLU won its first victory in under one week. Workers, primarily women, organized in area churches and arranged picket lines filled with hundreds of people. At the same time, TSLU organized workers in nearby factories, creating pressure throughout Richmond's tobacco industry. Carrington and Michaux agreed to raise wages between 10 and 20 per-

African American women laboring at Richmond tobacco factory, ca. 1900.

a week did not make a living wage. Black women, who worked nearly exclusively as hand stemmers removing the central stems from tobacco leaves, reported making half that amount.

After striking, the plant's 300 African American workers contacted two major trade unions to represent them: the Congress of Industrial Organizations and the American Federation of Labor. Concerned both with a primacy for organizing white workers and a desire not to disrupt the South's legal segregation, those unions showed little interest in supporting strikers of color. Instead, the recently formed Southern Negro Youth Congress (SNYC) stepped in. Organized in Richmond three months earlier, SNYC leadership formed the strikers into the independent Tobacco Stemmers and Laborers Union (TSLU) to negotiate terms with factory owners.

cent, limit the workweek to five eight-hour days, pay time and a half for overtime, and recognize the TSLU as the sole bargaining agent for its workers. This strike represented the first in an intensely active three-year period of labor organizing in Richmond, particularly among the city's African American tobacco workers.

Subsequent strikes also led to significant concessions on the part of employers. Such was the case just two months later on June 30, when more than 2,000 TSLU members gathered at the Tobacco By-Products and Chemical Plant in Fulton to support 160 African American workers who went on strike to receive higher wages as skilled laborers. They marched through the city in a show of solidarity with Richmond's 5,000 Black tobacco factory workers. After weeks of striking and negotiations, owners agreed to officially allow Black workers to be classified as "skilled" laborers, which ensured higher wages.

Victories were also tempered by setbacks. In 1940, tobacco factories increased mechanization overseen exclusively by white employees, eliminating many Black workers from employment in the industry. This factory building no longer exists, but another factory is now located at this site.

**TO LEARN MORE**

Gellman, Erik. *Death Blow to Jim Crow: The National Negro Congress and the Rise of Militant Civil Rights.* Chapel Hill: University of North Carolina Press, 2012.

Love, Richard. "In Defiance of Custom and Tradition: Black Tobacco Workers and Labor Unions in Richmond, Virginia, 1937–1941." *Labor History* 35, no. 1 (1994): 25–47.

## 5.6 Rudd's Trailer Park

2911 Richmond Highway

In 2015, thirty-two mobile home owners brought a federal discrimination lawsuit, in conjunction with the Legal Aid Justice Center, against the city of Richmond. The fed-eral Fair Housing Act prevents housing discrimination based on national origin, which includes discrimination when enforcing housing codes. The plaintiffs argued that the city's recent code enforcement campaign discriminately targeted Latino residents of mobile home parks with abusive code enforcement campaigns aimed at displacing families from their homes. At Rudd's, 75 percent of residents are immigrants from Mexico and Central America, and at neighboring Mobile Towne, over 90 percent of immigrants are from that region. Most residents speak Spanish or Mixtec. Mobile homes are the most affordable home ownership option in the area. However, mortgage interest rates are higher as lenders classify these homes as movable property and, therefore, riskier investments. Taxes also can be higher, as some Virginia locales apply both real estate and personal property (typically applied to vehicles) taxes to mobile homes.

In 2014, the city launched inspections of its nine mobile home parks, issuing hundreds of violation notices to residents and park owners while condemning some homes on the spot. While no one disputed the poor housing conditions, residents noted that violations were issued in English with no translation services made available and that the city issued notices

Rudd's Trailer Park, 2020.

for repairs that were not immediate safety and health problems, despite knowing the financial burdens the residents faced. Melody Scrugg's mother lived in a forty-year-old trailer at the time of the lawsuit. Scruggs noted: "My mom's on a fixed income, and it's hard to find a place in her price range . . . Most of these trailers are so old, it's really hard to get them up to code." Her mother's trailer passed inspection with the addition of a smoke detector, but it still had other electrical problems and contained mold.

In 2016, the U. S. Department of Housing and Urban Development (HUD) approved the city's settlement agreement for the lawsuit. As part of the settlement, the city paid $30,000 in financial damages, conducted language-appropriate community outreach, assisted residents with payment for needed repairs, hired a fair housing compliance officer, and established a comprehensive housing nondiscrimination policy.

**TO LEARN MORE**

Eshleman, Tina. "A Solid Community." *Richmond. com,* January 15, 2017.

"An Assessment of Central Virginia's Manufactured Housing Communities: Understanding the Conditions, Challenges, and Opportunities." *project:HOMES,* November 2016.

Southwood Apartments, called "La Mancha" by its residents, 2020.

## 5.7 La Mancha (Southwood Apartments)

4602 Southwood Parkway

Between 1990 and 2020, the U. S. South experienced the highest population growth of immigrants from Latin America. In Central Virginia, this led to a threefold population increase and a rising number of Latino immigrant communities in southside Richmond and north Chesterfield County. Diverse peoples from Latin America have made Richmond their home while creating community networks of mutual aid and support. La Mancha, as its residents call Southwood Apartments, emerged as one of the area's first centralized communities of diverse Latino life and culture. Built in 1960, this large apartment complex contains 1,286 units around a square-mile radius near the Chesterfield County border. Now the largest Latino neighborhood in the city, the complex has been deemed "La Mancha" by its residents. The term translates into English

PERSONAL REFLECTION

**JOSÉ "TITO" HENRÍQUEZ**
**Documentary Photographer, Writer,**
**and Journalist**

Both my parents are Salvadorans. I decided I wanted to study photography. I was delving into my own personal and family history trying to learn as much as I could about El Salvador and my parents, why they came here. I got a grant to go, and I did a project there. I was looking for that in Richmond. It started with me driving through Southside, and eventually I came across a market, barbershops, restaurants. I just began talking to people: "I'm a college student trying to document Latino culture in Southside. Can I take your picture?" I took portraits: the cheese worker at the market, the stylist at the Dominican hair salon, the barber. I was drawn to the photographers of the industrial age documenting working-class people in real conditions.

Eventually, I heard about Southwood. They call it La Mancha. I drove to that neighborhood one day, got out, and I just started walking. Immediately I felt that connection to the apartment complexes that I grew up in. I was drawn to the unsupervised kids playing soccer, running around in the neighborhood, in the playgrounds. They were playing in the creek. I started talking to them, told them what I was doing, and they took an interest in it. So, I started photographing them. I started photographing the neighborhood. I started taking audio and video, so it became this multimedia collage. I talked to their parents and built relationships in the community. I got trust. Almost a year I was in the community doing that. That's the work I like doing. I like being immersed. I came to this work with a social justice passion: What is it that I can do? How can I change this thing I'm documenting?

as "the stain," exemplifying the community's complicated relationship with property owners, management, and the broader Southside community, formerly dominated by African American and white working-class residents.

Wanda Hernández calls La Mancha "a ground zero for incoming immigrants" to Richmond. Hernández curated the region's first bilingual exhibit and oral history project at The Valentine, a museum dedicated to telling Richmond's history. This 2017 exhibit, *Nuestras Historias: Latinos in Richmond,* was the first of its kind to document Latino history in Richmond. José "Tito" Henríquez, a local multimedia artist, spent a year working in La Mancha on social projects alongside

residents, documenting life and interviewing children to highlight the community life of the neighborhood. This attention, coupled with organizing among tenants, like Hilda Villatoro, and community organizers Elena Camacho and Claudia Arevalo from New Virginia Majority, garnered increased attention from the public alongside both state and local policy makers.

In fall 2021, the *Richmond Times-Dispatch,* spurred by accounts of tenant mistreatment, initiated a lengthy investigation into Southwood Apartments, LLC. The inquiry found appalling living conditions alongside an active tenant movement of residents and advocates. Out of a hundred tenants inter-

PERSONAL REFLECTION

**WANDA HERNÁNDEZ**
Curator of Nuestras Historias: Latinos in
Richmond exhibited at the Valentine History
Museum, Doctoral Candidate in American
Studies, University of Maryland

What was so beautiful about Richmond was
the indigeneity of Latinx residents. There's
probably a significant amount overlooked
in this Latinx conglomerate. For Indigenous
Latinxs, Spanish may be their second language and English their third—if Spanish
and English are languages they adopt. Organizations tend not think about that enough.
Working with the Latinx community is more
complicated than English-Spanish translation.

I wanted the exhibit to be a mirror for
people from all walks of life. Oral histories
were the way to center people that aren't
necessarily centered in day-to-day life. Often the landscape tells me that we've been
here, but history books don't. I see all these
Latino businesses. I see us in landscapes,
but not in texts. So oral histories seemed
like what made the most sense. Making
those connections and capturing those
real conversations was important. Seeing
people from police officers to landscapers
and presidents of chambers of commerce
to laborers; people starting programs, businesses, creating culture. I saw people working to make things happen, and lots of mutual aid work in solidifying community.

With such a significant amount of the
Latinx community either dealing with racism
in the United States or in their countries of
origin, war, poverty, or what have you, I think
it could be a good practice to use oral histories—where it's not extractive—to process
for healing. That's why we went that route.

I'm eternally grateful to The Valentine for
trusting me even though I was new and ea-
ger to learn. They needed someone to lead
the project, and that's how I ended up there.
It set me on the path I'm on now.

viewed, eighty-eight had mice in their units,
seventy-two reported having both rodents
and roaches, and sixty had mold. Residents
told stories of leaky toilets, filthy ducts,
exposed wiring, and wastewater backing up
into their apartments when neighbors used
the bathroom. When tenants requested a
meeting, the property manager repeatedly
refused and responded in writing by blaming
residents from "third world countries" for
the conditions in their units.

Between 2015 and 2018 Southwood processed evictions for 1 in 4 of its residents.
In 2020, 1 in 20 evictions in Richmond were
from La Mancha. Despite the influx of $3.2
million for COVID-related rent relief, the
third-largest amount in the state, both evictions and substandard living conditions
remain. Ongoing outreach and mobilization endures. In late 2021, two residents, supported by two dozen tenants, filed formal
complaints to management. Hilda Villatoro
rallied fellow residents and advocates with a
bullhorn from the passenger seat of her car:
"If we do not raise our voice, this is going to
continue. They receive the money for rent
relief, but that doesn't mean they are listen-
ing to us."

The residents' local city council representative, Michael Jones, worked alongside residents

to push the State Attorney General's Office of Civil Rights to investigate. In January 2022, the spokesperson for Southwood publicized a goal of individually assessing every unit. It remains to be seen whether Southwood Apartments, LLC will follow through on its promises and whether the Attorney General's Office will investigate. As community organizer and fellow immigrant Elena Camacho tells the residents she works alongside at Southwood: "If you and your neighbor and everybody get together, we don't have to be scared."

**TO LEARN MORE**

Clark, Mary Lee. "'Nuestras Historias' Tells the Story of Richmond's Latino Community." *Richmond Times-Dispatch,* July 25, 2017.

Henriquez, José. "Professor Leads Outreach to Latino Communities." *Commonwealth Times,* March 4, 2014.

Robinson, Mark, and Sabrina Moreno. "In Richmond's Largest Latino Neighborhood, People Live among Mold, Mice, Roaches. The Landlord Says Tenants Are to Blame." *Richmond Times-Dispatch,* December 30, 2021.

Visit José "Tito" Henríquez's website "The Core Is Deep" for images, audio, and commentary from La Mancha community members: https://thecoreisdeep.squarespace.com/la-mancha

View The Valentine's online exhibit of *Nuestras Historias: Latinos in Richmond,* created and curated by Laura Browder, Patricia Herrera, and Wanda Hernandez. https://artsandculture.google.com/exhibit/nuestras-historias-latinos-in-richmond-pt-1/CgIiL_6KVwNNLg

### 5.8  Broad Rock Sports Complex

4802 Warwick Road

Since 2000, this park has become a site of informal gathering for the area's Latino communities, who come to play soccer, cook food, and build community. In 2004, the city started hosting the IMAGINE Multicultural Festival annually here, a bilingual event that features diverse local ethnic groups who offer food, dance, and music. The park also hosted the area's first Latino farmers market, La Plaza, a weekly market that opened in 2012 with a specific intention to serve Southside's Latino households. While most area farmers markets then catered to middle-class white consumers with goods supplied by white farmers and artisans, La Plaza

Playground at Broad Rock Sports Complex.

became a place for Latino food producers to sell directly to Latino residents in an area considered a food desert, given its lack of access to grocery stores and fresh produce.

The La Plaza Farmers Market eventually languished at the park, but the owners of La Milpa, Martin Gonzalez and Monica Chavez, relaunched it at their restaurant and market in 2019. Gonzalez, originally from Mexico City, opened La Milpa in 2000. It is a beloved local institution, a twenty-four-hour restaurant and market that hosts annual festivals to celebrate some of Mexico's most important traditions, like Día de Los Muertos (Day of the Dead) and Día de la Virgen de Guada-

lupe (Day of the Virgin of Guadalupe). The space functions as an important cultural center, and in 2017, it closed for "A Day Without Immigrants," a protest and boycott held on February 16, 2017, to highlight the contributions of the nation's immigrants, which also signaled opposition to harsher federal immigration policies enacted by the Trump administration.

In addition to the relaunch of the farmers market, Gonzalez and Chavez started Colibri, an eight-acre garden near La Milpa; it supplies produce to the restaurant and market. According to Gonzalez, "We are putting the pieces together so La Milpa will

(Above) La Milpa Restaurant.

(Left) Celebrating La Fiesta Latino in 1984 at what would later become Broad Rock Sports Complex.

be a place with longevity. I'm very happy because it's connecting the whole idea— farming, the restaurant and bringing people together. When you are able to make connections, you want to support them—the farmer and the owner, you are supporting something larger. That's what's happening here." La Milpa sits just across Richmond's border in Chesterfield County. Since La Milpa's founding in 2000, Chesterfield's Latino population has increased by more than 250 percent, as evidenced by the extensive growth of successful Latino-owned and Latino-serving businesses in this area. Latino-owned restaurants like La Milpa and public spaces like Broad Rock Sports Complex play important roles in providing space for community formation and growth.

**TO LEARN MORE**

Mellon, Eileen. "A Fresh Start." *Richmond Magazine,* May 8, 2019.

**TO VISIT NEARBY**

**LA MILPA RESTAURANT AND MARKET** at 6925 Hull Street, Chesterfield County.

## 5.9 City of Richmond/ Chesterfield County Boundary

Hull Street at Chippenham Parkway

This location marks the demarcation line between the city of Richmond and Chesterfield County as established in 1970. That year, at the height of whites' fears around school desegregation and Black voting rights, the city annexed twenty-three square miles of north Chesterfield, which included 47,000 residents. Since north Chesterfield consisted almost entirely of white families, the annexation changed the city's voting demographics from a Black majority of 52 percent to a Black minority of 42 percent.

Activist Curtis Holt challenged the annexation in court. Having run and lost a campaign for a city council seat, Holt sued, arguing that the annexation and the city's at-large electoral system purposefully diluted African American voting strength. Some white residents of the newly annexed area supported Holt, fearing that their formerly white schools would become integrated if their neighborhoods became part of the city.

The U.S. Supreme Court ruled in *Holt v. City of Richmond* that the annexation was racially motivated in order to dilute African American voting power. In order to keep its annexed land, the city had to convert its electoral system to a single-member district system, meaning that voters elected representatives based on the areas in which they lived rather than at-large. From 1970–77, the city was not allowed to hold elections as various lawsuits made their way through the court system. This seven-year stretch may represent the longest any city has been prevented from holding local elections. When again allowed to hold elections on March 1, 1977, the city elected its first Black-majority city council, who in turn elected the city's first African American mayor, Henry Marsh III.

**TO LEARN MORE**

Campbell, Benjamin. *Richmond's Unhealed History.* Richmond: Brandylane, 2011.

Hayter, Julian. *The Dream Is Lost: Voting Rights*

*and the Politics of Race in Richmond, Virginia.*
Lexington: University Press of Kentucky, 2017.

Moeser, John, and Rutledge M. Dennis. *The Politics of Annexation: Oligarchic Power in a Southern City.* Rochester, VT: Schenkman Books, 1982.

## 5.10  McDonough Community Garden

3300 McDonough Street

McDonough Community Garden lies at the intersection of two southside Richmond neighborhoods with vastly different demographics: Reedy Creek and Woodland Heights. Reedy Creek is a majority–African American neighborhood with a median household income much lower than the city's overall rates, whereas Woodland Heights is an affluent majority-white community. This garden serves as a community gathering space for both neighborhoods as well as a sustainable food source run by and for community residents. Its unique location pushes community members to navigate boundaries of power and difference while encouraging relationship building and engagement.

Community activist Duron Chavis first established and facilitated work in the garden alongside community members and local nonprofits. This work negotiates ongoing citywide tensions to address food access, health, wellness, and social justice. Chavis initially worked to create sustainable agriculture in order to address food insecurity by establishing Happily Natural Day, an annual summer festival centered on health and social change in Richmond's African American communities. After moving to the city's southside in 2012, he noticed a neglected plot of city land situated at this intersection. He initially applied for and received a small grant and land donated by the city, which grew into the McDonough Community Garden, a space for community gathering that hosts a variety of food justice programs.

McDonough Community Garden.

PERSONAL REFLECTION

**DURON CHAVIS**

**Executive Director of Happily Natural Day, Founder of Resiliency Gardens, and Longtime Community Activist**

In the history of my work, McDonough is a catalyst. Certain efforts are turning points. McDonough is one of those. I was getting ready to get this apartment, and I saw this triangle plot, and I thought, "That would be a great space for a community garden." I was actively thinking about starting a community garden, because I was in the headspace of doing this community garden as a longitudinal community-engaged practice if we really want to transform community.

Will Allen, an urban agriculture pioneer, came to Richmond so I went and sat next to the person in charge of the city's community garden program. A month later we would pitch the project to Feast RVA. We got 700 bucks. We used that to get wood and soil and build the first twelve raised beds. All that was so serendipitous. Lightning struck, [and] we ended up starting that space.

We've been talking about community change, consciousness raising, poverty mitigation, but the moment that we put shovel to dirt to metamorphize space, all that we needed to do that work becomes available. As an activist, it made me look at how our work revolved around tangible transformation in the built environment.

The community garden becomes a space where you have to reconcile power. The land being owned by the city automatically puts it in this place where community members are in control of the aboveground improvements, but there are rules and city influence trying to push back and evolve the space. The challenges of perception, who lives in the neighborhood versus what happens in the space. People and places, it's who is in those spaces that defines how the city engages with the place.

The food justice movement centers not only communities' lack of access to healthy, affordable food but also issues of racial equity and land ownership, often long-denied to communities of color. Food deserts are areas where residents have limited access to healthy, affordable food, and often lack adequate access to transportation to buy food elsewhere. Richmond is the largest food desert in the United States relative to its population, meaning it has a high concentration of residents with little access to healthy, affordable food and limited transportation to access food outside of the neighborhoods where they live. Richmond's food justice movement has been organizing to address food deserts through sustainable agriculture and community-controlled gardening initiatives since the early 2000s. Today, this garden is an active site of community engagement as well as an intervention against local residents' food insecurity.

**TO LEARN MORE**

Modlin-Jackson, Cat. "Fighting for Food Justice in a Gentrified Richmond." *RVA Magazine,* April 23, 2019.

Small, Leah. "Food Justice for All." *Richmond Magazine,* April 14, 2020.

Happily Natural Festival: https://thenatural festival.com/

Huguenot High School.

## 5.11 Huguenot High School

*7945 Forest Hill Avenue*

Huguenot High School is the largest school in the Richmond Public School (RPS) system, serving over 1,200 students. By 2017, Huguenot had the largest high school Latino population in the Richmond metro region, as it serves Richmond's Southside, where most of the city's Latino residents live. Repeated incidents of school administrators' intimidation of Latino students here highlight both the growth of Latino communities in local schools and RPS's struggle to successfully support and serve this rapidly growing student population.

Between 2013 and 2015, students and parents protested school administrators' discriminatory actions against Spanish-speaking students at Huguenot. In an initial 2013 incident, the school principal searched the backpacks of Latino-appearing students and threatened them with reprisal related to their families' immigration status. In response, Latino parents, students, and support organizations like the local branch of the NAACP staged a protest over students' treatment, with that year's valedictorian, Jessica Osornio, leading the way. As parent Mayra Alvarado reported: "We want justice and we want for our children's rights to be respected. I think that we all deserve respect because we are all equal."

Students and parents demanded adequate ESL (English as a Second Language) and translation services as well as an end to all implied or verbal threats of deportation originating from school employees. RPS superintendent Dana Bedden issued an apology in February 2015, two years after the initial incident took place. RPS continues to struggle to meet the needs of its Latino students, as illustrated by its abysmally low Latino graduation rate, which was 33 percent in 2020. Also, demands by parents and activists revealed that in 2019, RPS undercounted the number of students needing ESL support by 800, meaning that 800 students who needed these services did not receive them. Thus, community efforts to demand equitable educational access continue.

## TO LEARN MORE

Nash, Tom. "Failure to Communicate." *Style Weekly,* September 23, 2014.

## 5.12 Philip Morris USA

3601 Commerce Road

Continuing the region's centuries-long ties to the tobacco economy, Philip Morris USA opened this manufacturing center in 1973. Its Marlboro cigarette has been the world's best-selling cigarette since then. The company manufactures all of its cigarettes here, producing half of all cigarettes sold in the U.S. In 2004, the company moved its corporate headquarters from New York City to 6601 W. Broad Street in Richmond. It remains one of the region's largest employers.

In *United States v. Philip Morris USA Inc.* (2006), a federal judge found several major tobacco companies, including lead defendant Phillip Morris, guilty of engaging in fraud to deceive consumers in order to downplay nicotine addiction and the adverse health effects of cigarette smoking. In a landmark, 1,700-page ruling, the Court found overwhelming evidence that these companies coordinated efforts to knowingly and willfully deny the known adverse health effects of smoking and the addictiveness of nicotine, manipulate nicotine content in cigarettes, and design their marketing to specifically target youth in order to recruit new smokers. The Court also found that the companies actively suppressed and destroyed incriminating information related to the hazards of smoking.

This large cigarette rendering stands outside of Philip Morris USA alongside Interstate 95.

As a result, tobacco manufacturers cannot use brand descriptors like "low" or "mild" to create a false impression that some cigarettes cause less harm to smokers. They also must issue corrective communication statements related to addiction, the adverse health effects of smoking and the inhalation of secondhand smoke, their manipulation of nicotine content, and the adverse health effects of products previously labeled as "light" and "low tar" cigarettes. Due to document suppression and concealment that resulted in defrauding the public, the companies must maintain public repositories and websites to make all industry documents disclosed as part of this litigation publicly available. They also must issue more transparent marketing data, especially as it relates to efforts aimed at youth. The language of the corrective statements was not finalized until 2017, and as of 2022, the question of whether those statements must be posted at retail establishments where cigarettes are sold remains unresolved.

## TO LEARN MORE

Tobacco Control Legal Consortium. "The Verdict Is In: Findings from *United States v. Philip Morris*." 2006.

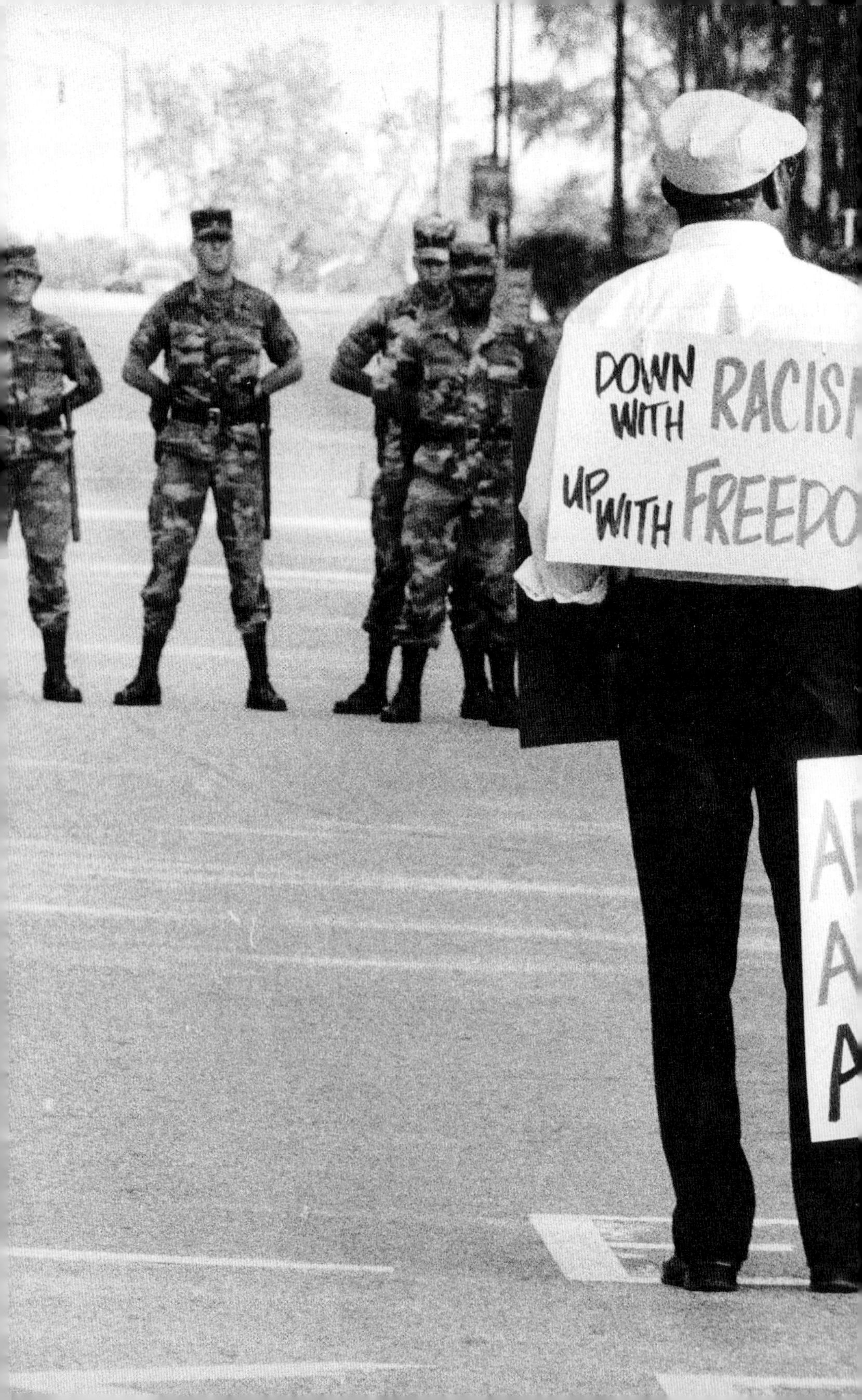
DOWN WITH
UP WITH

# 6

# Peters- burg and Points South of Richmond

# Introduction

**THE AREA SOUTH OF RICHMOND COMPRISES** Chesterfield County and the Tri-Cities region. The Tri-Cities lie near the path of the Appomattox River and include the towns of Petersburg, Hopewell, and Colonial Heights. Chesterfield County, with a population in excess of 370,000 residents, is the largest municipality in Central Virginia. It neighbors both the city of Richmond and the Petersburg area. Here, in Midlothian, the nation's first coal mining started during the colonial period, worked by white laborers as well as free and enslaved Black miners. One of the first railroads built in Virginia facilitated transporting the coal mined here to the James River and shipped worldwide.

Chesterfield County has the area's fastest-growing population and owes much of its growth to suburban development over the last fifty years. Its population nearly doubled between 1970 and 1980 due to the effects of white flight out of Richmond accompanied by extensive highway-building and suburbanization projects that connected commuters to areas farther afield, alongside businesses and services that supported residential growth. Today, Latino communities and businesses line the corridors between the city of Richmond and Chesterfield County along the major thoroughfares of Route 1, Hull Street, and Midlothian Turnpike. In 1972, the Zajur family opened the region's first Mexican restaurant, La Siesta, along Route 1. Fifty years later, this corridor has blossomed into a residential, economic,

and cultural destination for diverse Latino communities, including Mexicans, Salvadorans, Guatemalans, Hondurans, Puerto Ricans, Colombians, and others. Taquerias, tortillerias, pupuserias, dulcerias, and mercados line these streets, and entrepreneurs run food trucks alongside Latino day laborers to serve them at local construction sites. While historically a white suburban enclave, almost 10 percent of Chesterfield County's population identified as Latino in 2020 and that number is expected to more than double by 2030.

Petersburg lies just outside of Chesterfield County twenty miles south of Richmond. It served as a trading post between whites and Indigenous communities during colonization, and like Richmond, in the early industrial era it developed extensive trade in flour, cotton, and tobacco alongside a thriving port. Pocahontas Island, a peninsula within the city, likely held the South's largest free Black community prior to the Civil War. Its residents established First Baptist Church (1774) and Gillfield Baptist Church (1797), two of the oldest Black congregations established by Black parishioners in the country. This large free Black community, with access to the city's port, made it an important link on the Underground Railroad, a loose network of people who helped the enslaved escape north.

After the Civil War, when Black and white Virginians briefly governed together before Jim Crow laws curtailed Black vot-

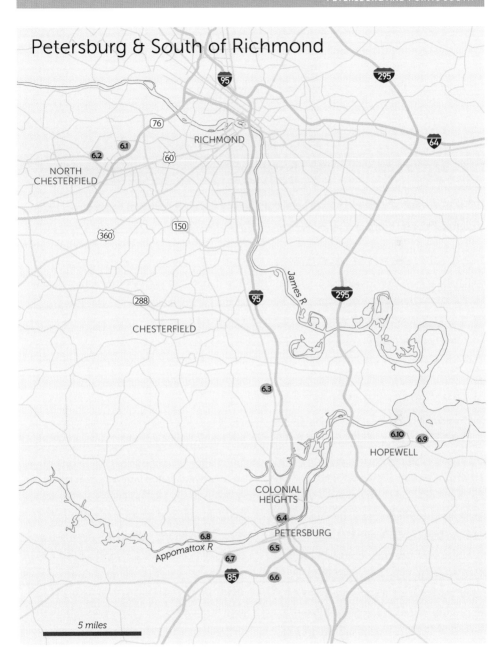

## Petersburg & South of Richmond

ing rights, the General Assembly invested in Black education and welfare, which led to the establishment of two prominent public institutions in Petersburg. In 1882, the state legislature founded what became Virginia State University, one of the nation's first publicly funded four-year historically Black colleges and universities (HBCUs). It also moved the Central Lunatic Asylum to its new campus in Petersburg. It was the only facility in the country solely dedicated to the psychiatric care of African Americans.

Petersburg became a major site of civil rights activism in the mid-twentieth century due to its deep communal roots of protest, resistance, and survival against entrenched white power structures. The Petersburg Improvement Association, founded in the 1950s by Gillfield Baptist Church pastor Rev. Wyatt Tee Walker and modeled after Dr. Martin Luther King Jr.'s Montgomery Improvement Association, served as a regional catalyst for civil rights organizing and direct action. By the 1960s and 1970s, much of Petersburg's industry and manufacturing had left town; residents followed. School desegregation and other African American demands for equal rights also fueled the outward movement of white residents. Long-term divestment in favor of surrounding counties, which began during this time, has stalled economic and population growth in Petersburg today.

White residents who formerly lived in Petersburg incorporated the neighboring town of Colonial Heights in 1948. Its population swelled by more than 50 percent between 1960 and 1970, the height of racial desegregation battles. The 1970 census listed only fifty-nine African Americans among the town's 15,000 residents. Colonial Heights did not record its first Black high school gradu-

Hopewell's City Point in 1861.

ate until 1986, and local civil rights leaders like Rev. Curtis Harris called out the town well into the 1990s for actively discouraging Black residency and upholding racist development policies.

Nearby Hopewell developed into an industrial center after chemical giant DuPont opened a gunpowder plant there in 1914. Other munitions industries followed during World War I, and in 1917, the U.S. Army opened nearby Fort Lee, situated between Petersburg and Hopewell, with 14,000 soldiers in residence after a sixty-day construction period. Chemical industry growth continued after both world wars. Hopewell's boosters proudly called the town the "chemical capital of the South." In the 1970s, a toxic pesticide produced at a plant here injured dozens of workers and catastrophically contaminated the James River. In the 1980s, this small town that occupies only eleven square miles produced 25 percent of the hazardous chemicals released into Virginia's air and waterways. As a result of Hopewell's chemical plants and its proximity to Petersburg, it became a stronghold

Old Towne Petersburg as photographed by Carol Highsmith, 2019.

for civil rights and environmental justice activism in the 1960s and beyond. In recent decades, it has suffered rapid out-migration and rising poverty rates as the growth of surrounding counties offers more amenities that have drawn Hopewell's middle-class residents, with the added benefit of allowing them to escape the town's continued pollution. Billowing smokestacks along Randolph Road greet visitors and residents on most days.

Sites in this region echo themes of community survival and resistance amidst industrial development and entrenched policies and practices of racial injustice. Also conspicuous within this geography are the effects of community disinvestment and environmental degradation, which continue to be a focus of community action.

## 6.1 Islamic Center of Virginia

1241 Buford Road, North Chesterfield

Fifteen hundred people gathered on the lawn of the Islamic Center of Virginia in February 2017 for an interfaith event to promote unity in response to the "Muslim travel ban." Created via an executive order issued by President Trump, the ban targeted people from seven Muslim-majority nations: Iran, Iraq, Libya, Somalia, Sudan, Syria, and Yemen. The ban took effect from January 27 until March 6, 2017, when it was superseded by another executive order designed to better withstand legal challenges.

Muslim American Seema Sked, who immigrated to the U. S. from Pakistan when she was two years old, attended her first protest against the ban in Richmond. Sked soon founded the Fight the Muslim Ban

The Islamic Center of Virginia plays a key role in supporting Muslim immigrants settling in the area.

campaign. She coordinated the sending of thousands of handwritten notes to congressional representatives in an effort to lessen the ban's effects. The group educated the public about the ban, advocated for its removal, and worked with asylum seekers to exercise their rights. Sked continues to organize locally on behalf of Muslim rights: "Organizing is about building relationships. I really like busting stereotypes. If nothing else, people have now met a Muslim, somebody who doesn't fit their idea of a Muslim. I have the opportunity to change somebody's perspective."

The Muslim population in the Richmond metro region continues to grow, in part due to a robust resettlement program for Muslim refugees greatly supported by organizations like the Islamic Center. In the 2010s, three new mosques were constructed in the area to better serve this community. In Virginia, Arabic speakers represent one of the fastest-growing language groups in the state, with a 63 percent increase between 2010 and 2019. In both Chesterfield and Henrico county school systems, both of which border the city of Richmond, Arabic is the most-spoken second language after Spanish.

**TO LEARN MORE**

Toben, Taylor. "Fight the Muslim Ban Founder, Richmond Resident Says She Likes Busting Stereotypes." *Commonwealth Times,* October 15, 2019.

## 6.2  La Siesta Restaurant (former)

9900 Midlothian Turnpike, Chesterfield County

The Zajur family, immigrants from Mexico City in the early 1960s, opened their first restaurant, Michel's Lunch, at 3rd and Broad as a desegregated restaurant in downtown Richmond when nearly every other restaurant offered segregated seating only. As Michel Zajur Jr. shares, "I am very proud of my father for opening one of the first restaurants on Broad Street for everyone Black and White despite the flack he got for doing so." In 1970, the family took over a restaurant called Sam's Diner at 8101 Richmond Highway and converted it into Richmond's first Mexican restaurant: La Siesta. It later moved to this Midlothian Turnpike location, where it operated until 2009.

Excerpt from La Siesta menu, ca. 1990s.

had lines out the door. The spices we grew out back. You couldn't find cilantro, or even jalapeno peppers, or tomatillos. They just didn't carry that anywhere in Richmond. That tells you how different it was." The restaurant became an intercultural gathering space for local residents and a hub for people in the Latino community. They asked for directions on how to start a business, find a place to live, or get a job. "We just pointed them in the right direction, go here, talk to this person, go there."

The family took their role in promoting Latino culture and food seriously; many locals learned about Latino language and culture alongside their food through programming the restaurant provided. One of the most successful reached over 100,000 students from counties throughout Virginia. Local schools took field trips to the restaurant where they were introduced to Spanish as a second language through an interactive program called "Siesta Town."

Eldest son Michel Zajur Jr. saw a need for community outreach and support. Given the limited resources and services available to Spanish-speaking immigrants at the time, he sought to build a bridge between communities. In 2000, he founded the Virginia Hispanic Chamber of Commerce to help people start

Members of the Colombo-American Association of Richmond dance at La Siesta, 1994.

In opening La Siesta, the Zajurs found themselves introducing the local community to authentic Mexican food, which was hard to get. The restaurant rapidly grew and became very popular. As Zajur states: "We

PERSONAL REFLECTION

## MICHEL ZAJUR

**Executive Director of the Virginia Hispanic Chamber of Commerce, Community Advocate, and Former Owner of La Siesta Restaurant**

Being in Richmond at that time, it was different. There weren't that many people who spoke Spanish in the community. When I emigrated from Mexico, my family stuck out like a sore thumb. We did not fit in. We were different. When my parents came here, they didn't speak English. We spoke English at school and Spanish at home. I often acted as a translator when I was young. There was a man I remember that would come over and help my parents. He helped [my father] to learn English and open his first business.

I never had the ambition of starting a chamber [of commerce]. I didn't know what a chamber did, but I knew that there needed to be a better way to help individuals new to the community get connected. That's what helped my parents when they came here. I saw the chamber as a bridge between communities.

There are barriers: cultural barriers, institutional barriers, language barriers. No organization was doing this with cultural competency and language proficiency. I started the chamber to pay it forward and help people build their American dreams here, like my family did. This is a new community. Hispanics start businesses at quicker rates than mainstream America. There are two different sides of it. One for the community, based in education, and also helping businesses grow and create opportunities.

Through the VA Hispanic Foundation, we've partnered with the schools. We've helped thousands and received numerous honors. We are very active and are helping students to have a vision that they aspire to be. We help them to do that. We are making a difference in the community: building hope, building a future, and a legacy for everyone.

and grow their businesses. It was the first organization of its kind in Virginia. Later in 2003, he established the Virginia Hispanic Foundation to provide further education, information, and resources after seeing the community challenges that began with the work of the restaurant.

Much of this southside area along Richmond Highway, Midlothian Turnpike, and Hull Street in the city of Richmond and north Chesterfield County has become a focal point for Latino business, culture, and community development. In the twenty-first century, abundant taquerias, supermercados, and cantinas line these thoroughfares, and La Siesta set the stage for these communities to develop and flourish decades ago.

## TO LEARN MORE

Kelleher, Michael. "Building Bridges and Sharing Ladders: Hall of Fame Inductee Person of the Year Michel Zajur, Virginia Hispanic Chamber of Commerce Founder." *Richmond Times-Dispatch,* December 18, 2018.

Machacek, Rachel. "Trailblazer: Michel Zajur of La Siesta." *Richmond Magazine,* June 1, 2013.

Former Colbrook Motel in 2019 prior to lot clearance in 2020.

### 6.3 Colbrook Motel (former)

13916 Richmond Highway (Route 1), Chester

Colbrook Motel opened to African American travelers in 1946. It consisted of a cabin-style motel and may have been the only lodging available to African Americans along U. S. Route 1 in Chesterfield County at the time. U. S. Route 1 was a major north–south thoroughfare along the East Coast before Interstate 95 opened in the late 1950s. In 1922, Virginia's General Assembly named Virginia's portion of Route 1 after the president of the confederacy, Jefferson Davis, at the request of the Daughters of the Confederacy. Most locals still refer to the route as "Jeff Davis Highway," although in 2021, Virginia mandated that all localities change the name of their portion of the road by year's end.

Two Black businessmen, William Brooks and Courtland Colson, developed the Colbrook property, combining their last names to form the motel's name. Brooks eventually bought out Colson, expanding the property and creating a popular restaurant that

became a gathering space for local African Americans. In 1947, the motel began to be featured in the popular *The Negro Motorist Green Book,* a guidebook published specifically for African Americans to help direct them to places that would safely accommodate and welcome them, particularly in segregated areas. Victor Green, a Harlem postal worker, conceived of the book after experiencing racial discrimination while traveling. Green published the guide for nearly three decades, beginning in 1937.

The original cabins no longer exist, but the site represents the importance of recognizing that well into the 1960s, African American travelers in Virginia had to carefully seek out specific accommodations, since they would not be admitted to white establishments, and in some areas, the number of Black-serving accommodations were few to none. They also risked their personal safety in trying to find lodging and restaurants to use in areas unfamiliar to them. Today, the site is being developed into an affordable housing community that will utilize the Colbrook name.

## TO LEARN MORE

Bruder, Anne, Susan Hellman, and Catherine Zipf. "Notes from the Road: Documenting Sites Listed in The Negro Motorist Green Book." *Arris: Journal of the Southeast Chapter of Architectural Historians,* 2018.

Griset, Rich. "Local 'Green Book' Motel Was a Haven for Black Travelers during Jim Crow: An Affordable Housing Project Seeks to Honor That History." *Chesterfield Observer,* October 14, 2020.

*The Architecture of The Negro Travelers' Green Book,* a website hosted by the University of Virginia: http://community.village.virginia.edu/greenbooks/

## 6.4 213–215 Witten Street

Pocahontas Island, Petersburg

The house at this address, located on Pocahontas Island, purportedly served as a stop on the Underground Railroad for enslaved people headed north. While it is nearly impossible to confirm or deny exact railroad locations today, Petersburg served as a well-established conduit along this path to freedom. Enslaved people began settling on Pocahontas Island, a seventy-acre peninsula on the banks of the Appomattox River in Petersburg, in the 1730s. Pocahontas Island became a notable freedom colony prior to the Civil War as the first predominantly free Black settlement in the state. At the start of the Civil War, more than half of Petersburg's population was Black, and one-third of that community consisted of freemen and women. Pocahontas Island represented one of the largest free Black communities in the nation, and likely the largest one in the South.

In 1856, Virginia passed a law requiring that all ships traveling north be inspected due to an escalation in the number of enslaved people sailing toward freedom. The General Assembly passed the law specifically in response to actions conducted by people like Captain William Baylis, a white ship captain who resided in Delaware. Baylis had recently sailed out of Richmond with an enslaved person who worked in one of the city's oyster houses hidden on his ship.

Using this Witten Street location as a site of congregation, Baylis again planned to transport a group of enslaved people north. On May 29, 1858, the schooner *Keziah* left the Petersburg port with a cargo of wheat and five enslaved people: Gilbert, Sarah, William, John, and Joe. Baylis set sail one day after 2,000 white residents in Norfolk and Portsmouth gathered to demand stricter oversight of the waterways following an attempted escape by an enslaved person named Anthony, who was found hiding aboard the ship *Francis French* in the James River. Unfortunately, the *Keziah* ran aground soon after leaving port. The enslaved people were found by a search party authorized by Petersburg's mayor after their enslavers raised the alarm that they were missing. Everyone on board returned to Petersburg under guard. There, Baylis, well known for his work helping the enslaved reach freedom, received a forty-year jail sentence for abduction. He remained in prison until the end of the Civil War. John was sold south for

This building is believed to have been a key site on the Underground Railroad prior to the Civil War. As an active port with a large presence of free Black residents, Petersburg served as a linchpin of the system to help enslaved people escape north to freedom.

(Above) Inside Richard Stewart's Pocahontas Island Black History Museum.

(Left) Richard Stewart sits on the porch of his Pocahontas Island Black History Museum, where he carefully preserves the community's history.

$1,150. The fates of Gilbert, Sarah, William, and Joe remain unknown.

Today, this house still stands, although it has significantly deteriorated. In the 1970s, residents worked to prevent the city of Petersburg from condemning 250 homes on Pocahontas Island in favor of industrial building. They later secured the creation of the Pocahontas Island Historic District after a tornado devastated the area in 1993. A few key ancestral community keepers, like Richard Stewart who runs the Pocahontas Island Black History Museum out of his home, take great care and responsibility in stewarding the rich history of this site. According to Stewart, "My ancestors always had confidence in me that one day, I'd grow up and be the man to lead this community and tell our history. You go into Washington, DC museums, but you can't walk on the fertile ground, the same ground that my ancestors walked. When you come here, you see things that are a glance into our past that allow you to touch that past. I want people to see this history so that they can pass it on to future generations."

*A note on the name:* Pocahontas Island acquired its name when it was incorporated as a town in 1752; it became part of Petersburg in 1784. The name itself is part of a long history of settler colonialism. Archeologists acknowledge this site as a key Indigenous settlement dating from 6500 BCE. The Appomattoc lived here at the time of European contact, and like many Indigenous communities in the area, they became tributaries to Powhatan at the turn of the seventeenth century. They numbered 100–150 and were continually driven from their lands by the English, due to both war and settlement. By the 1720s, no tribal members remained. Thus white colonizers, after eradicating local Indigenous communities, named this area after an Indigenous woman, paramount chief Powhatan's daughter, Pocahontas, whose own story and life had been deeply misconstrued and manipulated by the English.

**TO LEARN MORE**

Kneebone, John T. "A Break Down on the Underground Railroad: Captain B. and the Capture of the Keziah, 1858." *Virginia Cavalcade* (1999): 74–83.

Schneider, Gregory. "One Man's Quest to Preserve the Haunting Black History of Pocahontas Island." *Washington Post,* September 26, 2016.

Steger, Martha. "Island Time." *Richmond Magazine,* March 2, 2021.

**TO VISIT NEARBY**

POCAHONTAS ISLAND BLACK HISTORY MUSEUM at 224 Witten Street, Petersburg. Call ahead (804–861–8889) to schedule a visit.

## 6.5 Beaux Twenty Club (former)

464 Byrne Street, Petersburg

This building originally housed a United Services Organization (USO) for African American soldiers during World War II. When the USO closed, local Black businessmen opened the Beaux Twenty Club, a social club, at this location. Founders included Hermanze Fauntleroy Jr., Petersburg's first Black mayor, selected by the city council in 1973. Over the decades of its existence, the

Beaux Twenty Club in 2020 prior to its restoration.

club morphed from a social and civic organization into a nightlife venue. It closed in
the 2010s. This part of Petersburg, known as
the Heights, distinguishes it from the city's
mostly low-lying areas. A community of
free Black people lived and owned property
here prior to the Civil War. John Shore, a
neighborhood resident and barber, served as
one of the city's first Black city councilmen
in the 1870s. In the early twentieth century,
the community's Black residents worked in
the city's major industries, including tobacco
factories and railroad yards. Once lauded for
its high rates of home ownership, the neighborhood suffered divestment after World
War II, due to racist housing, urban renewal,
and community development policies. Today,
residents of the Heights are mostly elders
with strong generational community ties.

Like most of Petersburg, the neighborhood lies within a floodplain, and as organizer Queen Zakia Shabazz notes, it had
been plagued by water issues: "Boil water
warnings, flooding, and even shutting off
customers' water who couldn't pay their
bills during the COVID-19 pandemic." Residents of the Heights, along with neighboring communities, have poor drainage fields
and lack access to shelter and evacuation in
the event of flooding. Advocates are working to list the former Beaux Twenty Club
building on the National Register of Historic
Places to protect it from demolition. Community partners, residents, and organizers
are creating a neighborhood resiliency hub
in the building. The solar-powered space will
offer residents shelter in the event of power
outages during hot or cold weather as well

PERSONAL REFLECTION

**QUEEN ZAKIA SHABAZZ**
Environmental Justice Advocate and Founder
of United Parents Against Lead

I became an activist in 1996 when my
son was poisoned by lead, and as a result,
I founded United Parents Against Lead
(UPAL) to advocate for children and families affected by lead poisoning, which few
people were talking about at the time.
Lead poisoning causes permanent and
irreversible brain damage so any child that
is poisoned, it impedes their development.
Communities, especially communities
of low income, are left to fend for themselves because they have old, deteriorating housing, often owned by slumlords
that either don't have the means or the
care to fix the properties so that families
have a safe place to live. Because all of
the properties are distressed, it leaves little
housing choices for families with lower
incomes and makes them at risk for lead
poisoning and other environmental hazards. It's a silent trend that will continue
if we do not raise our voices, if we do not
point it out and call it out. Amid the CO-
VID-19 pandemic, I'm so tired of hearing
that our communities and our people are
disproportionately impacted because this
isn't new. Our communities are not disad-
vantaged; they have been divested. Leaders have intentionally pulled resources
and funding from them so they, of course,
are disproportionately impacted.

as access to food and skills training. A leading community partner, United Parents
Against Lead (UPAL), has worked in Richmond and Petersburg since 1996 to conduct
lead remediation in dozens of residents'

homes and to advocate for safe living conditions for all community members, regardless of race or income. Its work is integral to the resiliency hub, which will incorporate community safety, health, and security into the foundation of its mission.

This site represents an example of how to revitalize historic properties in long-neglected communities in ways that center the needs of community members by welcoming them into the process of creating the spaces that benefit them, unlike much of the profit-driven development work that fails to prioritize local communities, especially if they are lower income or racial minorities.

## 6.6  Legends Historical Park and Wilcox Lake

Baylors Lane off of Defense Road, Petersburg

The city of Petersburg created this park near newly developed affluent white suburbs in 1921. The city initially named the space Lee Memorial Park, in honor of confederate general Robert E. Lee, a name that it held for ninety-nine years. As part of a women's relief program of the Works Progress Administration (WPA) during the Great Depression, white women oversaw the work of unemployed Black women who cleared the land, created ravines,

built trails, and planted 365,000 flowers and shrubs, as well as a million honeysuckle roots, to create the Lee Park Wildflower and Bird Sanctuary. The project employed more than a hundred women at any given time. The NAACP and other Black organizations complained about the obvious labor disparities between the work conducted by the Black women and their white female supervisors, but the inequities continued until the project ended in 1940. After World War II, the park, with its trails and swimming lake, was one of the most popular recreational spaces in the area, but it was for white use only.

In 1953, thirty-two African American residents petitioned Petersburg's city council for equal use and access to city-owned facilities. Within a month of the lawsuit's filing, the all-white city council closed the park, including its lake and swimming facilities, rather than integrate. A federal judge dismissed the lawsuit in 1955 since the city had permanently closed the facility.

Wilcox Lake remains closed to recreational activities, 2020.

Willcox Lake and Bathing Beach, Petersburg, Va.

6A491-N

Postcard ca. 1950 showing white families enjoying Wilcox Lake.

The city later opened and integrated many of the park's facilities, but the lake remains closed to the public. In 2020, the city council renamed the park Legends Historical Park to honor notable local Black basketball players Moses Malone, Mark West, Frank Mason, and Quinton Spain, all of whom played at the park in the 1970s.

**TO LEARN MORE**

Adam, John. "Calming the Waters at Wilcox Lake." *The Progress-Index,* September 23, 2018.

## 6.7  Central State Hospital (formerly the Central Lunatic Asylum for Colored Insane)

26317 W. Washington Street, Petersburg

Founded in 1870 to serve Virginia's African American patients, the Central Lunatic Asylum for Colored Insane became the first institution in the nation to provide mental healthcare solely for African Americans. Renamed Central State Hospital in 1894, the

state initially founded the asylum on the site of a former Freedmen's Bureau just outside of Richmond. The facility moved to Petersburg in 1885, due to the need for more space and the dilapidated condition of the initial site.

At its founding, patients included an equal number of "insane persons" and "paupers." The asylum admitted its first patient, Edith Smith, because she had few resources and no place to go. Many others arrived due to civil commitments, meaning that a judge found them to be a danger to themselves or others and ordered them to be involuntarily confined. Officials removed others from local jails and criminally committed them.

The establishment of the asylum greatly increased African Americans' access to publicly funded mental healthcare. However, the question of what kind of care they received lingers. Dr. William Drewry, the institution's fourth superintendent who served for twenty years, delivered a speech at a 1908 conference in which he detailed his belief in the relationship between African Americans'

A building no longer in use at Central State Hospital, 2020.

granted funding for significant expansions, both in buildings and services, during the 1960s. The facility desegregated in 1970.

King Davis, the first African American to lead the Virginia Department of Mental Health and Professor Emeritus at University of Texas at Austin, saved many of the facility's records by transporting 800,000 documents detailing the hospital's hundred-year history from Petersburg to Austin to preserve them. These records offer a rare picture into a mental institute that served African Americans immediately following emancipation and throughout the Jim Crow era, since nearly all facilities that served Black patients closed soon after desegregation and destroyed or lost their records. He hopes to encourage current and future scholars to study these records, recalling, "I wish I had more time." Today, Central State Hospital still operates on these grounds.

emancipation and their rising numbers of insanity. Basing his reasons on prevailing racist beliefs, he depicted freed people as "emotional in nature," "weak minded," and prone to idleness. As one example, records listed the cause of patient Godfrey Goffney's psychosis as "freedom." Patients were stigmatized by race, presumed or real mental illness, and gender. A report from the asylum's first year of operation described patient Georgiana Page's condition simply as a "useless old harlot."

The Virginia Sterilization Act of 1924 gave superintendents at state mental institutions the authority to sterilize any patient "afflicted with hereditary forms of insanity that are recurrent: idiocy, imbecility, feeble-mindedness or epilepsy." Over 8,000 patients in the state's colonies were sterilized, including 1,634 Central State residents.

In the 1950s, the hospital experienced severe overcrowding as it supported nearly 5,000 patients. Reports noted that one large room housed over 300 patients, and elsewhere, patients slept on floors. The state

## TO LEARN MORE

Dietrich, Alicia. "UT Scholar Tells Forgotten Story of African-American Psychiatric Patients." *Alcalde*, January 17, 2014.

Foltz, Caitlin. "Race and Mental Illness at a Virginia Hospital: A Case Study of Central State Asylum for the Colored Insane, 1869–1885." Virginia Commonwealth University thesis, 2015.

Giddens, Tharon. "Hope, Healing and Ghosts." *Richmond Magazine*, October 7, 2019.

(Above) Former site of Matoaca Manufacturing Company along the Appomattox River.

(Left) Matoaca millworkers photographed by Lewis Hine in 1911.

## 6.8 Matoaca Manufacturing Company (former)

Pickett Avenue at Appomattox River, Chesterfield County

Chartered as a cotton and paper mill along the Appomattox River in 1836, Matoaca Manufacturing Company (MMC) was one of six Petersburg area mills that employed several hundred white women by the mid-nineteenth century. These mill workers represented the South's first industries to employ white women for wage labor. Water-powered mills primarily employed white women and children. While white men worked as managers, mechanics, and packers, women spun and wove cotton.

Prior to the Civil War, mill owners found it more profitable to employ poor white laborers than to buy a labor force of enslaved workers. Textile mills throughout the South maintained that strict color line after the Civil War as well. Mill owners instead used the threat of hiring cheaper Black laborers, a fear that many white elites in the South relied upon to keep pay low among white working communities following the abolition of slavery.

Laborers worked twelve or more hours six days each week. Owners paid low wages, and employees often lived in company-controlled tenement housing. Children as young as eight labored alongside older girls and women. The mill also introduced its employees to a new, rigid schedule. Worker Anthelia Holt wrote that she was at the mill "until seven oclock every night and until four oclock on Saturday . . . know that I am in the penitentiary for we won't see anything outdoors, only on Sunday." Most women were single and sent a portion of their meager wages back home to their families, who lived on local farms. Still, the mill afforded them the opportunity to live apart from their families, which some workers found beneficial, and to control some portion of their own wages. MMC, isolated from newer facilities and technologies available in nearby Petersburg, closed in the 1920s. No remnants of the former mill remain.

**TO LEARN MORE**

Barnes, Diane. *Artisan Workers in the Upper South: Petersburg, Virginia, 1820–1865*. Baton Rouge: Louisiana State University Press, 2008.

English, Beth. "'I Have . . . a Lot of Work to Do': Cotton Mill Work and Women's Culture in Matoaca, Virginia, 1888–95." *Virginia Magazine of History and Biography* 113, no. 3 (2006): 226–53.

## 6.9 Life Sciences Products Company (former)

905 E. Randolph Road, Hopewell

In 1974–75, workers at the Life Sciences Products factory manufactured Kepone, a toxic, nonbiodegradable insecticide used to bait ants and roaches. Allied Chemical patented Kepone in the 1950s and contracted with the Life Sciences Products factory to produce it in 1974. From March 1974 to July 1975, this plant in Hopewell was its sole manufacturer. Several workers exhibited symptoms of being poisoned by Kepone. They reported tremors, headaches, breathing problems, and vision impairment, conditions workers recognized as the "Kepone shakes." Delbert White noticed hand tremors soon after he began work there, and while he suspected he had been exposed to a hazardous chemical, the plant's supervisors and co-owners assured him that nothing in the factory would cause him harm. By the time he quit eleven months later, his exposure had been passed on to his children and wife, all of whom exhibited dizziness, tremors, and enlarged livers. At least twenty-nine workers were hospitalized during one year of production.

While some local doctors failed to recognize the poisoning, Dr. Yi-Nan Chou suspected it and sent a patient's blood sample to the Centers for Disease Control in Atlanta.

Contemporary industry in Hopewell, located where the Life Sciences Products Company once operated.

There, an employee called to verify the legitimacy of the sample, given how much chemical content it contained. An investigation into the plant began. In addition to exposing the workers to this health hazard, water containing Kepone infiltrated local sewer drains. When Hopewell's water treatment plant began to fail, officials traced it back to the presence of Kepone in the waste water.

The Virginia Health Department closed the plant in the summer of 1975. Subsequent investigations found poisoning in the water from the James River in Hopewell to the Chesapeake Bay eighty miles away. Kepone was found in air samples twenty miles north at the Richmond airport. That December, Virginia's governor closed the James River to all fishing after Kepone was found in a wide variety of marine life. In 1976, 120 fishermen, crabbers, and oystermen filed the first of several civil lawsuits against Allied by victims seeking compensation for lost wages, either due to direct poisoning or the poisoning of the wildlife on which they earned their living. Former workers filed suit seeking $173 million in damages. Allied settled these claims out of court. In the landmark environmental case *United States v. Allied Chemical Corp.*, Allied paid over $13 million for illegally dumping Kepone in the river in violation of the Clean Water Act. The state implemented fishing bans that were not lifted in full until 1988. Concerned citizens pointed out that Kepone does not disappear; it simply gets buried in river sediment. Two fenced-off toxic dump areas still exist at the site.

## TO LEARN MORE

Foster, Richard. "Kepone, 'The Flour Factory.'" *Richmond Magazine,* July 8, 2005.

Reich, Michael, and Jacquelin Spong. "Kepone: A Chemical Disaster in Hopewell, Virginia." *International Journal of Health Services* 13, no. 2 (1983): 227–46.

Wilson, Gregory. "Toxic Dust: The History and Legacy of Virginia's Kepone Disaster." Virginia Museum of History & Culture. Lecture, October 5, 2017.

Hopewell Municipal Building.

## 6.10 Hopewell Municipal Building

300 N. Main Street, Hopewell

In 1966, Rev. Curtis Harris organized a march to protest the building of a landfill in Hopewell's African American neighborhood of Rosedale. Harris, who had pastored Union Baptist Church since 1959, was a local civil rights leader who helped form the Hopewell Improvement Association, an affiliate of Martin Luther King Jr.'s Southern Christian Leadership Conference. The association pushed for the desegregation of Hopewell's public facilities, including its cemetery, city pool, and library.

Harris and a few dozen protestors marched from the site of the proposed landfill in the Rosedale neighborhood three miles downtown to the Hopewell Municipal Building. There, the group was met with an equal number of Ku Klux Klan members, dressed in robes, who flanked them as they made their way inside to deliver their let-

ter of protest to the city manager. The letter asked not only to stop the landfill but also to appoint a committee that included Black residents to find another site for the landfill. Curtis wrote, "It is regrettable that in this enlightened age 20 percent of any community could be systematically excluded from every committee and commission of any significance within the community."

Upon returning outside, they began singing civil rights anthems while KKK members led racist chants. Harris started to pray, and a Klan member declared that everyone had the right to pray and went silent. When Harris finished, a member of the Klan began to pray. Then the Klan members quietly disassembled. Having dispersed the Klan, Harris's group then marched to Union Baptist Church, a landmark of civil rights organizing in Hopewell. While this action did not stop the city from building the landfill, Harris went on to run for Hopewell's city council seven times, eventually winning after working to change the way in which the city elects its council members into a more democratic process. He became the city's first Black mayor in 1998. While built at the time, the landfill has since been closed, and Harris's legacy lives on. Hopewell renamed the city's post office after him in 2020 to memorialize his decades-long activism on behalf of the city's African American residents.

## TO LEARN MORE

Lee, Lauranett. *Making the American Dream Work: A Cultural History of African Americans in Hopewell, Virginia*. New York: Morgan James, 2008.

View Rev. Curtis Harris's oral history at VCU's Voices of Freedom Digital Collection: https://digital.library.vcu.edu/islandora/object/vcu%3A38562?search=curtis%2520harris

## TO VISIT NEARBY

**DRIVE BY THE HOME** where Harris and his wife, Ruth, lived for nearly six decades at 209 Rev. C. W. Harris Street. The Hopewell city council renamed the street in honor of Harris in 2014.

# 7

# Charlottesville and Points West of Richmond

# Introduction

**CHARLOTTESVILLE AND SURROUNDING**
Albemarle County lie in Virginia's Piedmont region, just east of the Blue Ridge Mountains. The Monacan occupied the Piedmont and parts of the Blue Ridge prior to white colonization. A well-worn Indigenous trading and game trail spur off of the major East Coast north–south Indigenous path paralleled today's Interstate 64. It linked communities to locations both east and west. By the 1700s, white settlers called this route Three Notch'd (now Three Chopt) Road; it extended east to Richmond and west across the Blue Ridge Mountains. Today, it is U. S. Route 250.

Thomas Jefferson, the nation's third president, looms large in Charlottesville's historic memory and landscape, as he located both his plantation home, Monticello, and the university he founded, the University of Virginia (UVA), here. He enslaved more than 600 people during his lifetime, freeing only a select few, mostly relatives. Thousands of enslaved laborers built and labored at UVA until the abolishment of slavery. They were owned or hired out by the university, faculty, and staff. Jefferson's deliberate university architecture design hid much of this work, even though enslaved laborers outnumbered students on campus during UVA's early years.

At the time of the Civil War, more than half of Albemarle County's population were enslaved. Throughout the South, areas with majority-Black populations faced strong resistance from local whites after emancipation regarding basic citizenship rights like voting, access to housing, and education. By the 1920s, Charlottesville's civic leaders had erected monuments to confederates and colonizers to demarcate white space. Local Ku Klux Klan chapters formed both in town and at UVA at a time when the town's Black citizens pushed for greater rights, like equal pay for Black and white teachers.

Simultaneously, UVA became the intellectual heart of the state's eugenics project, serving as the "scientific" knowledge base behind racial segregation. Eugenicists maintained white supremacy through a pseudoscience that claimed whites as the master race, and UVA faculty in the sciences and at the medical college spread the ideology and practice of eugenics. Scholar Lisa Woolfork notes in *Charlottesville 2017: The Legacy of Race and Inequity* that from the 1920s to the 1950s, "UVA was a veritable powerhouse of white supremacist ideology, scientific racism, and massive resistance to segregation." This work greatly contributed to how ingrained eugenics thinking became as its supporters passed heinous legal acts in Virginia that included legalizing the sterilization of "epileptics and the feebleminded" without consent in 1922 and further entrenching the privileges of whiteness.

After World War II, demands for equal rights from Black citizens reached a crescendo. In particular, Black citizens demanded more and better public education

# Charlottesville & West of Richmond

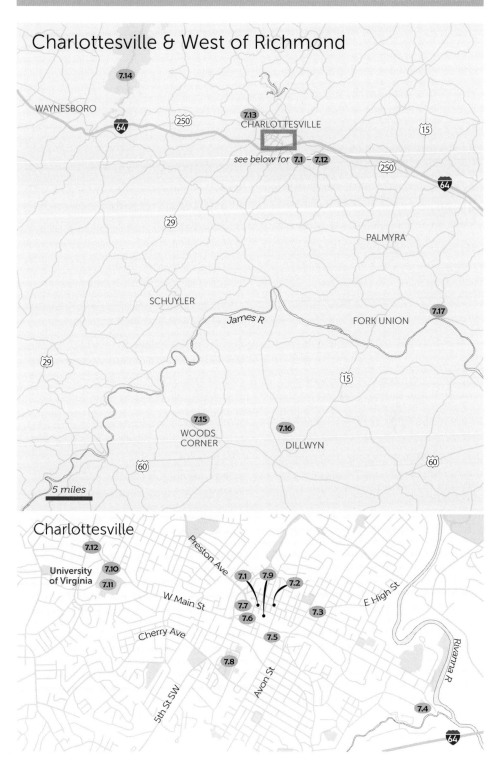

WAYNESBORO

CHARLOTTESVILLE

*see below for* 7.1 – 7.12

PALMYRA

SCHUYLER

*James R*

FORK UNION

WOODS CORNER

DILLWYN

5 miles

## Charlottesville

University of Virginia

Preston Ave

W Main St

Cherry Ave

E High St

Rivanna R

Avon St

5th St SW

opportunities. While the courts granted their demands for desegregation, Governor Lindsay Almond closed schools in Charlottesville from September 1958 to February 1959 rather than desegregate them. While the city and state could not ultimately prevent school desegregation, the city utilized a host of racist housing policies and urban renewal schemes to destroy most of the Black neighborhoods near the city center. To create areas like the downtown mall, a pedestrian avenue catering to affluent white locals and tourists, the city razed several Black neighborhoods, then built public housing outside of the city's core to replace the homes many African Americans owned, and lost, in this process.

As the town that houses the state's flagship university, Charlottesville has promoted itself as a center of liberalism in recent decades. A vibrant New Left movement emerged in the 1970s, which built upon activism by the city's Black activists in the 1950s and 1960s. Scholar Thomas Hanna named UVA as one of the four most prominent collegiate centers of New Left activism in the South, with student movements mobilizing for greater racial equity and against the Vietnam War. This student-driven activism challenged the university's entrenched conservative leadership and began to reshape campus culture. As well, these movements aligned with long-established activism in the city. Since the 1980s, Charlottesville has been the site of important LGBTQ activism and community making, and Black residents in Charlottesville and Black students at UVA continued to resist the city's and university's white supremacist

practices. But that veneer of white liberalism has eroded in recent years. When Charlottesville's city council voted to remove two prominent confederate monuments in 2017, the city became ground zero for white supremacist activity, much of it organized by two UVA alumni: Richard Spencer and Jason Kessler. Kessler still resides in Charlottesville. The 2017 Summer of Hate included marches and rallies by white supremacist organizations that culminated in the Unite the Right Rally on August 12, 2017, which resulted in the death of Heather Heyer, an attendee who stood in support of human rights.

On July 10, 2021, the city removed two prominent confederate statues, an important win in reshaping the city's visual landscape. But removing statues does not resolve histories of racist policy, as made evident in Charlottesville's long-term affordable housing crisis. A 2020 report by the Charlottesville Low-Income Housing Coalition noted that between 2012 and 2021, housing values rose by as much as 50 percent. Since 2000, Black home ownership in the city has fallen by 24 percent while white homeownership has risen by 20 percent. Thousands of families have unmet housing needs, a continued effect of discriminatory housing policies the city began implementing more than a century ago. While Charlottesville's prioritization of housing and business development for the affluent continues, its connected histories of racism and poverty often remain invisible in the city's present-day landscape.

Similar histories of fighting for racial justice and economic well-being also shape the rural areas of the surrounding Piedmont.

Market Street Park in 2020 prior to the removal of the Lee statue.

South of Charlottesville lies rural Buckingham County. There, Dominion Energy targeted Union Hill, a town founded by formerly enslaved people after the Civil War, for a natural gas pipeline compressor station in the mid-2010s. Like their counterparts in Charles City County to the east, rural majority-minority communities often find themselves targeted by the fossil fuel industry to push through pipelines and gas plants at a time when the state claims it will reach carbon neutrality by 2045. Other racial justice issues, such as health and safety conditions in local prisons, came to a head during the COVID-19 pandemic. The sites in this chapter feature Indigenous people's fight for sovereignty under settler colonialism, organizing for racial and environmental justice, and mobilization to support and grow LGBTQ communities. It features people working for change in their communities to dismantle unjust systems of power and centers people's struggles, both past and present, for racial equity and environmental justice.

# Charlottesville and Points West of Richmond Sites

## 7.1 Market Street Park

101 E. Market Street, Charlottesville

In 1924, Charlottesville's city leaders unveiled a statue of Robert E. Lee and christened this site Lee Park. Over ninety years later, localities around the country began to reconsider their confederate memorial landscape following the murder of nine African American members of the Emanuel African Methodist Episcopal Church in Charleston, South Carolina, in 2015. Locally, high school student Zyahna Bryant, founder of Charlottesville High School's Black Student Union, submitted a petition to the city to remove this statue. Bryant recalls: "In the spring of 2016, I did something that scared me, but something that I knew needed to be done. I wrote the petition, a letter to the editor and

Informal memorial to Heather Heyer near Market Street Park, 2020.

city council, calling for the removal of the Robert E. Lee statue and the renaming of the park . . . I was 15." As a partial result, in February 2017, Charlottesville's city council voted to remove the Lee statue from the park, but a subsequent lawsuit brought by members of neo-confederate organizations, including the Sons of Confederate Veterans, prevented its removal. Frustrated with the delay, in June 2017, the city council voted unanimously to rename the park Emancipation Park. Renaming the park, along with the vote to remove the Lee statue, served as a catalyst for white supremacists to gather in Charlottesville in August 2017. Publicity for the gathering included a photo of Lee's face with the words "They will not replace us" superimposed over the image.

Tensions had been mounting over these decisions for months. White nationalists led a "Take Back Lee Park" rally in May 2017, and in July, fifty Ku Klux Klan members rallied in town. They were met with more than a thousand counter-protesters and left within an hour of their arrival. On August 12, 2017, the Unite the Right Rally, organized by white supremacist Jason Kessler, took place with a stated purpose to oppose the removal of the Lee statue from this park. The previous night, a hundred white nationalists had marched through the University of Virginia's campus wielding tiki torches and yelling racist and antisemitic chants. As white supremacists, neo-Nazis, neo-confederates, and various militia groups gathered, so did counterprotesters. That morning, Governor Terry McAuliffe declared a state of emergency, and Virginia state police declared the assembly unlawful. That afternoon, white supremacist James Fields Jr. rammed his car into a group of counterprotesters, killing Heather Heyer and injuring nineteen others. The rally garnered international attention and showcased the violence spurred by actions to de-center memorials and other symbols foundational to the maintenance of white supremacy.

In December 2017, African American activist Mary Carey submitted a petition to the city council to again rename the park, stating that as long as the statue of Lee remained, she and others did not see it as an emancipatory space. In July 2018, the city council renamed the park after its geographic location on Market Street. Three years later, on July 10, 2021, the city removed the Lee statue in this square as well as the nearby Stonewall Jackson statue in Court Square Park, located at 405 E. High Street.

## TO LEARN MORE

Southern Poverty Law Center's *Hate Map* chronicles the actions and geographies of hate groups across the country. https://www.splcenter.org/hate-map

The grassroots group *#TakeEmDownNOLA* in New Orleans pioneered effective action to remove confederate monuments in the South. http://takeemdownnola.org/

## 7.2　Congregation Beth Israel

301 E. Jefferson Street, Charlottesville

Congregation Beth Israel.

Charlottesville saw a number of German Jewish immigrants establish roots here in the mid-nineteenth century as part of a larger movement by Germans of many faiths to emigrate to America amidst political and economic turmoil at home. In 1870, German Jewish merchants Isaac Leterman and Bernard Oberdofer purchased property to create a Jewish cemetery on behalf of the Charlottesville Hebrew Benevolent Society. That society began holding meetings as Congregation Beth Israel in 1882. The congregation built the original synagogue at the corner of Market and Church (now Second) Streets in 1883. In 1902, the U.S. government requested that Congregation Beth Israel sell that land so that a post office (now a library) could be erected. Work began on the present-day synagogue in 1903.

On August 11–12, 2017, white supremacists gathered in Charlottesville to protest the city council's decision to remove the city's prominent confederate statues. On the evening of August 11, a group marched across the University of Virginia grounds chanting racist and antisemitic slogans. Prominent white supremacist, Holocaust denier, and UVA alumnus Richard Spencer was part of this group. The next morning, armed white supremacists wearing military fatigues and carrying semi-automatic weapons loitered outside of Congregation Beth Israel as worshippers gathered for Shabbat prayers. The congregation had requested that a city police officer be posted at the synagogue that morning to protect worshippers, as it was well known that the groups included violent neo-Nazi leaders. The police refused this request, and instead the congregation hired a private security guard.

With forty congregants inside, groups parading by shouted antisemitic slogans, performed Nazi salutes, and loudly pointed out the location of the synagogue. Some carried flags with swastikas and other Nazi symbols alongside confederate ones. Like the previous night, groups chanted "Jews will not replace us," recreated scenes from Nazi propaganda films, and wore shirts displaying Adolf Hitler quotes.

After services, Beth Israel's worshippers left in small groups from a back exit to avoid detection. Later, they learned that websites affiliated with white supremacist groups in attendance called on rallygoers to burn the synagogue. That afternoon, a vicious car attack that killed human rights advocate Heather Heyer occurred two hundred feet from the building.

## TO LEARN MORE

Nelson, Louis, and Claudrena Harold, eds. *Charlottesville 2017: The Legacy of Race and Inequity*. Charlottesville: University of Virginia Press, 2018.

Urofsky, Melvin. *Commonwealth and Community: The Jewish Experience in Virginia*. Richmond: Virginia Historical Society, 1997.

## 7.3  AIDS Services Group (former)

315 10th Street NE, Charlottesville

A group of healthcare advocates founded the nonprofit AIDS Services Group in 1986 to provide care and advocacy for individuals living with AIDS. The University of Virginia (UVA) Hospital recorded Charlottesville's first AIDS case four years earlier in 1982. Similar to hospitals around the country, patients reported issues like food trays being left outside of their rooms because staff were afraid to enter them. Many patients had no support, either disowned by their families or still closeted to them. Many of those who contracted AIDS faced fear, alienation, and abandonment.

When Blaise Spinelli, a medical tech at UVA Hospital, received a call from hospice about an AIDS patient who the organization could not serve, he and others formed a grassroots group to provide that care. The group became the AIDS Services Group of Charlottesville (ASG). Trained by Washington DC's Gay Men's Health Clinic, the group met weekly and grew to include local medical professionals and others who wanted to help. ASG soon secured funding for a director and served seventy-five clients within its first two years. Over the decades, ASG adapted to keep pace with the changing needs of people living with HIV / AIDS.

In 2013, ASG transitioned to Thrive. The organization expanded to offer HIV-informed primary healthcare to anyone who needed it, alongside a range of mental health services. It also provided healthcare for transgender people seeking affordable or no-cost hormone therapy. The agency permanently closed in 2015, one of four former AIDS service organizations in Virginia to close that year as the need for support specific to HIV / AIDS declined alongside funding for this work. Grassroots organizations like ASG led the fight to ensure AIDS patients received proper care and treatment while also working to reduce stigma and provide care and comfort to individuals who were often abandoned by their families, and marginalized by traditional healthcare institutions, while very sick or dying. Today, another nonprofit occupies this space.

**TO LEARN MORE**

Brashear, Graelyn. "Charlottesville AIDS Care Center Announces Closure." *C-ville Weekly,* April 3, 2015.

Long, Preston. "Across 30 Years and an Epidemic, Charlottesville's Gay and Lesbian Communities Came Out Together." *C-ville Weekly,* November 13, 2012.

## 7.4 Charlottesville Woolen Mills

E. Market Street at Pireus Row, Charlottesville

On February 5, 1918, eighteen workers, twelve men and six women, threatened a work stoppage at the woolen mills. With the onset of World War I, the mills experienced difficulty acquiring supplies from abroad, and received no government contracts to help offset the slowdown. In August 1917, Congress passed a law to regulate fuel prices and distribution. In January 1918, the federal government ordered a five-day "holiday" to be followed by ten weeks of Monday "holidays," all of which would require the mills to close in order to conserve fuel. On the day following this five-day federally mandated shutdown, these workers demanded pay for the days of lost work. Most had worked at the mills for decades. When they threatened a work stoppage, their manager fired them on the spot, advertising for their replacements in the afternoon newspaper.

In an emergency meeting, the board governing the mills granted the manager permission to raise wages. While all eighteen workers soon returned, the company did not

While some of the historic Woolen Mills site has been converted for contemporary use, ruins like this building remain, 2020.

raise wages until March. By 1920, mill wages aligned with other Charlottesville industries, after decades of lagging behind. Like many textile mills, the woolen mills had long sought to develop strong kinship ties among its workers. Owners rented housing units to workers and established both a church and a school, creating the feel of a company-run town. The mills did not hire children under the age of thirteen, an unusual prohibition in an industry known for its exploitation of child labor. The owners hoped this benevolent paternalism would create a stable workforce by facilitating community building and social ties to retain its workers despite paying low wages. This walkout is significant because such action was uncommon in Virginia, a state historically hostile to unions and labor demands. It represents one of the few successful walkouts and one that included both men and women, unusual due to the sex segregation at many industrial job sites at the time. The mills closed in 1962, but the four-story brick building, rebuilt after a fire in 1882, still stands as a converted loft space for residential and commercial occupancy. It anchors a newly designated historic district.

**TO LEARN MORE**

Myers, Andrew. "The Charlottesville Woolen Mills: Working Life, Wartime, and the Walkout of 1918." http://historicwoolenmills.org/pages/andy_myers.html

*The Daily Progress.* "Labor Dispute at Woolen Mills Leads to Worker Strike." February 6, 2017.

## 7.5 Martha "Mattie" Thompson Residence (former)

500 Garrett Street, Charlottesville

Martha "Mattie" Thompson, a woman listed as "mulatto," indicating mixed race, in the federal census, bought a property at what was the southeast corner of Garrett and 5th Streets in 1885. She turned the three-story property into a brothel, which she operated for more than forty years. Both white women and women of color worked for Thompson, several of whom went on to run their own brothels.

The Garrett Street neighborhood, just south of Water Street, contained Charlottesville's red-light district in the late nineteenth and early twentieth centuries. It was one of the only areas in town where white women, living in brothels as sex workers, resided in the same neighborhood as working-class African Americans during legal segregation. While illegal, most people chose to ignore the brothels except for those who went looking for them until after World War II, when the city targeted the neighborhood for urban removal. Police did occasionally take action. On October 29, 1912, for example, they raided eight brothels and arrested twenty-five women, charging them with prostitution. Despite the presence of many men frequenting the brothels, the police only arrested women, targeting them for selling sex but not men for buying it.

When Thompson died in 1925, she left the property to Bernard Samuels. She had been enslaved to Samuels's great grandfather from her birth in 1850 until the Civil War. Samuels buried her

Mattie Thompson's Garrett Street brothel, 1915.

at the family grave plot in Front Royal, Virginia. The gravestone described her as an "aunt" and a "servant" of the family. Placing her grave at a ninety-degree angle to the others, Samuels buried her at the feet of the family to whom she had been enslaved. Her life showcases the intricate ways in which women of color negotiated the complex terrain of life during the Jim Crow era.

This residence no longer exists; 5th Street no longer exists at this location. The city demolished this neighborhood as part of its urban renewal plans in the 1970s, destroying a large and vibrant African American neighborhood.

**TO LEARN MORE**

Bluestone, Daniel. "Charlottesville's Landscape of Prostitution, 1880–1950." *Buildings & Landscapes: Journal of the Vernacular Architecture Forum* 22, no. 2 (2015): 36–61.

### 7.6 Muldowney's Pub (former)

212 W. Water Street, Charlottesville

Bostonian Joan Schatzman moved to Charlottesville in 1976, a twenty-four-year-old out lesbian. Concerned with the lack of inclusive gathering spaces, she quit her job at the Pepsi plant in 1980 and opened Muldowney's. Prior to its opening, a handful of gay and lesbian friendly spaces operated in Charlottesville, but none were specifically cultivated for gay and lesbian patrons. Muldowney's could not function as a standalone bar. Virginia's Alcoholic Beverage Control (ABC) agency does not allow any establishment to serve alcohol alone, although it has made some recent exceptions in relation

to beer and wine. A substantial amount of sales at all establishments selling liquor, both in the past and today, must come from food sales. Thus, Schatzman had to create a restaurant alongside a bar. ABC was notorious for its prosecution of bars thought to welcome a gay and lesbian crowd. It revoked and suspended licenses if establishments "became a meeting place and rendezvous for users of narcotics, drunks, homosexuals, prostitutes" and others. It also forbade places from employing anyone suspected of being gay. ABC enforced these statutes with zeal until the federal courts declared them unconstitutional in 1991.

Flyer for punk music at Muldowney's Pub, mid-1980s. Death Piggy later became the popular Richmond-based heavy metal band GWAR.

Muldowney's was known anecdotally as being "straight 'til 8," and while ostensibly illegal, it functioned as Charlottesville's first gay and lesbian bar. It also provided a space for others to find community in Charlottesville, hosting drag nights on Saturdays and punk shows toward the end of its existence. Schatzman sold Muldowney's in 1985 to five gay men who reopened it as The Silver Fox under the same concept of maintaining a gay and lesbian friendly space. It closed in 1991. These spaces provided critical community and support during a time when many LGBTQ folks could not openly be themselves, and during the AIDS crisis, when being gay was further stigmatized.

only Black elementary school, Jefferson School, resided there as did many Black fraternal orders, churches, and businesses.

The neighborhood's close proximity to downtown did not bode well for its long-term survival. In 1960, a city referendum narrowly passed to redevelop Vinegar Hill at a time when many African Americans were still disenfranchised; this referendum, for example, passed at an election that required voters to pay a poll tax. Those in favor of demolition pointed to the substandard housing in the area, although that same year, an outside analyst stressed that the problem was not one of housing but of wages. Residents simply could not afford upkeep on

**TO LEARN MORE**

Long, Preston. "Across 30 Years and an Epidemic, Charlottesville's Gay and Lesbian Communities Came Out Together." *C-ville Weekly*, November 13, 2012.

## 7.7 Omni Hotel

212 Ridge McIntire Road, Charlottesville

Built in 1985, the Omni stands in what once was the African American neighborhood of Vinegar Hill. The neighborhood occupied twenty acres of land at the center of Charlottesville. It grew when formerly enslaved people entered the city following the Civil War. As segregation solidified in the early twentieth century, Vinegar Hill became a thriving Black mixed-income neighborhood filled with both residences and businesses. The neighborhood functioned as a center of Black social and economic life. The city's

The Omni Hotel anchors the west end of Charlottesville's Downtown Mall, an upscale stretch of restaurants, music venues, and stores.

Children playing in Vinegar Hill, ca. 1960.

their properties given the dismal wages they received at work.

This urban renewal project completely demolished the neighborhood. It disrupted twenty-nine primarily Black-owned businesses, and it displaced 158 families. Childhood resident Kathy Johnson Harris, whose family moved out in 1965, remembers: "We were the last family to leave Vinegar Hill. My memories are fond because this is all I know about my childhood . . . I wonder how many people understand how big urban renewal was. It wasn't just the housing. It was people's businesses, people's livelihoods. It was their wealth."

The city declared most residents eligible for public housing, and some moved into the newly built Westhaven Public Housing Project, named after former Vinegar Hill resident and Black entrepreneur John West. The move west isolated residents from the city center and further concentrated poverty. The Omni, which anchors the west end of the Downtown Mall, a highly trafficked commercial corridor and outdoor space, represents this displacement and gentrification. No visual cues remain to mark this transformation of space.

### TO LEARN MORE

Saunders, James Robert, and Renae Nadine Shackelford. *Urban Renewal and the End of Black Culture in Charlottesville, Virginia: An Oral History of Vinegar Hill.* Jefferson, NC: McFarland, 1998.
*That World Is Gone: Race and Displacement in a Southern Town.* Field Studio Films, 2010.

### TO VISIT NEARBY

**BENJAMIN TONSLER HOUSE** at 327 6th Street SW. Tonsler was a well-known Black educator who served as principal at Jefferson School, the city's first public school for Black students. A park that bears his name, Tonsler Park, is located at 500 Cherry Avenue.

**JEFFERSON SCHOOL AFRICAN AMERICAN HERITAGE CENTER** at 233 4th Street NW is housed in the original 1926 Jefferson High School building, the city's first high school for Black students.

Oakwood Cemetery with new housing development in the background, 2020.

## 7.8 Oakwood Cemetery

727–849 1st Street S., Charlottesville

The gravesite of Carrie Buck (later Carrie Buck Detamore) resides in this city-owned cemetery in central Charlottesville. In 1927, doctors forcibly sterilized Buck under the Virginia Sterilization Act of 1924. Virginia's General Assembly was the second state to pass this type of legislation and the first to implement it as part of a national upsurge in policies to preserve the "purity" of the white race.

Carrie Buck became the first documented eugenics case in the country, and the first of over 8,000 Virginians sterilized without their consent by the state between 1927 and 1972. Only California sterilized more of its residents than Virginia. Buck's mother had been committed to the Virginia State Colony for Epileptics and the Feeble-Minded in 1920. State officials placed seventeen-year-old Carrie there as well after giving birth out of wedlock to her daughter Vivian, a result of rape by her foster mother's nephew, in 1924.

In 1927, the U. S. Supreme Court declared the Virginia Sterilization Act constitutional in the case *Buck v. Bell,* with Justice Oliver Wendell Holmes Jr. infamously and enthusiastically noting that "three generations of imbeciles are enough." The state could legally sterilize any patient institutionalized in one of its five mental institutions "with hereditary forms of insanity that are recurrent, idiocy, imbecility, feeble-mindedness or epilepsy" without consent. In practice, most patients were simply poor and, in two cases out of three, women and girls.

After sterilization, the state released Buck from the State Colony. Colonies initially hired former patients out to families as domestic help, taking a cut of their pay. Buck married twice; her second husband was Charles Detamore. Buck's grave is listed under this name. Charles's name is listed first and hers is listed underneath as "Carrie E." Both she and her daughter Vivian are buried here. Vivian, who state officials forcibly removed from Buck at birth, was an honor roll student at her local elementary school before her death at the age of eight from colitis.

In the early 2000s, both the General Assembly and Governor Mark Warner expressed "profound regret" for the state's role in the eugenics movement. The state instated a limited compensation program for victims in 2015 after years of activism on the part of victims and their families.

**TO LEARN MORE**

Catte, Elizabeth. *Pure America: Eugenics and the Making of Modern Virginia*. Cleveland: Belt, 2021.
Cohen, Adam. *Imbeciles: The Supreme Court, American Eugenics, and the Sterilization of Carrie Buck*. New York: Penguin, 2017.
Lombardo, Paul. *Three Generations, No Imbeciles: Eugenics, the Supreme Court, and* Buck v. Bell. Baltimore: Johns Hopkins University Press, 2010.

**TO VISIT NEARBY**

The Daughters of Zion Cemetery at the corner of Oak Street and 1st Street South lies adjacent to this property. Members of the Daughters of Zion benevolent society, made up of African American women, purchased this plot in 1873, as the public Oakwood Cemetery was segregated until the 1960s. A group of descendants organized to pressure the city to better preserve the cemetery in the 2010s. Many of the group's initial goals have been met, and their work serves as a model for grassroots preservation efforts.

## 7.9 Hemings Family Residence (former)

Intersection of E. Main and E. 2nd Streets, Charlottesville

In the 1780s, Thomas Bell leased Sally Heming's sister, Mary, from prominent planter and enslaver Thomas Jefferson. Bell later bought and freed Mary and their two children. Mary inherited Bell's properties, including this residence, upon his death in 1800. Sally Hemings, mother to four of Jefferson's children, relocated here after Jefferson's death in 1826.

Sally Hemings, enslaved to Jefferson, bore seven children by him, four of whom lived into adulthood. Teenaged Sally traveled to France in 1787 as an attendant to one of Jefferson's two daughters born to his wife, Martha, who died in 1782. According to the memoirs of their son Madison, Sally did not want to return to the United States, given she could gain freedom in France. However, Jefferson "promised her extraordinary privileges" that he would free their children when they turned twenty-one. With this promise but no legal guarantee that he would keep it, Sally returned to Jefferson's plantation, Monticello, in Charlottesville. In 1802, during Jefferson's presidency, James Callender of the *Richmond Recorder* publicly named Sally as the president's enslaved "concubine," inciting local scandal and making the relationship international news.

Their two oldest children, Beverly and Harriet, left Monticello secretly when they reached adulthood. Both passed as white, entered white communities, and married white spouses.

**CHET'LA SEBREE**
Poet and Director, Stadler Center for Poetry
and Literary Arts, Syracuse University

**"Extraordinary Privilege, August 1792"**

*She refused to return [to Virginia] with him.*
*To induce her to do so he promised her*
*extraordinary privilege.* —Madison Hemings

I smashed his favorite pale blue pinwheel
    pearlware—
a gift—a soup tureen for whomever I am
    serving
pound of meat, peck of cornmeal.

In white pipe, I light a little tobacco,
watch smoke unfurl, curl from bone.
Etched the antlered buck, this

honeycombed structure was rendered
for my pleasure—a fleeting thing. My body
whet his scent, a wet I won't wish away—

for no other dare take a journey with me—
though he will never give me his name.

So I circle a fishpond—thick summer wind
pricking fair hair on skin, false foxglove
    sprouting—

pace day and night,
wonder if my decision was right.

—from *Mistress* (2019)

Jefferson made provisions in his will to
free the two youngest, Madison and Eston,
when they became adults. He carefully
veiled his reasoning, and did not mention
Sally in the document. Jefferson verbally told
Mary Randolph, his daughter by Martha,
to free Sally as well. Jefferson died in 1826,
and eight years later, Randolph directed
that Sally be "given time," a practice used

to emancipate enslaved people without having to request permission for them to legally remain in Virginia. Sally had been living as a free person since Jefferson's death, residing at various Main Street residences, including this one.

While the relationship was well known at the time, Thomas Jefferson and his white family never acknowledged it. Many historians also dismissed it until DNA analysis confirmed it in 1998, and it became widely publicized in the work of historian Annette Gordon-Reed. This residence no longer exists, and it is not formally memorialized.

**TO LEARN MORE**

Gordon-Reed, Annette. *The Hemingses of Monticello: An American Family.* New York: Norton, 2008.
Stanton, Lucia. *"Those Who Labor for My Happiness": Slavery at Thomas Jefferson's Monticello.* Charlottesville: University of Virginia Press, 2012.
"The Memoirs of Madison Hemings," as published by the *Pike County Republican,* March 13, 1873.

## 7.10 The Rotunda, University of Virginia

1826 University Avenue, Charlottesville

The Rotunda, modeled after the Roman Pantheon, opened in 1826. Built by enslaved laborers, it was designed by Thomas Jefferson to facilitate intellectual engagement between faculty and students. It is a center of campus student life and also a site of contestation when students' needs conflict with that of administrators.

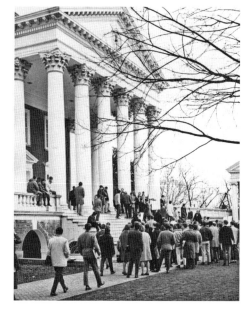

(Above) The Rotunda is a frequent site of student action at the University of Virginia.

(Left) Students gather for a civil rights rally at the Rotunda in 1968.

The National Day of Silence, a student-led movement held annually in April to protest the bullying and harassment of LGBTQ students, started at the University of Virginia (UVA). In April 1996, student Maria Pulzetti gathered 150 of her peers at the Rotunda to commit to a day-long vow of silence to protest LGBTQ bullying in schools across the nation. The following year, her classmate, Jessie Gilliam, coordinated con-current Day of Silence protests at over one hundred colleges and universities. Within five years, hundreds of educational institutions participated as it expanded beyond colleges to include high schools and middle schools.

Pulzetti organized the event during her first year at UVA after taking a class with civil rights leader Julian Bond in which she learned about student-initiated nonviolent protest. She appreciated how the pledge of silence took an action generally considered passive and transformed it into collective community action. According to Pulzetti, "People were pretty supportive. That's kind of how the Day of Silence grew in the beginning, because it was a safe thing for our straight allies to participate in. By participating, you weren't necessarily coming out at all. You were just protesting homophobia and the silencing of the queer youth experience." Locating the action at the Rotunda embodied significant symbolic power, directly challenging traditions of homophobic, patriarchal, white supremacist institutional culture.

This action inspired a global movement. The Gay, Lesbian, and Straight Education Network continues to coordinate the annual event, in

The Memorial to Enslaved Laborers at the University of Virginia, which sits adjacent to the Lawn.

which thousands of schools worldwide participate. The day is often the first LGBTQ-affirming event that students experience in schools. It is also not without its controversies. Students in K–12 schools in Florida, Tennessee, and elsewhere have faced suspension and other forms of administrative discipline for their participation in recent years, and state policy makers across the country continue to pass bills that impede LGBTQ-affirming public education.

**TO LEARN MORE**

Mazina, Dina, and Rebecca DiBrienza. "National Day of Silence." Outhistory.org, 2008.
Virginia Department of Historic Resources. "LGBTQ Heritage in Virginia." 2018. https://www.dhr.virginia.gov/survey-planning/lgbtq-heritage-in-virginia/

### 7.11 The Lawn at the University of Virginia

*400 Emmet Street S., Charlottesville*

The Lawn at the University of Virginia (UVA) is a large, grassy court designed to be the central outdoor gathering space on campus. Historically, it served as the staging ground for numerous actions protesting segregated spaces, mobilizing for racial justice, and organizing for higher staff wages. The university calls it the most popular gathering space on campus. It is lined by highly desired campus living space.

Prior to the abolition of slavery, thousands of enslaved people toiled on the grounds of the University of Virginia (UVA). Enslaved workers made and laid the bricks that cover the Academical Village that frames the Lawn. Isabella Gibbons, who worked in the kitchens of Pavilions V and VI on the Lawn while enslaved to two professors, wrote in a letter post-emancipation: "Can we forget the crack of

Living wage protests on the Lawn at UVA, 1999.

By 1968, Black students made up only 0.4 percent of UVA's student body, despite African Americans making up more than 20 percent of all Virginians. That fall, student council president Bud Ogle and James Roebuck, who succeeded Ogle as president to become the council's first African American president in 1969, presented a series of civil rights demands to university officials. Hundreds of students marched on the Lawn to support these demands in February 1969. Their petitions included the establishment of an African American Studies department, the racial integration of athletics, the addition of African American admissions officers, a ban on "Dixie" and confederate flags at official school events, and a living wage for all workers, as they knew that the lowest-paid campus workers were Black.

the whip, the cowhide, the whipping post, the auction block, the handcuffs, the spaniels, the iron collar, the negro-trader tearing the young child from its mother's breast as a whelp from the lioness? Have we forgotten those horrible cruelties, hundreds of our race killed? No, we have not, nor ever will." After slavery's abolition, UVA continued to employ a large number of Black campus workers who were still denied a living wage.

UVA officially desegregated in 1950 when Gregory Swanson won a court victory to attend the law school. However, he could not reside on campus, and he left after one year, citing social ostracization. UVA functions centered white Greek Life and football games, where students waved confederate flags and sang "Dixie," a racist song considered a de facto confederate anthem. Of the three Black men who first entered UVA as undergraduate students in 1955, only one, Robert Bland, stayed until graduation.

The university approved the establishment of African American Studies in 1970, a year that saw thousands of students march on the Lawn in solidarity after National Guard members killed four students peacefully demonstrating against the Vietnam War at Kent State University. For ten days in May, students boycotted classes and occupied buildings. They called for the removal of all law enforcement from campus. They demanded that more people of color be admitted to the university and that it open admission to women, which it did that fall, after eighteen-year-old Virginia Scott sued for admission. They also demanded more women and people of color in administrative and faculty positions. They again called for raising the pay of UVA's lowest-paid staff.

Protests and marches on the Lawn to demand a living wage for UVA employees continued for decades. UVA has long been the area's largest employer, and in 2020, it finally raised its minimum wage to $15 per hour for full-time employees. However, part-time workers do not qualify and other needs, such as Charlottesville's ongoing affordable housing crisis, continue to strain hourly wage workers.

**TO LEARN MORE**

Nelson, Louis, and Claudrena Harold, eds. *Charlottesville 2017: The Legacy of Race and Inequity.* Charlottesville: University of Virginia Press, 2018.

McInnis, Maurie, and Louis Nelson, eds. *Educated in Tyranny: Slavery at Thomas Jefferson's University.* Charlottesville: University of Virginia Press, 2019.

**TO VISIT NEARBY**

**THE MEMORIAL TO ENSLAVED LABORERS.** UVA students first proposed this monument in 2010, and it opened in 2019. It is situated northeast of the Rotunda and Lawn.

**THE FORMER SITE OF CATHERINE "KITTY" FOSTER'S HOME** in front of Gibson Hall near the corner of Jefferson Park and Brandon Avenues. Kitty, a free Black woman, purchased the property in 1833. Members of her family created a free Black community there known as Canada.

## 7.12 Memorial Gym

210 Emmet Street S., Charlottesville

On the evening of August 11, 2017, a hundred khaki-wearing white supremacists gathered here on the University of Virginia (UVA) campus. Organized by alumni Jason Kessler and Richard Spencer, the group marched across the Lawn holding tiki torches, a carefully chosen symbol from Nazi propaganda films, shouting slogans that included "White Lives Matter" and "Jews will not replace us." They gathered around the campus statue of Thomas Jefferson, whose history and ideology, in their view, aligns with their own. This march served as a prelude to the next day's deadly Unite the Right rally.

The Memorial Gym was an intentionally chosen gathering space for white supremacists. In 1921, the Ku Klux Klan (KKK) donated $1,000 to assist UVA in building the gym, which opened in 1924. Also in 1921, the KKK opened a local chapter in Charlottesville, and shortly after, a separate campus chapter formed at UVA. In 1924, the city used the gym for events celebrating the confederacy when it erected a monument to confederate general Robert E. Lee at **Market Street Park** (page 171).

Charlottesville's Summer of Hate in 2017 witnessed a number of white supremacist events. In May, Richard Spencer led a rally at the Lee statue to protest the city's decision to remove it. Another white supremacist gathering took place on July 8 at the Stonewall Jackson statue. Afterwards, its attendees drove through the city's public housing communities, dumping trash and yelling racist insults at residents. While media outlets often portrayed these gatherings as fueled by outsiders, they were organized by Jason Kessler, a UVA alumnus and Charlottesville resident, and fellow UVA graduate Richard Spencer, who the Southern Poverty Law Center calls "one of the country's most successful young white nationalist leaders."

One month after the deadly events of August, forty students placed a black shroud over the Jefferson statue on campus. In explaining the event via email to alumni, UVA president Teresa Sullivan described it as "desecrating ground that many of us consider sacred." While police arrested none of the white supremacists marching on campus the evening of August 11, they arrested three enrolled students who peacefully unfurled a banner stating "200 Years of White Supremacy" at a celebration of UVA's bicentennial that fall. These contestations over the power to occupy space unimpeded matter, and they persist. As UVA professor Lisa Woolfork asks: "Why has UVA arrested more people for protesting white supremacy than for promoting it? And what might this discrepancy reveal about the weight that white supremacy continues to bear on university life?"

Memorial Gymnasium continues to operate as a gym and houses UVA's wrestling and volleyball teams. No formal memorialization of its racist origins or connection to white supremacy exists in the landscape.

**TO LEARN MORE**

Nelson, Louis, and Claudrena Harold, eds., *Charlottesville 2017: The Legacy of Race and Inequity.* Charlottesville: University of Virginia Press, 2018.

Provence, Lisa. "Skeletons in the Closet." *C-ville Weekly,* July 12, 2017.

## 7.13 Wood's Crossing

Farmington Drive at Ivy Road, Albemarle County

At this railroad crossing, a white mob pulled John Henry James from a train on July 12, 1898, and lynched him. The day prior, a white woman accused a Black man of sexually assaulting her and officials arrested James, who they believed fit her description, when they found him sitting inside Dudley's bar in Charlottesville. As word spread, a white mob formed at the jail where James was being held. The sheriff snuck James out of the jail after nightfall and took him by train to Staunton to spend the night as a safety precaution. The next morning,

Present-day Wood's Crossing.

officials escorted James back to Charlottesville to face a grand jury. A few miles outside of town at a scheduled stop, an armed
mob of 150 white men pulled James from
the train and brutally killed him. Despite
the presence of many officials, no one was
charged for the murder, and when informed
of his death, the grand jury issued a posthu-
mous indictment against James.

Between the 1870s and 1930s, white Virginians lynched more than seventy African American men, although these numbers only reflect publicly reported lynchings.
Rarely had the victims committed a crime.
Whites instead used the accusation of criminal activity to perpetuate lynching as a
means to instill terror into Black communities at a time when African Americans sought
to exercise their full rights of citizenship,
from voting in elections to owning property.
Activists, clergy members, historians, and
local officials held a ceremony of remem-
brance for James at this site in July 2018.

**TO LEARN MORE**

Equal Justice Initiative. "Lynching in America:
    Confronting the Legacy of Racial Terror."
    https://eji.org/reports/lynching-in-america/
Heim, Jo. "Sacred Ground, Now Reclaimed."
    *Washington Post,* July 7, 2018.
Wolfe, Brendan. "The Train at Wood's Crossing."
    http://brendanwolfe.com/lynching/

## 7.14 Skyline Drive and Shenandoah National Park

To access Skyline Drive, take Interstate 64
exit 99 or Route 250 near Waynesboro and
head north

Skyline Drive runs 105 miles along the entire
length of Shenandoah National Park. It contains seventy-five overlooks where visitors
can view the Shenandoah Valley to the west
and the Piedmont to the east. It also allows
access to numerous hiking trails, including
the Appalachian Trail, which runs along the
top of the Blue Ridge Mountains.

In 1926, Congress established Shenandoah National Park, and two years later, Virginia's General Assembly passed the Public Park Condemnation Act, which allowed
the state to take land from landowners and
tenant farmers for the project. Creating the
park displaced nearly 500 families, over 2,000
people, as officials sought to present a pris-
tine uninhabited parkland for visitors. Most
families knew nothing about the project until
state survey crews arrived at their homes. As
part of the displacement campaign, sociolo-
gists and others noted the squalor in which
these families lived, describing them in popular publications as "backward," "illiter-
ate," and "crossbreeding degenerates." Photographers duplicitously posed residents in
front of dilapidated buildings, which viewers
wrongfully assumed were residents' homes.
These campaigns garnered support for the
forced removal of hundreds of families. In
reality, families lived off of the land through
logging, cultivating orchards and gardens,
raising and curing meat, and working as
masons, carpenters, and blacksmiths.

Looking west from Charlottesville toward Skyline Drive.

Park construction began in the summer of 1931. Later, Civilian Conservation Corps workers dismantled families' homes and planted nonnative vegetation. Most displaced residents did not qualify for compensation as most did not own the land their families had occupied for several generations. Of those who did receive compensation, it was low, due to plummeting real estate values amidst the Great Depression.

Today, the park attracts one million visitors annually, with minimal acknowledgment of its controversial origins in forced displacement. Most think of the park as previously uninhabited wilderness rather than an area where government actions removed families who had once worked, lived, and occupied the land for generations.

**TO VISIT NEARBY**

Visit the **MEMORIAL** built to recognize the sixty-seven Albemarle County families displaced by the building of the park at 6610 Blackwells Hollow Road in Crozet. Similar memorials are planned for neighboring counties by the Blue Ridge Heritage Project: http://www.blueridgeheritage project.com/

**TO LEARN MORE**

Eisenfeld, Sue. *Shenandoah: A Story of Conservation and Betrayal.* Lincoln: University of Nebraska Press, 2014.

Powell, Katrina. "Time to Leave." *Virginia Living,* November 22, 2010.

Listen to oral histories of families displaced by the park at James Madison University's Shenandoah National Park Oral History Collection: https://commons.lib.jmu.edu/snp/

## 7.15 Union Hill Baptist Church

Route 663 north of Woods Corner, Buckingham County

Beginning in 2014, Union Hill, a community located in Buckingham County, became the target of a proposed sixty-eight-acre compressor station for the Atlantic Coast Pipeline. The members and leaders of Union

Union Hill Baptist Church.

Hill Baptist Church actively organized resistance to the pipeline. As the church's pastor, Rev. Paul Wilson, told his congregation: "They [pipeline proponents] want to shut us up. This church is too loud. It's too vocal. It's getting to be a problem for Dominion."

Dominion Energy, the region's energy monopoly, and Duke Energy planned to construct a 600-mile pipeline that would bring fracked gas from West Virginia to Virginia and North Carolina. Compressor stations control the flow of gas through the pipeline, and alongside other concerns of pipeline leaks and explosions they also create significant air pollution.

Freedmen and women founded the Union Hill community following the Civil War when a Freedman's Bureau office and school for freedpeople were established at the Buckingham County courthouse. Many current town residents are these founders' descendants. Community members saw the proposed compressor station project as intentionally targeting a rural low-income African American community. An estimated

85 percent of residents identify as African American, and community members have a lower life expectancy than the state average.

Residents used a number of methods to counter the building of this pipeline. They relied on decades of research conducted and preserved by Charles White and other African American residents who co-founded their own historical society when Buckingham County's society refused to incorporate a focus on Black history in the 1970s. After the pipeline proposal, community researchers went door to door to collect evidence of environmental injustice experienced by community members since historic courthouse records had been lost due to fire.

After six years of protest, Dominion and Duke Energy canceled the pipeline project in July 2020, citing innumerable delays and expenses related to lawsuits brought by environmentalist and environmental justice groups concerned about the grave impact of an extensive fossil fuel project at a time when many want to see these energy giants embrace clean, renewable energy sources. In December 2020, in a landmark decision, a federal appeals court unanimously revoked the required air permit for the station. Activists like those at Union Hill Baptist were essential to translating community concern into action to defeat the pipeline.

**TO LEARN MORE**

Fjord, Lakshmi. "Union Hill Community Household Study Site and Methods Report," 2018. http://www.friendsofbuckinghamva. org/friends/wp-content/uploads/2018/12/ Fjord-Union-Hill-Community-Household

-Study-12–17–18-Lakshmi-Fjord.pdf

Sokolow, Jonathan. "Echoes of a Dark Past at Virginia's Standing Rock." *Huffington Post,* July 19, 2017.

Thomson, Vivian. "Breathing While Black." *Washington Post,* January 25, 2019.

## 7.16  Dillwyn Correctional Center

1522 Prison Road, Buckingham County

Dillwyn Correctional Center is a state-run prison for men that incarcerates over 900 people. Buckingham Correctional Center, a higher security prison that houses more than 1,100 individuals, sits across the street. In

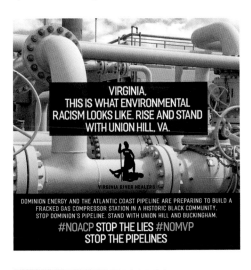

May 2020, Dillwyn was the site of Virginia's worst coronavirus outbreak, with more than 200 imprisoned men contracting the virus. Buckingham reported only slightly lower infection numbers. Families complained that the administration refused to take action to stop the virus's spread and would not communicate with them.

On May 2, a group of imprisoned men began protesting when prison officials attempted to add thirty beds to an already crowded space being used to house prisoners who had tested positive for COVID-19. The men created a barricade to prevent guards from moving more beds into the area; officials threatened to tear-gas them. At the same time, prisoners housed elsewhere in the facility started a hunger strike. The men cited overcrowding, lack of hygiene supplies like soap and hand sanitizer, and a guard's refusal to wear a mask as the impetus for their action. Afterwards, the Department of Corrections transferred several prisoners out of the facility to higher-security prisons, citing questionable reasons of safety.

By July 2020, Dillwyn reported 347 COVID-19 cases among the 907 people imprisoned there. Across the street at Buckingham, 165 of those imprisoned were

(Above) Flyer for Action to Stop the Building of the Atlantic Coast Pipeline, 2017.

(Left) Dillwyn Correctional Center.

infected. With both facilities housed in rural Buckingham county with a total population of 17,000, the county consistently ranked among the locales with the highest per capita infection rates in the country in summer 2020. This site shows the ways in which those who push against the constraints of imprisonment utilize methods available to them to advocate for safer, healthier living space during a global pandemic. It challenges notions of prisoners' supposed lack of power within a totalizing system of incarceration while also revealing the risks involved when officials ignored their demands for more humane conditions by isolating or transferring many of them to more restrictive higher-security facilities.

**TO LEARN MORE**

Hausman, Sandy. "Prisoners Protest as More Than 700 Contract COVID-19." RadioIQ, May 12, 2020.

Hitchcock, Ben. "'A Total Disaster:' COVID Runs Rampant in Buckingham State Prisons." *C-ville Weekly,* May 26, 2020.

### 7.17  Rassawek

Point of Fork, Fluvanna County. View this site from the Columbia Boat Ramp by the James River off of Columbia Road. Look across the river to the landmass opposite it.

Rassawek is the historic capital of the Monacan Indian Nation. The Monacan have occupied this site for more than four thousand years. The Nation once covered half of Virginia, and its tributaries gathered here to pay annual tribute. The Smithsonian Institute began documenting the site's extensive burial grounds in the 1880s. Today, with over 2,600 tribal members, the Monacan Indian Nation is the largest of Virginia's recognized tribes.

In 2015, the James River Water Authority (JRWA), a joint project of Louisa and Fluvanna counties, obtained a state permit to withdraw water from this site. JRWA sought to build a pump station and pipeline here to deliver water to support development at Zion Crossroads twenty miles away. The project's site in Rassawek drew immediate criticism from the Nation, who officials did not consult.

The Monacan engaged citizens and organizations across the nation in its battle. As a result of this mobilization, the Army Corps of Engineers received more than 12,000 objections to the project site. As well, in 2018, Congress granted the Nation federal recognition. That designation includes the right for the Nation to consult on federal policies and projects that impact them, and the Nation used that leverage against JRWA's project.

In 2020, Virginia disqualified JRWA's archeologist, and the Nation filed extensive legal documentation with the Army Corps of Engineers as to why the project should not proceed. Meanwhile, the National Trust for Historic Preservation named Rassawek to its annual list of the country's most endangered historic sites. After these developments, JRWA agreed to hire archeologists approved by the Nation, who produced reports showing a nearby alternative location that posed little risk of disturbing ancestral remains, despite JRWA's insistence that an alternative site did not exist. The Nation provided JRWA with a letter officially supporting the alternative site located two miles away, and the JRWA voted unanimously on March 15, 2022 to abandon its plans at Rassawek in favor of the alternate site.

The Nation issued a Public Statement of Gratitude to thank the large, diverse coalition it built to preserve Rassawek. Tribal chief Kenneth Branham noted: "This rare victory for the preservation of tribal sacred places comes after more than four years of determined public advocacy by the Nation and our many allies across Indian Country and the United States. Our ancestors may now rest in peace. This outcome is a triumph for Native people, but also for all Virginians and Americans who seek to understand our shared human history and culture."

## TO LEARN MORE

"Rassawek Saved from Destruction." Monacan Indian Nation press release, March 16, 2022. http://www.culturalheritagepartners.com/saverassawek/

Vogelsong, Sarah. "Water Authority Abandons Plans to Site Pump Station at Rassawek." *Virginia Mercury,* March 16, 2022.

The Historic
**Tri-
angle**
and
**Points
East** of
Richmond

# Introduction

**THIS EXPANSIVE GEOGRAPHIC AREA ROUGHLY** follows the path of Interstate 64 east of Richmond, and includes the towns of Williamsburg, Jamestown, and Yorktown, collectively known as the Historic Triangle in both tourist material and local knowledge. Utilizing the widely known naming convention of the Historic Triangle allows for a direct engagement with triumphant, white-centered narratives about the founding of North American colonies by European colonizers and, by extension, the United States. The Historic Triangle lies less than thirty miles west of Point Comfort in Hampton, where enslaved people of African descent arrived in 1619, formally establishing enslavement in the colony when sold to white colonizers at Jamestown, the first permanent site of English settlement, established in 1607.

The areas within the chapter profiled outside of the Historic Triangle do not derive significant revenue from tourism. Some are rural and isolated; others have been sites of contentious environmental battles, ranging from water access to projects that would grow the region's fossil fuel imprint amidst deep concerns of environmental and climate injustice. Many

Indigenous sites are located in rural areas because colonization pushed these communities away from their original homelands in favor of white settlement, development, and trade. Indigenous communities, in other words, were and are isolated by design, yet continue to survive due to their resilience and ability to collectively mobilize.

This region is an epicenter for both Indigenous displacement and African enslavement in what would become the United States. Tourist sites and their accompanying businesses often built entire economies on the backs of these injustices. The development of Colonial Williamsburg and Yorktown Battlefield, part of the Colonial National Historic Park, intentionally displaced African American residents and communities in the twentieth century to establish historical

Duke of Gloucester Street in 1902 prior to the restoration of Colonial Williamsburg in the 1930s.

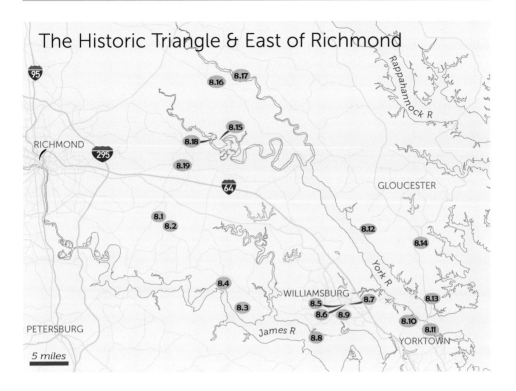

# The Historic Triangle & East of Richmond

RICHMOND

GLOUCESTER

WILLIAMSBURG

PETERSBURG

YORKTOWN

*James R*

*York R*

*Rappahannock R*

5 miles

interpretative sites focused on white colonial-era histories. The federal government
played a leading role, via the National Park
Service and the expansive military instal-
lations developed here during both World
Wars I and II.

Prominent sites like Colonial Williamsburg, Jamestown Settlement, and the American Revolution Museum at Yorktown, often
described as living history museums, represent the height of "edutainment," sites that
deliberately blur historical and educational
components with entertainment as a way
to draw in a large number of tourists. Other
businesses driven by tourism, like mini-golf,
all-day pancake houses, and outlet malls,
have initiated additional economic development and population growth. Between 3

to 4 million tourists visit the area annually,
and according to the Williamsburg Tourism
Council, the town gained $730 million from
tourism revenue in 2020.

Tourist sites in the Triangle often focus
narrowly on the founding of the nation as
a triumphal achievement of white colonists
who overthrew tyrannical English overlords,
thereby winning their freedom and creating
the United States. Historically, Indigenous
communities factored into these narratives
only as superficial accessories to white-centered narratives, with the story of paramount chief Powhatan's daughter Pocahontas exemplifying how these histories have
been sensationalized for mass media consumption and predominantly white tourist
audiences. Enslaved Africans, until recently,

have not factored into these whitewashed histories at all. Increasingly, sites interpret selective elements of Black history, due to the activism of African Americans, including the work of Black interpreters working at these sites, as well as the desire of organizations to attract African American tourist dollars. But Black histories, like Indigenous histories, are often not prioritized as central to the stories these sites tell.

Both Indigenous and African American communities here have struggled for the right to exist and to be afforded the same rights as white communities since Virginia's colonial era. Thus, these sites emphasize the long-term impact white settlement had on Indigenous communities as well as the arrival of enslaved Africans and the role their presence had in establishing, among other things, codified differential treatment based on racial identity. Seventeenth-century legislators at Jamestown decreed that a child born to an enslaved mother followed her status, thus protecting white inheritance from claims by mixed-race children while also ensuring the steady growth of a domestic enslaved population. English and Indigenous leaders signed treaties that required some Indigenous communities to pay tribute to Virginia's governor while making them subjects of the English Crown. While some Indigenous rights to land for living and hunting were supposedly guaranteed as well, in practice, English encroachment was never-ending. Two of the oldest reservations in the nation are located here: the Pamunkey and the Mattaponi. Despite being recognized as Indigenous communities for more

than a century before the establishment of the United States, neither tribe received federal recognition until the second decade of the twenty-first century.

One current site, the National Park Service's Werowocomoco, represents a disruption in past historical practices, as it is being developed in close consultation with Virginia Indian tribes. Werowocomoco, in present-day Gloucester, was the seat of paramount chief Powhatan at the time of the arrival of the English colonizers. The Powhatan and their tributaries occupied lands extending from the coast west to present-day Interstate 95, south to the North Carolina border and north beyond Fredericksburg. The site's specific location was not recovered until 2003. Emblematic of the power of settler colonialist narratives, the site of Jamestown is widely known and preserved, while this prominent, older, and more populated Indigenous site of power and governance has only recently been located.

Today, the region serves as a midpoint between two major economic centers: Richmond to the west and Hampton Roads, which includes several significant cities, to the east. Its economy is driven by tourism and the military, although residents also settle in smaller communities, drawn to more rural and suburban settings, and commute to cities farther afield for work. A few rural residents still make their living through farming and fishing, but it is increasingly difficult for that work to sustain families' economic needs due to land development for residential, commercial, and military use.

# The Historic Triangle and Points East of Richmond Sites

## 8.1 Proposed Site of Chickahominy Gas Power Station

Chambers Road near the Roxbury Road Corridor, Charles City County

Proposed site of the now-abandoned plan to build the Chickahominy Gas Plant, 2020.

This proposed facility in Charles City County would have increased the carbon footprint of Virginia's electrical grid by 20 percent even though the state has set a goal to reach carbon neutrality by 2045. Charles City County is a majority-minority county; 45 percent of its residents are African American and 7 percent are Virginia Indian. Balico, the facility developer, noted that the power station's name is intended to honor the Chickahominy, who have lived in the area for centuries.

Local residents learned of the permitting process for air emissions related to the Chickahominy Station only days before the State Air Control Board met to make its decision in June 2019. Despite short notice, more than a dozen county residents testified about major health concerns related to the station; many more had hoped to participate but could not due to how the bureaucratic permitting process inhibited public notification and participation. The board granted the permit, a board reconfigured by Governor Northam in 2018 when he replaced two members who had raised environmental justice concerns about a compressor station planned for Buckingham County with others more favorable to fossil fuel industries.

After the air board hearing, residents quickly formed the Concerned Citizens of Charles City County, abbreviated as C5, to share information and demand transparency from local government officials and state regulators, including the Department of Environmental Quality (DEQ). C5 compelled the DEQ to hold information sessions and ultimately forced the special exception request for extracting water from the Potomac Aquifer to go before the State Water Control Board for citizen review. While citizens submitted more than 1,400 public comments to the board in opposition to the project, it issued a groundwater withdrawal permit to the Chickahominy Station in an unanimous vote in June 2020. As community resident and C5 member Benita Cotman-Lewis recounts: "The local and state process for this power plant has left us out from the beginning . . . At a time when deep, ongoing racial injustice is finally being revealed and discussed, we, here in Charles City County, can see that this power plant proposed for our community is clearly an environmental injustice."

Despite state and industry collusion to build this facility, Balico officially ended its plans in March 2022. NOVI Energy had also been pursuing the building of another plant, C4GT, within one mile of the proposed Chickahominy Station. The state issued all of the necessary regulatory permits for the C4GT plant prior to community knowledge about the project. However, due to pressure generated by local citizens and the changing energy market, NOVI Energy canceled plans for this plant in July 2021. Both developers cited "opposition from outside interests and regulations" in the cancellation of their projects; much of that opposition came from local community members who organized strategically and successfully across complicated levels of local and state bureaucracies to help end these projects.

**TO LEARN MORE**

Finley-Brook, Mary. "The Hidden Power behind the Chickahominy Gas Power Plant Proposal." *Virginia Mercury*, October 9, 2019.

Kreydatus, Beth. "Virginia Needs a More Transparent Regulatory System for Fossil Fuel Investments." *Richmond Times-Dispatch*, December 15, 2019.

Vogelsong, Sarah. "Chickahominy Power Cancels Plans for Natural Gas Plant in Charles City." *Virginia Mercury*, March 17, 2022.

## 8.2 Samaria Indian School (former)

*8130 Lott Cary Road, Providence Forge*

This entry highlights the continuing struggle for access to education among Virginia Indians, and the particular challenges faced by nonreservation tribes such as the Chickahominy. Only two tribes, the Mattaponi and the Pamunkey, have reservations in Virginia. They both negotiated treaties with colonial-era Virginia leaders when England claimed this land as its colony; no future government entity created additional reservations.

In 1870, Virginia created a statewide system of free public schooling, but it excluded Indigenous communities. They could not attend schools for white students, and schools for Black children often either were not located near their communities or they did not want to attend them as students who identified as Virginia Indians. As a result, the Chickahominy opened the tribe-funded Samaria Indian School, an elementary school, in 1901. In 1917, Virginia opened and funded elementary schools for the Mattaponi and Pamunkey, tribes that had lived on reservations since the seventeenth century, but it did not allocate school funding for nonreservation communities like the Chickahominy. In 1922, the state agreed to pay a portion of Samaria's teachers' salaries after years of pressure from the tribe for the state to meet its obligation to provide free public schooling to all Virginia children. If Indigenous students attended high school, they left the state to do so. Most traveled twelve hundred miles to Bacone Junior College in Oklahoma, where they could complete high school and earn the equivalent of an associate's degree. While the difficulty of relocating so far away precluded most people from attending, some did. Most of Samaria's teachers, for example, trained there.

In the mid-1940s, the federal government allowed some Virginia Indian students to attend high school 450 miles away at the federally run Indigenous school in Cherokee, North Carolina, but they only granted permission to children living on reservations, again excluding communities like the Chickahominy. Subsequently, Samaria began offering high school classes with government funding, as the school officially became part of the local public school system in 1950. After decades of pressure from Virginia Indian tribes not on reservations, the state finally offered and funded this education. In 1963, Virginia opened its formerly whites-only public schools to all students, including Virginia Indians. Samaria Indian School closed in 1968.

Although they were one of the first Indigenous communities encountered by the white colonizers who settled at Jamestown, the Chickahominy were not granted state recognition by Virginia until 1983. The Chickahominy did not receive federal recognition until 2018, thus highlighting the even greater barriers they faced in exercising sovereignty without a government-recognized land base.

**TO LEARN MORE**

Adkins, Elaine and Ray. *Chickahominy Indians– Eastern Division: A Brief Ethnohistory.* Xlibris, 2007.

Rountree, Helen. "The Indians of Virginia: A Third Race in a Biracial State." In *Southeastern Indians since the Removal Era*, ed. Walter Williams. Athens: University of Georgia Press, 1979.

**TO VISIT NEARBY**

**CHICKAHOMINY TRIBAL CENTER** at 8200 Lott Cary Road. The Chickahominy host an annual fall festival and powwow in late September. Everyone is invited to attend to learn about the community's histories and traditions.

## 8.3 Sandy Point

Juncture of Sandy Point Road (Route 613) and Wilcox Neck Road (Route 623), Charles City County

On August 9, 1610, governor and captain-general of the Jamestown colony Thomas West, known as twelfth baron De La Warr, sent a military expedition to this location six miles upriver from Jamestown. Here, the Paspahegh lived. The Paspahegh had recently attacked an English guardhouse that restricted their entrance to the peninsula, where one of their communities was located, from the mainland.

Previous to this action, De La Warr had issued a summons for Powhatan, the paramount chief, to return English subjects and property seized in previous fights or face attack. Warriors loyal to Powhatan had raided the English's Jamestown fort throughout the winter, denying the colonizers access to outside food. By spring, 75 percent of Jamestown's population was dead due to starvation and disease, a period often referred to in historical documents as "the starving time."

Powhatan, who had made it clear that the English should either remain within their fort or leave the area, did not respond to De La Warr's summons. In retaliation, English soldiers invaded the Paspahegh village, setting fire to structures, destroying the village's crucial supply of corn, and killing villagers. The English captured and killed at least one woman and her children, including the relatives of werowance Wowinchopunck, which violated tribal custom. The Paspahegh did not recover; they abandoned the area.

From this time forward, English raids on Indigenous communities continued indefinitely. This attack and its aftermath are often noted as the beginning of the First Anglo-Powhatan War. During this time, which lasted until 1614, the English terrorized Indigenous communities in a number of ways, including randomly slaughtering people of all genders and ages, murdering captives, and razing entire villages.

**TO LEARN MORE**

Fausz, Frederick. "An 'Abundance of Blood Shed on Both Sides': England's First Indian War, 1609–1614." *Virginia Magazine of History and Biography* 98, no. 1 (January 1990): 3–56.

Rountree, Helen. *Pocahontas's People: The Powhatan Indians of Virginia through Four Centuries*. Norman: University of Oklahoma Press, 1990.

## 8.4 Wilson's Wharf

13150 Sturgeon Point Road, Charles City County

In 1864, African American Union soldiers built an earthen fort at Wilson's Wharf called Fort Pocahontas. The name references paramount chief Powhatan's daughter Pocahontas, whose own story and life had been deeply misconstrued and manipulated by the English during her lifetime in the early seventeenth century; those misrepresentations endure today. This fort protected Union vessels on the river and guarded the wharf's landing. The fort served as a supply depot and a strategic part of the U.S. Army's Overland Campaign to capture the confederate capital of Richmond, forty miles away, and force an end to the war. After its completion, the fort became a refuge for local enslaved people who sought freedom by escaping to the fort.

Over a thousand men, nearly all U.S. Colored Troops (USCT), guarded the garrison. On May 24, 1864, they beat back an attack by 2,500 confederate cavalrymen. It was the only Civil War battle in Virginia in which nearly all of the Union troops were Black. Many of those defending the fort were formerly enslaved people who had lived on the area's plantations. Confederate troops expressed humiliation at being defeated by Black Union soldiers, and the victory proved to be both a psychological and military success for the USCT members.

The USCT were regiments of Black soldiers in the U.S. Army. They enlisted more than 178,000 men, and by the end of the war the USCT constituted 10 percent of the

(Left) Earthworks at Wilson's Wharf, 2020.

(Below Left) United States Colored Troops fight at nearby Dutch Gap, November 1864.

been largely forgotten locally until its recovery in the 1990s.

### TO LEARN MORE

Besch, Edwin. *U. S. Colored Troops Defeat Confederate Cavalry.* Jefferson, NC: McFarland, 2017.
Fort Pocahontas: *fortpocahontas.org*. An annual reenactment is held at the former fort, usually during the first weekend in June.

## 8.5 The Brafferton

Wren Yard, College of William and Mary, Williamsburg

army's soldiers. The Union initially only used Black men as laborers, but that position changed as the war dragged on. The Emancipation Proclamation, issued on January 1, 1863, not only freed enslaved people in states in rebellion against the Union, but it also explicitly allowed Black men to enlist and fight for the Union. The Battle at Wilson's Wharf was the first significant engagement of USCT in Virginia. While Northern newspapers lauded the victory at the time, it had

The Brafferton opened in 1723 to house a school for Indigenous children that had been established in 1693 as part of The College of William and Mary's royal charter. The school intended to Anglicize its students, in hopes that its graduates would act as intermediaries and advocate on behalf of English interests.

Indigenous communities initially sent no students to the school. Some reasonably feared that their children might be enslaved rather than educated. Four boys formerly captured by a distant Indigenous tribe became the school's first pupils. Over time, various Indigenous communities sent students, although the school enrolled only a few students at any given time. The reasons Indigenous communities sent their sons to the school were complex. Some wanted to remain in good standing with the English. Others needed tribal members who could speak and write English to better negotiate with colonial governments. Some may have been forced to send students due to tribute requirements established by treaty agreements. Most students remained immersed in their communities' customs and practices during and after leaving the school. The British did not accomplish their goals of indoctrination; instead, students departed with critical knowledge about the English that helped their communities navigate and negotiate life among white colonizers. The school closed during the Revolutionary War in the 1770s.

Alumni showcase the many ways in which they used their schooling. John Nettles helped his tribe in North Carolina read treaties written by the British and served as an interpreter. Charles Murphy became a Cherokee interpreter for colonial leader Patrick Henry. Thomas Step of the Nottoway became a war captain for Virginia during the French and Indian War. Still others exploited divisions between powerful groups of whites as best they could. John Montour, a Delaware-Oneidan, initially served as an agent for the British during the Revolutionary War. After the British imprisoned him,

The Brafferton at the College of William and Mary. Today, the building houses administrative offices.

he allied with the Americans, but after witnessing a massacre of Indigenous people carried out by Americans, he again shifted his allegiance back to the British. In these ways, the impact the school had on its students served as a microcosm for the complex negotiations that Indigenous people traversed in order to survive settler colonialism.

**TO LEARN MORE**

Dietrich, Tamara. "'We Used to Be There': The Lost History and Legacy of America's Indian School." *Daily Press,* December 25, 2019.

Moretti-Langholtz, Danielle, and Buck Woodward. *Building the Brafferton: The Founding, Funding, and Legacy of America's Indian School.* Williamsburg: Muscarelle Museum of Art, 2019.

Palace Green in Colonial Williamsburg.

## 8.6 Palace Green

Intersection of Duke of Gloucester and Palace Green Streets, Williamsburg

Visitors and locals alike gathered here along Duke of Gloucester Street in March 1991. A fife and drum corps led a procession organized by Local 32 of the Food and Beverage Workers Union; among the marchers were more than a thousand of Colonial Williamsburg's hotel and restaurant workers. In December 1990, tensions mounted when Colonial Williamsburg and Local 32 could not agree on new three-year contracts. Union leaders demanded guaranteed pay raises, perfect attendance bonuses, and lower healthcare premiums. Instead, management would only agree to discretionary pay raises and merit raises. Employees saw merit raises as uncertain and out of their control. Between 1987 and 1990, the consumer price index rose 17 percent while wages for non-tipped employees at Colonial Williamsburg rose only 11 percent. Thus workers wanted a guarantee of equitable pay raises. During those three years, average annual income for all employees covered by the collective bargaining agreement fell below the poverty line while health premiums, for those who qualified, rose each year.

Given the timing of the dispute, workers chose to organize an informational picket line only. Colonial Williamsburg experiences its lowest annual visitation rates after the Christmas holidays; workers did not want to deter any tourist traffic during what is already a slow time when they work few hours. This informational picket included writing to organizations like the Virginia Bar Association, who held their large annual conferences on site, to make them aware of the dispute. As scholars Richard Handler and Eric Gable point out, workers used the Colonial Williamsburg Foundation's own rhetoric of freedom and liberty in their negotiations for better working conditions. For example, signs noted that workers could not have independence without a living wage. Ultimately, workers signed a new contract in April 1991. While they did not receive all of their demands, their employer agreed to more guaranteed pay raises, rather than merit-based increases, in the future. This site reveals how common labor struggles often remain invisible to visitors at high-volume, well-known tourist destinations unless made public by a march or demonstration.

**TO LEARN MORE**

Handler, Richard, and Eric Gable. *The New History in an Old Museum: Creating the Past at Colonial Williamsburg.* Durham: Duke University Press, 1997.

Steinberg, Mark. "Changing Times in Colonial Williamsburg." *Daily Press,* April 14, 1991.

## 8.7 Wetherburn's Tavern

406 E. Duke of Gloucester Street, Williamsburg

On October 10, 1994, Colonial Williamsburg staged its first, and only, reenactment of a slave auction on the steps of this tavern. The museum's Department of African American Interpretations and Presentations (AAIP) developed the program. However, local civil rights organizations questioned the museum's ability to sensitively depict a slave auction. The controversy surrounding the event drew more than 2,000 visitors to the reenactment.

Colonial Williamsburg, a self-identified "living history" museum, seeks to portray Virginia's colonial capital as it existed in the 1770s. At that time, African Americans made up half of the town's population, and most were enslaved. Yet the museum did not mention enslavement during its first fifty years of existence; it began interpreting slavery in 1979. AAIP director Christy Coleman viewed the event as an authentic rendering of difficult history. After the event, she took questions from the audience and detailed why each carefully chosen scenario had been included. For example, she discussed how the department deliberately chose to show a husband and wife being sold apart in order to highlight the real and frequent ways in which enslavers attempted to destroy families.

Others contested that the forty-five minute event seemed too much like entertainment that exploited a very painful history for African Americans to an overwhelmingly white audience. Museums like Colonial Williamsburg exist at the intersection of education and entertainment, with a need to attract a wide audience of visitors in order to stay in business. Those upset with the reenactment could not ignore the history of Colonial Williamsburg itself. The creation of the museum in the 1920s displaced nearly all remaining African American businesses on Duke of Gloucester street. The museum hired few Black employees until the late 1950s, and then employed them primarily as low-paid service workers.

Scholar Ywone Edwards-Ingram notes, however, that while African Americans were not hired or trained as interpreters prior to 1979, they still held important roles linked to interpreting the museum for visitors. From the 1930s to 1970s, African American coachmen, who drove visiting dignitaries and tourists alike, held highly visible roles as "accomplished workers who helped to

(Left) Wetherburn's Tavern, 2020.

(Below) Black coachmen drive visiting dignitaries at Colonial Williamsburg, ca. 1938.

pioneer standards that are still central to coach-driving practices at the museum." The coachmen "were included, not excluded, in the public face of Colonial Williamsburg during this period, despite the fact that the museum did not treat these interpretive areas as top priorities." As one visitor noted of Ben Spraggins, who became a coachman in 1937: "When you ride with Ben, you get the notion that Williamsburg is his town."

Colonial Williamsburg began incorporating slavery into its narratives in 1979, but by the 1990s, the museum still marketed itself through a triumphant patriotic storyline that centered white colonial leaders. The significance of African American history at the site often could only be accessed by attending a special tour at an additional cost, thus making Black history seem tangential, rather than essential, to the historical understanding of the colonial capital.

Sites like Colonial Williamsburg, which opened during legalized segregation and centered a whitewashed history of its subject matter, still struggle to tell authentic, nuanced, and abundant accounts of African American history. However, the work of Black interpreters at these sites challenges white-centered narratives; their work and the racist reception it sometimes receives by white visitors emphasizes the ways that contemporary race relations and white supremacy continue to shape these spaces.

**TO LEARN MORE**

Devlin, Erin. "Colonial Williamsburg's Slave Auction Re-Enactment: Controversy, African American History and Public Memory." College of William and Mary thesis, 2003.

Edwards-Ingram, Ywone. "Before 1979: African American Coachmen, Visibility, and Representation at Colonial Williamsburg." *Public Historian* 36, no. 1 (2014): 9–35.

Horton, James and Lois. *Slavery and Public History: The Tough Stuff of American Memory.* Chapel Hill: University of North Carolina Press, 2008.

Twitty, Michael. "Dear Disgruntled White Plantation Visitor, Sit Down." *AfroCulinaria,* August 9, 2019.

## 8.8  Jamestown Church

1369 Colonial Parkway, Williamsburg
The church lies within Historic Jamestowne, a fee-based site of historical interpretation.

The Jamestown Quarter Court, named because it met four times annually, gathered in Jamestown Church as part of the English's Jamestown settlement. In 1629, the Court heard a case of gender fluidity involving colonist Thomasine Hall. Hall was born in England around 1600. In Hall's early twenties, Hall accompanied her/his brother into the army; Hall cut her/his hair, wore men's clothes, and went by the name Thomas. After this service, Hall reverted to using the name Thomasine and wearing women's clothing.

In 1627, Hall again donned men's clothing and set sail for Virginia as an indentured servant. Initially, Hall dressed as a man and labored on a tobacco plantation, but soon Hall started wearing women's clothing and doing traditional women's work. The small community became uneasy, in part because of a rumor that Hall had sex with a woman, a crime of fornication if Hall was a man, but equally problematic if Hall was a woman. Three married women "inspected" Hall, declaring Hall to be a man. But the person to whom Hall was indentured disagreed. When asked about his/her sex, Hall answered that s/he was both male and female.

Archeology work to recover remnants from Jamestown's earliest seventeenth-century church buildings takes place in the foreground of the 1907 church structure, 2020.

Additional physical examinations took place without Hall's consent. The community determined that Hall was a man and should be punished for impersonating a woman. Ultimately Hall stood before Jamestown's Court in 1629, relating a personal narrative that confounded colonial notions of gender. Hall's gender determined not only how to dress but also what kind of labor Hall could perform. The colonial governor declared Hall to be both a man and a woman, and legally required Hall to wear both male and female clothing: the pants and shirt of a man and an apron and cap of a woman.

While Hall identified as both a man and a woman, Hall could never again blend into society. Hall had never mixed clothing, but at specific times, dressed and worked as a man, and at other times, as a woman. The ruling also did not determine what kind of work Hall could do, yet work in the colony was deeply divided along gendered boundaries, norms, and expectations. Hall's gender malleability transgressed rigid gender roles, and while the court opened the possibility for a different understanding of gender, it did not honor how Hall had lived in the past. Instead, it likely marked Hall as a societal outcast, endangering Hall's acceptance in the community and ability to earn a living.

The church that stands today was built in 1907, although remnants from six prior churches, some dating back to the mid-seventeenth century, can be found within the Historic Jamestowne site.

### TO LEARN MORE

Brown, Kathleen. "'Changed . . . into the Fashion of a Man': The Politics of Sexual Difference in a Seventeenth-Century Anglo-American Settlement." *Journal of the History of Sexuality* 6, no. 2 (1995): 171–93.

Vaughn, Alden. "The Sad Case of Thomas(ine) Hall." *Virginia Magazine of History and Biography* 86, no. 2 (1978): 146–48.

## 8.9 College Landing Park

1070 S. Henry Street, Williamsburg

College Landing Park provides access to College Creek, a tributary of the James River. At some point between 1559 and 1561, a party of Spaniards kidnapped a member of the Powhatan community named Paquiquineo from this area. Spanish colonizers took Paquiquineo to Mexico, where the Dominicans

College Landing Park.

baptized and educated him. Upon his baptism, he was christened Don Luis de Valasco, after his sponsor. He later traveled to both Spain and Cuba.

Paquiquineo eventually persuaded the Jesuits to establish a mission near his home community. In May 1570, an expedition that included Paquiquineo, eight Jesuits, and a young novice left Havana for the Chesapeake Bay. They sailed up the river that would become known as the James, landing at College Creek, five miles east of Jamestown Island. They later crossed the peninsula, settling on the York River. Once established, the Jesuits noted that Paquiquineo stayed in the village only a couple of days before moving back into his home community.

This mission arrived during a time of famine, and with few supplies they soon faced a host of life-threatening problems. Despite repeated messages urging his return, Paquiquineo did not. In February 1571, three missionaries sought him out to further pressure him. He again refused, and a group of Indigenous men killed the three Jesuits as they made their way back to the mission. Within a few days, Paquiquineo and a group of warriors killed the remaining five missionaries.

As a result, in August 1572, a Spanish force that included four warships and the governor of Cuba arrived. The Spanish indiscriminately captured and killed a number of Indigenous people. They sent word that the man they knew as Don Luis must return or more captives would be killed. While they released some captives, they hanged the others when he failed to show.

They then sailed for Cuba; the whereabouts of Paquiquineo remained unknown. As a result, many Indigenous communities in the area banded together as tributaries to the Powhatan in order to better collectively protect themselves. While Paquiquineo exerted ingenuity in finding his way home, the stakes of his resistance were high as colonizers killed many others when they could not find him.

**TO LEARN MORE**

Horn, James. *A Land as God Made It: Jamestown and the Birth of America.* New York: Basic Books, 2006.

Rountree, Helen. *Pocahontas's People: The Powhatan Indians of Virginia through Four Centuries.* Norman: University of Oklahoma Press, 1990.

## 8.10 Yorktown Naval Weapons Station

Route 238/Old Williamsburg Road at Baptist Road, Yorktown. This address takes you to the intersection near Gate 1. You cannot enter the facility, but you can drive by it.

The creation of the Yorktown Naval Weapons Station (NWSY) displaced three African American communities, including Charles' Corner, that took shape here during the Civil War. These communities first formed when enslaved people liberated themselves by setting up camp near Union army lines in this area. Families became self-sufficient, buying land, building homes, felling timber, fishing, growing crops, and harvesting oysters. After fifty years of Charles' Corner's existence, President Woodrow Wilson signed a proclamation in 1918 for the creation of NWSY, calling it a "military necessity" dur-

Naval Weapons Station Yorktown Gate 1 Entrance.

This site demonstrates that while African American residents labored for fifty years to create community stability and sustainability following the Civil War, the proclamation of a wartime president destroyed that work, forcing residents not only to find new homes but also new ways of living, surviving, and earning money. It also is not unusual in its history, as several nearby African American communities faced similar displacement. In 1918, the U. S. Army displaced another Black Yorktown community in order to build Fort Eustis. Communities in Williamsburg like Magruder were forcibly relocated in 1942 due to the creation of Camp Peary, a World War II training ground that became a CIA training facility after the war. Still others, like **Slabtown** (see page 212), were forcibly moved by the National Park Service in the 1970s. Some of these later community removals included residents and descendants who had originally been evicted from Charles' Corner during World War I.

ing World War I. The federal government gave residents of Charles' Corner thirty days' notice to relocate.

Residents noted the lack of available housing nearby, the difficulty in moving not only their families but also their crops, and the fact that many of their young men were away serving in the war. Most had placed their life savings into their property. While they would receive compensation from the federal government, it would come only after they vacated the property, meaning families had to find alternate living arrangements before they received payment. As well, the money they received did not account for their loss of access to valuable income-producing resources, most notably timber and oyster harvesting. This displacement shifted how community members supported themselves. Many had to turn to wage labor rather than working on their own lands and local waterways, which represented a loss of autonomy as they became more directly beholden to white business owners and supervisors.

### TO LEARN MORE

Heymann, Amelia. "The Community Displaced by the Yorktown Naval Weapons Station." *Daily Press,* February 26, 2018.

Mahoney, Shannon. "Community Building after Emancipation: An Anthropological Study of Charles' Corner, Virginia, 1862–1922." College of William and Mary dissertation, 2013.

Slabtown cemetery, which is now part of Yorktown Battlefield at Colonial National Historical Park.

## 8.11 Slabtown (former)

Off of Cook Road, just south of Goosley Road. Turn into the Grand French Battery Parking Lot.

This area represents what once was the heart of Slabtown, a community created by and for refugee, enslaved, and free people during the Civil War. Its cemetery is still visible here. This community occupied much of what is known today as Yorktown Battlefield. In 1861, three enslaved men escaped their confederate captors, making their way to the Union-held Fort Monroe in Hampton. The Union officially classified the men as "contraband of war" and refused to return them to the confederates. News of this decision traveled throughout enslaved communities, and refugees began seeking protection behind Union lines. When the Union captured Fort Yorktown in 1862, many African Americans took the opportunity to liberate themselves from slavery by traveling to the fort. By 1863, over 12,000

formerly enslaved people made their home around the fort. Union officials named the community closest to the fort Slabtown after the timber that residents used to build their homes. Eventually, Slabtown included six schools, two churches, and a seminary for freedmen. At its height in the late nineteenth century, this African American community rivaled the size of nearby Yorktown, a majority-white community.

This working-class African American community of people who farmed the land and worked on local waterways became threatened with the creation of what would become the Colonial National Historical Park in the 1930s. The National Park Service (NPS) established this park to commemorate the Battle of Yorktown, the last battle of the

Formerly enslaved Virginians creating Slabtown, May 1862.

Revolutionary War, fought in 1781. Slabtown existed in what had been the heart of the battlefield. Slabtown residents organized primarily through Shiloh Baptist Church to protect their community from the 1930s through the 1970s, but the NPS ultimately pushed out all of the residents. By 1977, the last Slabtown resident had been forced out, and the NPS razed all former homes in anticipation of the battle's 1981 bicentennial. As former residents have pointed out, this area remains empty and undeveloped to this day.

**TO LEARN MORE**

Deetz, Kelley. "Slabtown: Yorktown's African-American Community, 1863–1970." College of William and Mary senior honors thesis, 2002.

Torkelson, Jacob. "Where Shall We Go?: Race, Displacement, and Preservation at Slabtown and Yorktown Battlefield." University of Pennsylvania thesis, 2019.

**TO VISIT NEARBY**

**SHILOH BAPTIST CHURCH** at 105 Goosley Road, Yorktown. Rev. John Carey, a formerly enslaved man, and Rev. Jeremiah Asher, a former chaplain in the United States Colored Troops (USCT), founded this church in 1863 as Slabtown first developed. The congregation moved a mile away from its initial location when displaced by the National Park Service in 1971.

## 8.12 Werowocomoco

Ginny Hill Road, Gloucester County

On the north bank of what is now known as the York River, paramount chief Powhatan lived in a community called Werowocomoco. The Algonquian leader and his community occupied this land at the time of English settlement at Jamestown. The Powhatan encompassed much of coastal Virginia with a population in excess of 15,000 people. English colonizer John Smith met Powhatan at this site after he was captured by Powhatan's brother in 1607. It is from this meeting at Werowocomoco that John Smith likely invented the tale or misinterpreted events when he later recounted that Powhatan's daughter, Pocahontas, saved him from execution.

After a range of frustrating and sometimes hostile confrontations in which the English continually intruded into this area, Powhatan and his community abandoned it, seeking a less accessible site from which to withdraw from English colonizers. They initially moved to Orapakes, a swamp near the Chickahominy River, and then moved farther north.

While knowledge of the English settlement at Jamestown looms large in U.S. history and memory, the location of Werowocomoco and its importance to the area's Indigenous communities were soon lost to the English. It was not until 2003 that archeologists located the site. Virginia Indian tribes oversee this recovery work in conjunction with other entities, including the National Park Service (NPS). The NPS has noted that this is the first archeological project to take place under the sustained guidance and participation of Virginia Indians. Seven Virginia tribes have cultural and ancestral links to Werowocomoco: the Pamunkey, the Mattaponi, the Chickahominy, the Chickahominy Eastern Division, the

Rappahannock, the Upper Mattaponi, and the Nansemond. Ken Adams, Chief Emeritus of the Upper Mattaponi, notes that Werowocomoco "means something to all [Americans] because it is truly where America began. It didn't begin at Jamestown but here where Powhatan and John Smith connected and realized that there was a tangle of power between them . . . This historic place is now a part of us, a rediscovery, and we need to proclaim it as the huge part of American history that it is." Archeological excavations have uncovered evidence of a large town, including earthen ditches that date to the year 1400. An active archeology site, the National Park Service acquired it in 2016, and it is closed to the public as of 2022.

## TO VISIT NEARBY

Ten miles downriver sits **MACHICOMOCO STATE PARK** at 3601 Timberneck Farm Road. Opened in 2021, it is Virginia's newest state park and is intended to honor and interpret the histories and cultures of Virginia Indians.

## TO LEARN MORE

Custalow, Linwood "Little Bear," and Angela "Silver Star" Daniel. *The True Story of Pocahontas: The Other Side of History.* Golden, CO: Fulcrum, 2007.

Gleach, Frederic. *Powhatan's World and Colonial Virginia: A Conflict of Cultures.* Lincoln: University of Nebraska Press, 2000.

Wood, Karenne, ed. *The Virginia Indian Heritage Trail.* Charlottesville: Virginia Foundation for the Humanities, 2008.

"Werowocomoco: Finding and Investigating a Legendary Site." Virginia Museum of History & Culture lecture, February 23, 2016.

## 8.13 Hayes Post Office (former)

2425 Hayes Road, Gloucester County

*Washington Afro American* covers the Irene Morgan case.

On July 16, 1944, Irene Morgan, a twenty-seven-year-old African American woman who was visiting her mother in Gloucester County, boarded a Greyhound bus at a post office here, which no longer exists. Twenty-five miles later, near Saluda, two white passengers boarded the crowded bus. The driver asked Morgan and an African American woman sitting beside her to move to the long rear seat at the back. Virginia law required buses to segregate their passengers by race and designated bus drivers "special policemen" with powers that included the right to determine the race of passengers, demand seat changes, eject passengers, and even make arrests. Morgan refused. The bus driver then drove to the Saluda jail where the sheriff issued a warrant for her arrest. Morgan tore up the warrant, threw it out the bus window, and fought back when the sheriff attempted to physically restrain her. Authorities charged Morgan with resisting arrest; she pleaded guilty and paid a fine. However, she refused to admit guilt for violating Virginia's segregation laws. When convicted, she did not pay the fine. The **Law Offices of Oliver Hill** (see page 73) in Richmond represented her in court. In its 1946 *Morgan v. Virginia* ruling, the U. S. Supreme Court banned segregation on interstate travel. However, many southern states refused to comply, leading Black and white activists to conduct the Journey of Reconciliation across the Upper South in 1947, a precursor to the Freedom Rides of 1961, to highlight southern states' lack of compliance with federal law.

### TO LEARN MORE

Catsam, Derek, and Brendan Wolfe. "*Morgan v. Virginia* (1946)." *Encyclopedia Virginia*, 2014.

Catsam, Derek. *Freedom's Main Line: The Journey of Reconciliation and the Freedom Rides.* Lexington: University of Kentucky Press, 2011.

### TO VISIT NEARBY

Visit **MORGAN'S GRAVESITE AT ROSEWOOD CEMETERY**, 3609 Providence Road, Gloucester, VA.

## 8.14  Gloucester County High School

*6680 Short Lane, Gloucester County*

In 2017, Gavin Grimm graduated from Gloucester County High School. At the beginning of his sophomore year there, he and his mother notified school administrators of Gavin's male identity; they allowed him to begin using male bathrooms. After a few months without incident, the school board received parental complaints and changed the policy. The board voted 6–1 to create a policy restricting bathroom usage only to facilities that correspond to students' "biological sex."

As a result, the American Civil Liberties Union (ACLU) spearheaded a federal court case to argue that the school board's policy violated both Title IX legislation and the 14th Amendment. Upon appeal in 2016, the Fourth Circuit Court of Appeals found that the school board policy violated Title IX. This occasion was the first time that a federal court ruled that Title IX's prohibition against sex-based discrimination applied to gender identity.

The U. S. Supreme Court granted review of the case. One month before arguments were to begin in March 2017, the Trump administration revoked the previous guidance for the Department of Justice concerning transgender students. Since this guidance formed the core of the appeals court ruling, the Supreme Court vacated its decision to review the case. On August 9, 2019, the U. S. District Court in Norfolk, Virginia, ruled in favor of Grimm. It found that there was "no question that the school board's policy discriminates against transgender students on the basis of their gender nonconformity." Grimm repeatedly notes that this case is not "just about bathrooms. It's about the right for trans people to exist in public spaces," thereby situating its importance within the larger struggle for trans rights. Grimm has become a nationally recognized transgender advocate, making *Time Magazine*'s "100 Most Influential People" list in 2017. He was the youngest person on the list.

## TO LEARN MORE

Grimm, Gavin. "Fighting for the Rights of Transgender Students." *New York Times,* June 19, 2019.

Zaveri, Mihir. "Virginia Schools' Bathroom Rule Violates Transgender Students Rights, U. S. Judge Says." *New York Times,* August 9, 2019.

## 8.15 Pamunkey Pottery School and Guild

1054 Pocahontas Trail, King William County

The Pamunkey have lived on this land for thousands of years. They are one of two Virginia tribes that still retain some of the reservation land created by treaties signed with the English colonial government in 1646 and 1677. They gained federal recognition in 2015. The Pamunkey have produced earthenware ceramics for centuries, primarily for utilitarian purposes, although they also used them at times for trade with white settlers. The Great Depression hit the Pamunkey hard, and in 1932, the state established a pottery school on the reservation with the goal of teaching potters how to mass-produce pottery for tourists. This work included hiring white instructors who introduced simplified techniques and designs that could be more easily and cheaply produced for the tourist trade. They also introduced designs like Southwestern motifs, which were not authentic to the Pamunkey. Instead, whites viewed them as emblematic of Indigenous arts, thereby increasing their marketability to white tourists.

After the founding of the school, a group of Pamunkey women ran the Pamunkey Pottery Guild, which oversaw all aspects of creating and selling pottery. They organized the Display House (also known as the Trading Post) as the first building visitors passed as they entered the reserva-

Former Pamunkey Indian School later used by potters to sell their wares.

The Pamunkey Indian Museum and Cultural Center located on the Pamunkey Indian Reservation.

tion. In 1959, they converted the one-room building that had previously functioned as a school into a new site to display and sell pottery. Anthropologist and tribal member Ashley Atkins Spivey notes that while pottery made for tourist consumption held almost no resemblance to traditional Pamunkey pottery, potters still used clay formed by Pamunkey River deposits as well as forms and images that they preferred as much as possible. Potters recognized the value of producing an economic commodity that could benefit the entire community.

The 1970s brought a reclamation of Indigenous traditional arts, and Pamunkey potters began producing "blackware," notable for its polished black sheen. Today, Pamunkey pottery includes the methods introduced by the state as well as revitalized traditional methods. Spivey emphasizes that this adaptation, established in order to survive, underscores Pamunkey pottery as a "living tradition . . . an assertion about belonging to a place where the Pamunkey get to determine for themselves how they can change, how they can draw on their past, and how they can shape their future in the face of opposition." As potter Debra Martin notes: "We are still making pottery as did our ancestors, but it's not exactly the same as previous generations, and the next generation won't necessarily look like my generation's. I don't want the creativity of our people to fade away. I'm all about the future generations. That is my concern—to make sure that we continue on with our history and culture."

### TO LEARN MORE

Atkins, Ashley. "Pamunkey Pottery and Cultural Persistence." College of William and Mary thesis, 2009.

VPM. "Pamunkey Pottery School: The Arts Scene." November 25, 2019. *https://www.youtube.com/watch?v=b0KDYocb-FQ*

### TO VISIT NEARBY

The **PAMUNKEY INDIAN MUSEUM AND CULTURAL CENTER** at 175 Lay Landing Road contains a wealth of information related to tribal history and culture. Pamunkey pottery is on display and for sale there. It operates seasonally, so confirm hours before visiting.

The **PAMUNKEY INDIAN BAPTIST CHURCH**, also located on the reservation, is the oldest Indian church in Virginia.

## 8.16  King William County Courthouse

Route 619 off of VA-30, King William County

Constructed in 1725, King William County Courthouse is the oldest U. S. courthouse in continuous operation. Many cases have been heard here, including a set of decisions in the early twentieth century related to the position of Indigenous communities within segregated transportation systems. In July 1900, Virginia mandated that all railroad companies operating in the state provide separate coach cars for white and "colored" passengers, giving the power to train conductors to decide who should ride where. This law represented Virginia's first statewide act of legalized racial segregation.

As a result, a contingent of Pamunkey tribal members, some of whom had been forcibly evicted from white coaches, attended court at the King William County Courthouse to ensure their ability to ride in coaches reserved for whites. The court ruled that the Pamunkey had to ride in coaches designated for "colored" people. Undeterred, the Pamunkey hired lawyers and generated sympathetic press coverage. Less than a month later, the superintendent of the Richmond Division of the Southern Railroad ruled that the Pamunkey could ride in coaches designated for white riders.

As a result, the Pamunkey started issuing official certificates of tribal citizenship that they could use as identification when traveling, as they could now ride in white cars but might need to prove their identity as Virginia Indians to do so. State practices and policies at the time delineated and enforced a white and Black binary, with Black Virginians being treated as second-class citizens. Most policies left Virginia Indians in limbo, as segregation laws did not recognize their existence. The Pamunkey thus worked to cement their identity as Virginia Indians at a time when many white officials denied the existence of Indigenous communities in the state. Rabid anti-Blackness on the part of

white officials often forced Virginia Indian communities to claim proximity to whiteness when their own existence as Indigenous communities was denied by those same officials.

**TO LEARN MORE**

Adams, Mikaëla. *Who Belongs? Race, Resources, and Tribal Citizenship in the Native South.* Oxford: Oxford University Press, 2016.

## 8.17 Scotland Landing

Garnetts Mill Lane, King William County

It was here along the Mattaponi River that local administrators proposed to build a water intake and pumping station as part of the larger King William Reservoir Project. In 1987, officials in Williamsburg, Newport News, and York County devised a plan to address projected regional water shortages, a plan that intruded upon the land and waterways of the Mattaponi in an act that legal scholar Allison Dussias described as the "seemingly never ending non-Indian demands on tribal resources." In addition to the station at Scotland Landing, the proposal called for building a seventy-eight-foot-high dam along Cohoke Mill Creek and two pipelines to distribute water into existing reservoirs. Over a thousand acres of wetlands and wildlife habitat would be destroyed to allow for the extraction of up to seventy-five million gallons of water per day from the Mattaponi River, which forms the bound-

King William County Courthouse.

Mattaponi Indian Reservation, 2020.

In April 2009, a federal judge struck down the Army Corps of Engineers' permit for the project, citing undue environmental harm. After spending more than $50 million across two decades, the municipalities involved ended their pursuit of the project. While instrumental to the project's defeat, the Mattaponi recognized that the project ended due to general environmental harm rather than due to infringement upon the rights of Indigenous tribes, again showcasing their centuries-long struggle to exert tribal sovereignty within contradictory systems of settler colonialism.

ary of the Mattaponi Indian Reservation. The project also would flood Indigenous archeological and sacred sites while threatening the extinction of fish species like the shad, which exist in the area primarily due to tribal preservation efforts.

The Mattaponi recognized the project as an infringement on their rights guaranteed by the Treaty of Middle Plantation of 1677, which protected some Indigenous lands and resources from non-Indian intrusion. In lawsuits filed to protect tribal resources, lands, and waterways, the Mattaponi made it clear that the reservoir project prioritized providing resources for an ever-growing non-Indigenous population at the expense of Indigenous communities. Tribal members detailed the many ways in which this project threatened the tribe's livelihood when Army Corps of Engineers staff first arrived to evaluate the project. They expressed their opposition to the project to local, state, and federal officials, particularly during regulatory procedures when the project sought to gain specific permits necessary to proceed with its work, and they brought litigation against the project in both state and federal court.

**TO LEARN MORE**

Dussias, Allison. "Protecting Pocahontas's World: The Mattaponi Tribe's Struggle against Virginia's King William Reservoir Project." *American Indian Law Review* 36, no. 1 (2011).

**TO VISIT NEARBY**

The **MATTAPONI SCHOOLHOUSE** at 1314 Mattaponi Reservation Circle, West Point. The Mattaponi built this schoolhouse in 1929 and used it to educate children until 1966. Today, it is used for tribal council and community gatherings.

## 8.18 White House Landing

White House Road at the Pamunkey River, New Kent County

White House Landing, located directly across the river from the Pamunkey Indian

Federal encampment along the Pamunkey River near White House Landing, 1862.

Reservation, was the site of a major Union army supply base during the 1862 Peninsula Campaign, a Civil War Union offensive aimed at capturing the confederate capital of Richmond. In 1862, confederate detectives arrested eleven Pamunkey men on their reservation for working with the nearby Union army. One immediately escaped, and three others were discharged. The remaining seven were taken to Richmond and imprisoned at Castle Thunder, a former tobacco warehouse converted into a jail that housed prisoners of war. There, prison officials forced the Pamunkey men to build confederate fortifications. The men shrewdly argued that they had been forced into working for the Union. They sued for their freedom, arguing that as tributary Indians who had been officially recognized by the treaties of 1646 and 1677, they could not be conscripted by any military, Union or confederate. The confederates released them.

Throughout 1862, 100,000 Union troops gathered at White House Landing. The Pamunkey could not have avoided the Union army even if they had wanted to do so. Pamunkey men became river pilots and scouts; Pamunkey women did the soldiers' laundry and cooked for them. Some, like Terrill Bradby, joined the Union army and served through the end of the war. Despite their support, the Union army stripped the Pamunkey of their livestock, wood, and other materials essential to their survival.

As a result, the Pamunkey filed numerous claims with the Southern Claims Commission, an agency formed in 1871 to compensate those who remained loyal to the Union for their losses. These claims provide a detailed historical record of how the Pamunkey assisted the Union and why. As tribal member John Langston testified: "We are Pamunkey Indians. We all thought if the rebellion succeeded, [the confederates] would have turned us all into slaves." This fear was not unfounded. In 1857, white men confiscated tribal members' guns, arguing that the Pamunkey were Black, which would have made it illegal for them to own firearms. While the governor ordered the guns returned, he warned that any tribal member with more than one-quarter "Negro" blood would lose the right to bear arms. This incident showed how closely whites policed racial boundaries and frequently tried to apply the strict regulations that governed enslaved and free Black people to Virginia Indians as well.

This site represents the complicated negotiations the Pamunkey navigated between two warring white factions, when neither offered protection or recognition for Indigenous people. It also shows how the Pamunkey insisted upon asserting their Indian identity at a time when state officials increasingly only recognized people's racial identity as white or Black, deliberately denying the existence of Virginia Indians.

## TO LEARN MORE

Pamunkey Indian Tribe (Petitioner #323). "Proposed Finding for Acknowledgment of the Pamunkey Indian Tribe." Bureau of Indian Affairs (2014).

Woodard, Buck and Danielle Moretti-Langholtz. "Mattaponi Indian Reservation: King William County." Virginia Department of Historic Resources, 2017.

## 8.19 George W. Watkins School

6501 New Kent Highway, New Kent County

Now an elementary school, this school initially served all grade levels as New Kent County's all-Black school during segregation. Named after Rev. George W. Watkins, who served as a local minister and principal at the school, it became the site of one of the most important legal decisions of the civil rights era. The 1954 Supreme Court decision known commonly as *Brown v. Board of Education* desegregated public school education, but with no timeline. In a ruling the following year, the Court called only for desegregation "with all deliberate speed," a contradictory phrase at best.

Ten years later, New Kent County schools remained completely segregated, an intentional act by the county school board. Dr. Calvin Green, who became president of the New Kent County National Associa-

tion for the Advancement of Colored People (NAACP) in 1960, and other African American parents pressed the county to comply with the *Brown* decision in the early 1960s. When these efforts failed, the NAACP began a federal lawsuit to force compliance in 1965. They filed the suit under the name of Green's youngest son, Charles.

New Kent County began a "freedom of choice" plan in 1965, whereby students could petition the school board to request permission to switch schools, which placed the burden of desegregation on African American students and their parents. Some Black students successfully petitioned to attend the formerly all-white New Kent School, but no white students chose to attend Watkins. In its 1968 *Green v. County School Board of New Kent* decision, the Supreme Court ruled that it was the responsibility of school boards to create realistic and timely plans to eliminate all vestiges of state-imposed segregation. The decision was broadly applied and initiated an era of expanded school desegregation throughout the nation.

## TO LEARN MORE

Allen, Jody, and Brian Daugherity. "Recovering a 'Lost' Story Using Oral History: The U. S. Supreme Court's Historic *Green v. New Kent County* Decision." *Oral History Review* 33, no. 2 (2006): 25–44.

Daugherity, Brian. *Keep On Keeping On: The NAACP and the Implementation of Brown v. Board of Education in Virginia.* Charlottesville: University of Virginia Press, 2016.

# 9

# Thematic
# Tours

## Monuments and Murals Tour

From the end of the nineteenth century until 2020, Richmond was known for its confederate monuments, especially those that once lined Monument Avenue. Today, most of those monuments no longer exist in their original form or location, due to residents' activism to rid the city of prominent symbols of white supremacy. This tour centers more inclusive renderings of the city's past and present as well as work that offers anti-racist visions for the future. It features monuments that recognize Black leaders and histories, as well as contemporary murals that create art for racial justice. In a city filled with hundreds of public murals created by local and international artists alike, all of the murals in this tour feature the work of local artists. Many are part of the Mending Walls RVA Project, curated by Richmond-based artist Hamilton Glass. Visit *https://mendingwallsrva.com/* to learn more about them. This route is accessible by bike or car. If done as a driving tour, there is ample opportunity to walk between the sites featured in the downtown area and Jackson Ward.

**UNDERLINED SITES ARE DETAILED ELSEWHERE IN THE GUIDE**

Begin at the *I CAN'T BREATHE* mural (28 N. 20th Street). This piece represents a key work in the Mending Walls Project. It was initiated by local artist Hamilton Glass in the summer of 2020 in response to yet another murder of an African American citizen,

George Floyd of Minneapolis, by police and the ensuing uprisings sparked across the country. Created by Amiri Richardson-Keys and Emily Herr, the mural speaks to its location in Shockoe Bottom, the site of the city's nineteenth-century slave trading business where hundreds of thousands of enslaved people were sold. While the artists were creating the mural, police in Wisconsin shot Jacob Blake, an African American man. He survived but was paralyzed; his image, as well as that of abolitionist Solomon Northrup, who likely spent time imprisoned at **DEVIL'S HALF ACRE** (E. Franklin near N. 15th Street), a jail that confined enslaved people in Shockoe Bottom, appears in the mural.

From there, travel to the **RECONCILIATION STATUE** (corner of N. 15th and E. Main Streets). Erected in 2007 and situated along the city's Slave Trail, it represents Richmond's role in the triangular trade route. This route allowed enslavers to maximize their profits, as they shipped raw materials from North America to England, manufactured goods from England to west Africa, and enslaved people onward to American locales like Richmond.

Up the hill lies Capitol Square (bounded by N. 9th and Governor Streets to the east and west and E. Broad and Bank Streets to the north and south), where the monument landscape has been reconfigured significantly in the twenty-first century. The **VIRGINIA CIVIL RIGHTS MEMORIAL** (2008) commemorates the actions taken by Barbara Johns and her fellow students in Farmville, Virginia, when they walked out of their school in 1951 to protest the condi-

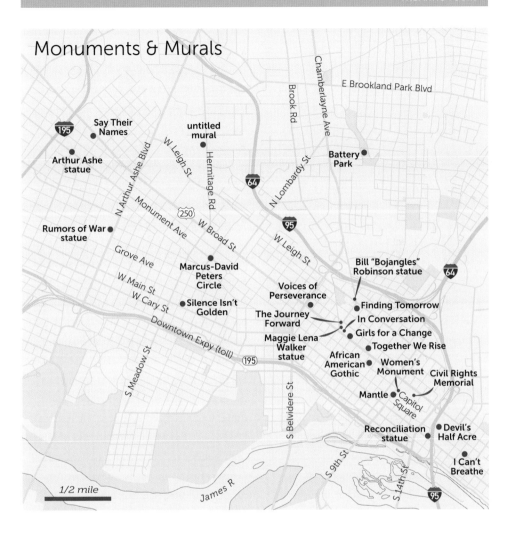

# Monuments & Murals

Say Their Names

untitled mural

Arthur Ashe statue

Battery Park

Rumors of War statue

Marcus-David Peters Circle

Bill "Bojangles" Robinson statue

Voices of Perseverance

Silence Isn't Golden

The Journey Forward

Finding Tomorrow

In Conversation

Maggie Lena Walker statue

Girls for a Change

Together We Rise

African American Gothic

Women's Monument

Civil Rights Memorial

Mantle

Capitol Square

Reconciliation statue

Devil's Half Acre

I Can't Breathe

Chamberlayne Ave

Brook Rd

E Brookland Park Blvd

W Leigh St

Hermitage Rd

N Arthur Ashe Blvd

Monument Ave

N Lombardy St

W Broad St

Grove Ave

W Main St

W Cary St

Downtown Expy (toll)

S Meadow St

S Belvidere St

S 9th St

S 14th St

James R

W Leigh St

1/2 mile

tions of their segregated high school. Richmond-based lawyers Oliver Hill and Spottswood Robinson III took their case to the U.S. Supreme Court. The **VIRGINIA WOMEN'S MONUMENT** (2019) commemorates twelve women, including seventeenth-century Pamunkey leader Cockacoeske, African American activist Maggie Walker, and African American educator Virginia Randolph. However, three of the white women depicted either legally enslaved people or

vocalized their support for enslavement, thus showcasing the continued struggles and failure to represent diverse histories without replicating deeply embedded structures of white supremacy. **MANTLE: A TRIBUTE TO VIRGINIA INDIANS** is the only abstract monument on the square, as its creators intended it to be experiential. Its name is taken from paramount chief Powhatan's Mantle, a large deerskin garment thought to be gifted to him by King James of England in 1608.

**AFRICAN AMERICAN GOTHIC** (404 E. Grace Street), created by Andre Shank and Sone-Seeré Burrell, is a play on Grant Wood's *American Gothic* and features two Black pioneers of the local food justice movement: Duron Chavis (see **MCDONOUGH GARDEN SITE**) and Nikiya Ellis. **TOGETHER WE RISE** (300 E. Broad Street), by Noah Scalin and Alfonso Perez, features two figures entangled in yellow tape emblazoned with the names of Black Americans killed by police, with Marcus-David Peters, who was killed by Richmond police in 2018, prominently displayed. Grab coffee next door at **URBAN HANG SUITE** (304 E. Broad), a space intentionally curated by owner Kelli Lemon to encourage conversation and connection among diverse groups of patrons.

Hamilton Glass's **GIRLS FOR A CHANGE** mural (E. Broad at N. 1st Street) was developed and created alongside local Black girls in order to celebrate them, and it borders the city's historic African American neighborhood, Jackson Ward. It also sits along the city's Arts District, which represents a diverse set of galleries, theaters, and artistic spaces. Walk down to **IN CONVERSATION** (4 W. Broad Street), by Hamilton Glass and Matt Lively, the first mural of the Mending Walls Project. This mural depicts two artists of different racial backgrounds, cultures, and upbringings coming together to engage in difficult dialogues related to race relations.

At the corner of the block is the **MAGGIE LENA WALKER STATUE** (corner of W. Broad and N. Adams Streets), unveiled on Walker's 153th birthday celebration in 2017. The city's first monument to a woman, it commemo-

rates the philanthropic and activist work of Walker, who was born in Church Hill and lived in Jackson Ward. Two blocks away is **THE JOURNEY FORWARD** (319 Brook Road), by Nadd Harvin and Humble, which reimagines Emanuel Leutze's *Washington Crossing the Delaware* as a Black child clutching a painter's palette and wearing BLM (Black Lives Matter)–emblazoned sneakers riding amidst waves of change.

**FINDING TOMORROW** (511 N. Adams Street), by Eli McMullen and Hamilton Glass, commemorates the life of Lorna Pinckney, founder of Tuesday Verses, a vibrant cultural space in the city that centers Black cultural workers and artists. Nearby is the **BILL "BOJANGLES" ROBINSON STATUE** (corner of N. Adams and W. Leigh Streets). Erected in 1973, the Robinson statue was the first to feature a Black Richmonder, and the only one to do so for two decades. The Astoria Beneficial Club, a Black mutual aid organization founded in 1901 to work toward achieving full citizenship rights for African Americans, envisioned and funded the statue. Robinson, who was raised in Jackson Ward, became a well-known Black entertainer in the first half of the twentieth century.

**VOICES OF PERSEVERANCE** (504 W. Broad Street), from Ed Trask and Jason Ford, represents multigenerational activists and leaders for civil rights and racial equity. **UNTITLED MURAL** (2500 Hermitage Road), by Mickael Broth and Andre Shank, pays tribute to the survival of Indigenous communities amidst the region's histories of colonization.

**SILENCE ISN'T GOLDEN** (1812 W. Main Street), by David Marion and MeMe, uses

African American writer Zora Neale Hurston's quote "If you are silent about your pain, they will kill you and say you enjoyed it" as their inspiration for this mural that interweaves water rights for both Indigenous and Black communities as integral to their freedom. It also features MeMe's family totem.

Kehinde Wiley's **_RUMORS OF WAR_** (200 N. Arthur Ashe Boulevard) sits on the grounds of the Virginia Museum of Fine Arts (VMFA). Wiley unveiled the statue in December 2019 amidst ongoing debates over the future of the confederate monuments along Monument Avenue, which lies four blocks north. In 2021, the state granted the VMFA millions of dollars to shape a community process to reenvision the avenue, including the activist and community–curated space of **MARCUS-DAVID PETERS CIRCLE** (1600 Monument Avenue). Activists declared their refusal to honor a process guided by an elite, white-led, and white-funded organization that has not dem-onstrated the ability to work with and in diverse local communities. As of this writing, the VMFA is no longer leading the effort, and the future direction of this work remains unclear. Monument Avenue, now with no confederate monuments, lies just north of the VMFA. The **ARTHUR ASHE STATUE** (Monument Avenue at Roseneath Road), erected in 1996, commemorates Richmond's African American tennis star and humanitarian. As a youth in the city, Ashe could not play on the tennis courts at Byrd Park because they were for whites only. Murals painted by Hamilton Glass that feature Ashe can be seen at **BATTERY PARK** (Overbrook Road at Hawthorne Avenue), where he played instead. On the way there, stop by **_SAY THEIR NAMES_** (3311 W. Broad), a mural created by Silly Genius and Nils Westergard, featuring the image of Richmond rapper and emcee Radio Blitz alongside the many names of Black people killed by police.

## Virginia Indians Tour

This tour charts the history and survival of Virginia's Indigenous communities since European colonization. Despite centuries of policies and practices aimed at their displacement and demise, alongside the spread of European disease, Virginia Indians continue to survive amidst settler colonialist legacies. Many historical sites lie within town and city centers while contemporary sites are situated in more rural locations, a direct result of the ways in which colonial and state policies pushed Virginia Indians out of the areas that whites sought for their own use and occupation. Those geographies still shape Virginia Indians' experiences, as it is harder to access resources and services, including employment and healthcare, in these rural areas.

This is a driving tour, and it will take the day to complete. It also includes when tribes hold their pow wows. These annual celebrations are open to the public and offer excellent opportunities for those who are not Indigenous to learn more about Virginia Indians.

**UNDERLINED SITES ARE DETAILED ELSEWHERE IN THE GUIDE**

Start in downtown Richmond at the **GOVERNOR'S MANSION** (Capitol Square near the corner of E. Broad and Governor Streets), where the Pamunkey and the Mattaponi have provided annual tribute to the governor since the seventeenth century. Once a requirement, today the occasion takes place the Wednesday before Thanksgiving and is a cultural celebration of all Virginia Indians. While on Capitol Square, visit **MANTLE: A STATE TRIBUTE TO VIRGINIA INDIANS**, located in the southwest corner of the square and dedicated in 2018. Then, head east to the battle site of **BLOODY RUN** (E. Marshall and N. 31st Streets, Richmond). Here, in 1656, a hundred Pamunkey warriors supported English colonizers against an attack by the Westo, a nonlocal tribe. The Westo killed the Pamunkey, and as a result they gained preferential rights with the English, highlighting the ways in which the presence of white colonizers heightened conflict among Indigenous communities.

From here, travel east to **SAMARIA INDIAN SCHOOL** (8130 Lott Cary Town, Charles City County), near the site of the present-day Samaria Baptist Church. The Chickahominy opened this tribe-funded school in 1901. The school closed in 1968 with the desegregation of public schools. The **CHICKAHOMINY TRIBAL CENTER** is located next door; the tribe hosts an annual fall festival and powwow the last Saturday in September. Next, travel to **SANDY POINT** (juncture of Sandy Point Road and Wilcox Neck Road, Charles City County). In August 1610, English soldiers invaded the Paspahegh community. The Paspahegh did not recover; they abandoned the area, and English raids on Indigenous communities persisted indefinitely.

Travel east to Williamsburg, which served as Virginia's colonial capital from 1699 to 1780. Visit **THE BRAFFERTON** (Wren Yard near the intersection of Jamestown and Richmond Roads, Williamsburg), which opened in 1723 to educate Indigenous chil-

## Virginia Indians

Upper Mattaponi Indian Tribe Headquarters

Scotland Landing

King William County Courthouse

Mattaponi Indian Reservation

Mantle

RICHMOND

Governor's Mansion

Pamunkey Indian Reservation

Bloody Run

GLOUCESTER

Samaria Indian School

Werowocomoco

Gloucester Visitor Center

Sandy Point

WILLIAMSBURG

The Brafferton

Machicomoco State Park

HOPEWELL

College Landing Park

PETERSBURG

YORKTOWN

Jamestown Island

Rappahannock R

York R

James R

5 miles

dren. The English hoped to Anglicize the children, but instead, students departed with critical knowledge that helped their communities navigate and negotiate life among white colonizers. The school closed in the 1770s. Nearby is **COLLEGE LANDING PARK** (1070 S. Henry Street, Williamsburg). Spaniards kidnapped Paquiquineo, a member of a local Indigenous community, from this area around 1560. Paquiquineo eventually persuaded the Jesuits to return and establish a mission here in 1570. Paquiquineo left, and he and a group of warriors eventually killed the missionaries from the mission. As a result, the Spanish captured and killed a number of Indigenous people, and Indigenous communities banded together as tributaries to the Powhatan to protect themselves against colonial intruders.

From here, **JAMESTOWN ISLAND** (Jamestown Road at Colonial Parkway) is a few miles away. More than a hundred English colonizers arrived here in May 1607. Within one month of their arrival, nearby Indigenous communities, who were tributaries to Powhatan, moved farther away. English and Indigenous leaders signed treaties here in 1646 and 1677. Both opened more land to English encroachment and created reservations for the Pamunkey and the Mattaponi; Indigenous leaders used what leverage they could to negotiate the best terms possible given their difficult situation, as English settlement and military power had increased substantially. The English abandoned the settlement in 1699 when the colonial capital moved to nearby Williamsburg. Today, the island is part of the Colonial

National Historic Park, which is accessible for a fee.

In 2021, Virginia opened **MACHICOMOCO STATE PARK** (3601 Timberneck Farm Road, Gloucester County), specifically established to honor and celebrate the legacy of Virginia Indians. The park is part of the larger preservation of Indigenous lands near Werowocomoco. Designed in collaboration with tribal representatives, park signs interpret the land, geography, and ecology using Algonquian language alongside English. Stop at the **GLOUCESTER VISITOR CENTER** (6509 Main Street) next. An exhibit interprets Werowocomoco, and includes archeological artifacts from the nearby site. Nearby **WEROWOCOMOCO** (Ginny Hill Road, Gloucester County) represents the seat of paramount chief Powhatan, and the political center of his chiefdom, at the time of English colonization. The National Park Service acquired the land in 2016 and is working in consultation with Virginia Indians to preserve it. *As of 2022, you can drive down Ginny Hill Road but a closed gate prevents access to the site.*

From here, travel west to the **PAMUNKEY INDIAN TRIBE AND RESERVATION** (Pocahontas Trail, King William County). The Pamunkey have lived on this reservation since the mid-seventeenth century. Their reservation includes the Pamunkey Baptist Church. Founded in 1865, it is the oldest Indian church in Virginia. **THE PAMUNKEY POTTERY SCHOOL** is here as well. The Pamunkey have produced earthenware ceramics for centuries. The **PAMUNKEY INDIAN MUSEUM AND CULTURAL CENTER** (175 Lay Landing Road) is an excellent source for learning more about the history and culture of the Pamunkey; it also displays examples of Pamunkey pottery. Call (804–843–4792) or consult the website (*http://pamunkey.org/reservation/museum-cultural-center/*) before visiting, as it operates seasonally.

To the north lies the **MATTAPONI INDIAN RESERVATION** (Indian Town Road at Mattaponi Reservation Circle, King William County), created by the colony of Virginia in 1658 on land long occupied by the Mattaponi. Due to continual white encroachment, the size of the present-day reservation is much smaller than originally established. From here, travel to **KING WILLIAM COUNTY COURTHOUSE** (King William Road at Horse Landing Road), where the original courthouse building from 1725 survives. Here, Virginia Indians undertook important activism to maintain their status as Indigenous people in the face of legal segregation beginning in 1900. Head north to **SCOTLAND LANDING** (Garretts Mill Lane, King William County) along the Mattaponi River where local administrators proposed to build a water intake and pumping station in 1987 that would have intruded upon the land and waterways of the Mattaponi. In 2009, a federal judge struck down the project.

Nearby are the **SHARON INDIAN SCHOOL** and **INDIAN VIEW BAPTIST CHURCH**, both of which are situated near the **UPPER MATTAPONI INDIAN TRIBE HEADQUARTERS** (13476 King William Road). The King William County School Board built the original elementary schoolhouse in 1919 for students in the Upper Mattaponi tribe, which operated until 1965. The building now houses the

Tribal Center. The tribe received federal recognition in 2018, and hosts an annual Memorial Day Weekend powwow.

## Black Freedom Struggles for Self-Determination Tour

This tour highlights sites where African Americans have liberated themselves and their communities from white supremacist rule since the first Africans arrived in the colony of Virginia under bondage at Point Comfort in 1619. The sites featured here are centered in Richmond, the former capital of the confederacy and the second-largest market for enslaved people prior to the Civil War. This driving tour will take half a day. Several Jackson Ward sites are located in close proximity to one another, allowing you to park and walk between them.

**UNDERLINED SITES ARE DETAILED ELSEWHERE IN THE GUIDE**

Start at **BRYAN PARK** (4308 Hermitage Road), where an enslaved blacksmith who became immortalized as "General Gabriel" and his co-conspirators planned a rebellion here in 1800 to abolish slavery in Virginia. From here, head east to **CHANDLER JUNIOR HIGH** (201 E. Brookland Park Boulevard, which today houses the Richmond Community High School). In September 1960, two African American students, Gloria Mead and Carol Swann, desegregated this formerly all-white school, marking the beginning of school desegregation in Richmond following a six-year delay after a 1954 Supreme Court decision declared segregated schooling illegal.

Travel to **OVERBY-SHEPPARD ELEMENTARY SCHOOL** (2300 1st Avenue) in Highland Park. Ethel Thompson Overby, one of the school's namesakes, became the first female African American principal of a Black Richmond school in 1933. She organized for pay equity between white and Black teachers and was a founding member of the Richmond Crusade for Voters. Created in 1956, the crusade registered thousands of Black voters, paid their poll taxes, and laid the groundwork for federal voting rights legislation.

Next, travel to **CREIGHTON COURT** (Nine Mile Road at Creighton Road), a hub of public housing tenant activism. Here, resident Curtis Holt organized tenants to resist oppressive housing policies in the 1950s and beyond. In addition, he filed a lawsuit challenging the city's 1970 annexation of a portion of Chesterfield County. The lawsuit's outcome helped to break the city's entrenched white leadership structure. Stop at the former site of the **RICHMOND COLORED NORMAL SCHOOL** (Twelfth and Leigh Streets), which educated the city's first generation of Black educators post-emancipation.

**VIRGINIA UNION UNIVERSITY** (1500 N. Lombardy Street), a center for Black empowerment and intellectual life, whose roots date back to 1865, has flourished at this Northside location since 1899. In 2020, it launched the Center for the Study of Historically Black Colleges and Universities (HBCUs), the first research institute of its kind in the nation.

At the **ST. LUKE PENNY SAVINGS BANK** (900 St. James Street), activist and entrepreneur Maggie L. Walker oversaw the Independent

# Black Freedom Struggles for Self-Determination

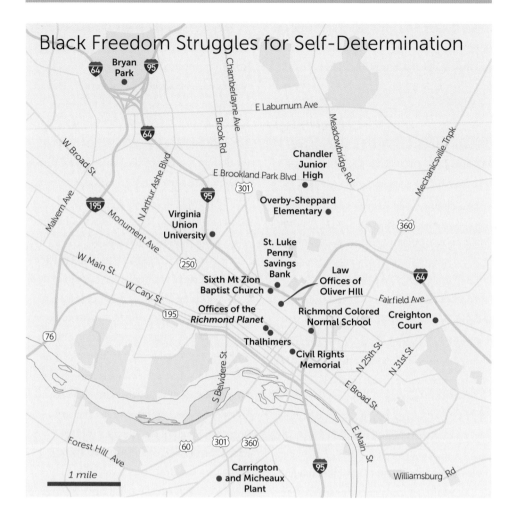

Bryan Park

Chamberlayne Ave

Brook Rd

E Laburnum Ave

Meadowbridge Rd

Mechanicsville Tnpk

W Broad St

N Arthur Ashe Blvd

Chandler Junior High

E Brookland Park Blvd

Overby-Sheppard Elementary

Virginia Union University

Malvern Ave

Monument Ave

W Main St

W Cary St

St. Luke Penny Savings Bank

Sixth Mt Zion Baptist Church

Law Offices of Oliver Hill

Fairfield Ave

Offices of the Richmond Planet

Richmond Colored Normal School

Creighton Court

Thalhimers

Civil Rights Memorial

N 25th St

N 31st St

E Broad St

S Belvidere St

E Main St

Forest Hill Ave

Carrington and Micheaux Plant

Williamsburg Rd

1 mile

---

Order of St. Luke in the early twentieth century. It housed the bank she founded, the first in the U.S. established by a woman. While in nearby Jackson Ward, visit the **MAGGIE L. WALKER NATIONAL HISTORIC SITE** (600 N. 2nd Street) and the **MAGGIE L. WALKER MEMORIAL PLAZA** (corner of Broad Street and N. Adams).

**SIXTH MOUNT ZION BAPTIST CHURCH** (14 W. Duval Street), founded in 1867 by John Jasper, was the first Black church established by a Black minister in Richmond. By

the late 1880s, Sixth Mount Zion had over 2,500 members and served as a critical space for religious and civic life in Jackson Ward. Today, the church continues to cultivate community connection and mutual aid. It welcomes visitors to its services, as well as to its **JOHN JASPER MEMORIAL ROOM AND MUSEUM**.

Civil rights attorney Oliver Hill practiced with partners from 1939 until 1998 at the former **LAW OFFICES OF OLIVER HILL** (623 N. 3rd Street). Hill became a prominent attorney at the forefront of fighting against legal segregation throughout Virginia. In 1948, he became the first African American elected to Richmond's city council in the twentieth century.

Nearby sits the former **RICHMOND PLANET OFFICES** (311 N. 4th Street). Led by John Mitchell Jr. from 1882 until 1929, the staff of the city's first Black newspaper worked tirelessly to expose white supremacy; the paper gained a national following. If you are hungry while in Jackson Ward, stop in at **MAMA J'S** (415 N. 1st Street), Velma Johnson's popular family-run soul food restaurant.

Travel to the former site of **THALHIMERS** (N. 5th and E. Broad Streets). This six-story department store covered an entire city block and became a prime site of desegregation protests during the civil rights era. The nearby **CIVIL RIGHTS MONUMENT** (Capitol Square, near E. Broad and N. 11th Streets) commemorates the actions of Barbara Johns and her classmates who, in 1951, led a walkout of their Black high school in Farmville to protest deteriorating conditions at their segregated school. It also commemorates civil rights lawyers Oliver Hill and Spottswood Robinson III, who pursued the subsequent court case that helped to end segregated schooling throughout the country.

South of the river, the former **CARRINGTON AND MICHAUX PLANT** (2200 Decatur Street) was a tobacco factory where 300 Black women, who worked the plant's dirtiest and lowest-paid jobs, went on strike in 1937 to demand better pay and working conditions. With the help of the Southern Negro Youth Congress, they formed their own union, since white unions would not work with them. As a result, the workers won increased wages, a forty-hour workweek, and additional pay for overtime work.

## Queer Cultures and Histories Tour

This tour centers sites of LGBTQ history, culture making, and resistance in Richmond, as well as sites that showcase the power that the state has harnessed at times to regulate and suppress LGBTQ rights and communities.

**UNDERLINED SITES ARE DETAILED ELSEWHERE IN THE GUIDE**

This tour starts at **ROBERT B. MOSS THEATRE** (1300 Altamont Avenue), which houses the Richmond Triangle Players (RTP). RTP began during the AIDS epidemic in 1993 to raise funds and awareness for LGBTQ issues. It was the first theater of its kind in the region.

Established in 1934, the **VIRGINIA DEPARTMENT OF ALCOHOLIC BEVERAGE CONTROL (ABC)** (2901 Hermitage Road) was based at this location between 1971 and 2021. The agency administers the state's ABC laws, and its agents have full police power. It functioned as a leading state adversary against LGBTQ communities as it actively sought to close alcohol-serving establishments catering to LGBTQ folks. In 1991, as a result of grassroots activism, federal courts declared the agency's anti-LGBTQ regulations unconstitutional. Stop by **DIVERSITY THRIFT** (1407 Sherwood Avenue), a large thrift store that

# Queer Cultures & Histories

Virginia ABC
(former location)

Robert B. Moss
Theatre

Chamberlayne Ave

Brook Rd

E Brookland Park Blvd

Monument Ave

N Arthur Ashe Blvd

W Leigh St

Hermitage Rd

N Lombardy St

Mulberry
House
(former)

Phoenix
Rising
(former)

Metropolitan
Community
Church

Carytown

W Cary St

W Main St

Grove Ave

W Broad St

W Leigh St

Fan Free
Clinic

Monroe
Park

Hippodrome

S Meadow St

Downtown Expy (toll)

S Belvidere St

Godfrey's

Byrd
Park

Brown's Island

S 9th St

S 14th St

Capitol
Square

1708
Gallery
(former
location)

1/2 mile

James R

---

opened in 1999. It is part of Diversity Richmond, an organization that has raised over one million dollars since its founding to support local LGBTQ initiatives. The space hosts entertainment like weekly bingo, art shows, and other community gatherings.

Travel to **THE HIPPODROME** (528 N. 2nd Street), a Jackson Ward nightlife venue that hosted nationally known Black artists in the first half of the twentieth century. Its entertainers often performed gay and les-

bian–themed material, and was known to be an LGBTQ-friendly space. Grab lunch at LGBTQ-owned **SOUL TACO** (321 N. 2nd) before leaving Jackson Ward.

Next, head downtown to the former location of **1708 GALLERY** (1708 E. Main Street). Opened in 1978 as an artist-run space, in 1990 the gallery sponsored an exhibit by Cuban artist Carlos Gutierrez-Solana that the state used to prosecute the gallery on obscenity charges. In court, the state lost its case, and the exhibit continued as a critical space for cultivating artistic freedom while centering AIDS awareness and education.

**GODFREY'S** (308 E. Grace Street) has served as an LGBTQ gathering space since 1997. It is well known for its popular Sunday drag brunches and has always been an 18+ entertainment venue, as its owners recognize the need for a supportive nightlife culture for LGBTQ youth. The annual statewide Virginia Pride event takes place on **BROWN'S ISLAND** (S. 7th Street at the river) on the third Saturday in September.

Richmond's Women's Alliance, including the Richmond Lesbian Feminists, sponsored women's festivals at **MONROE PARK** (620 W. Main Street) in the mid-1970s. In October 1977, community members and activists hosted a rally here in support of the city's gay and lesbian communities in response to Anita Bryant's arrival in Richmond. Bryant, who was giving a concert in town, was an outspoken opponent of gay rights.

In 1968, a nurse, two doctors, and a minister established what became Virginia's first free health clinic, the **FAN FREE CLINIC** (initially located at 1103 Floyd Street). It was instrumental in treating patients during the HIV / AIDS crisis in the 1980s and beyond. Parishioners established the **METROPOLITAN COMMUNITY CHURCH** (2501 Park Avenue) in 1978 as a safe worship space for LGBTQ Christians. The congregation moved into this church in 1993, where it hosts a variety of community events, including an annual Trans Day of Visibility event on March 31.

A group of lesbian, gay, bisexual, and straight Richmonders founded a commune known as **MULBERRY HOUSE** (2701–2703 W. Grace Street) in the early 1970s, where they cultivated tight-knit kinship ties at a time when many gay men and lesbians were closeted or shunned by their families. **BYRD PARK** (600 S. Arthur Ashe Boulevard) was the site of Richmond's first Lesbian and Gay Pride Day on June 23, 1979. Public events like this one educated the broader community, enabled a broader base of support for future organizing initiatives, and provided important community space for out LGBTQ folks to gather while also signaling to those who were closeted that there was a welcoming community for them to join.

**PHOENIX RISING** (19 N. Belmont Avenue) opened in 1993 as an independent bookstore carrying LGBT-themed books, magazines, and media. It also served as a space where patrons could connect to others in the local LGBT community. The bookstore closed in the mid-2010s due to competition from big box stores and online outlets. Less than two blocks south lies **CARYTOWN** (W. Cary Street between N. Thompson Street and Arthur Ashe Boulevard), a bustling shopping district known for its independent small businesses like LGBTQ-owned card and gift store **MONGREL** (2924 W. Cary). It has been the staging site for a number of LGBTQ marches and parades in the past. It also is home to **BABE'S OF CARYTOWN** (3166 W. Cary), an LGBTQ-owned space that has cultivated nightlife for LGBTQ community members for over three decades.

## Food Justice Tour

This tour centers sites of people organizing to combat the twin problems of racial injustice and food insecurity to create healthier, more equitable communities. The route travels through Richmond to north Chesterfield County, then farther south to Petersburg. Allow half to a full day for exploring by car.

**UNDERLINED SITES ARE DETAILED
ELSEWHERE IN THE GUIDE**

This tour begins at **OLD CITY HALL** (1001 E. Broad Street), where welfare recipients in 1969 demanded meetings with city leaders to protest their lack of access to quality food, among other essentials. They recruited prominent community members, and two African American city councilmen, to live on a welfare budget for a week, to show the meager resources available to them. From here, travel to *AFRICAN AMERICAN GOTHIC* (404 E. Grace Street). Part of the Mending Walls Project, it features two leaders in the local food justice movement: Duron Chavis and Nikiya Ellis.

Travel north to **CHARLES S. GILPIN COMMUNITY FARM** (intersection of St. Peter and W. Hill Streets). Community organizer and Gilpin Court resident Lillie Estes launched this project in 2019. She transformed a vacant lot into a space that brings healthy, affordable food to Gilpin Court, the city's largest public housing community.

Travel east to the **FOOD JUSTICE CORRIDOR**, maintained by Arthur Burton. It travels through four East End public housing communities and runs northwest along Creighton Road. The project fosters a culture of health that extends beyond food to include safe, affordable housing and quality education. Visit one of its gardens at **MARTIN LUTHER KING MIDDLE SCHOOL** (1000 Mosby Street).

Travel across the river to the **5TH DISTRICT MINI FARM** (2224 Bainbridge Road). Its founder, urban agriculturalist Randy Minor, works on the same land as his grandfather and emphasizes teaching community members how to grow their own food. Then travel to **MCDONOUGH COMMUNITY GARDEN** (3300 McDonough Street) and **BROAD ROCK COMMUNITY GARDEN** (404 E. Broad Rock Road). Duron Chavis and other community members have transformed these once neglected spaces into vital local gathering spaces that address systemic issues of racial injustice by broadening access to healthy, affordable food and accessible land in communities of color.

**ARCO IRIS** (6445 Midlothian Turnpike) was one of the first in a wave of Salvadoran markets and restaurants to open here in the early 2000s. In addition to hard-to-find grocery staples, it offered resources needed by the area's growing Latino communities, like wire transfer services. A few miles west sits the former site of **LA SIESTA** (9900 Midlothian Turnpike). Michel Zajur's family opened this restaurant, originally operating out of a dining car on Route 1, in 1972; it was the area's first Mexican restaurant. Five decades later, many Latino entrepreneurs run businesses, restaurants, and markets that serve the region's diverse Latino communities in this area.

# Food Justice

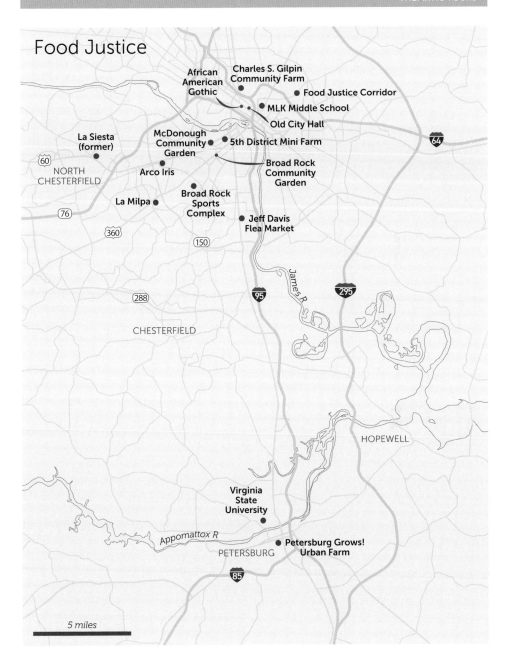

African American Gothic

Charles S. Gilpin Community Farm

Food Justice Corridor

MLK Middle School

Old City Hall

La Siesta (former)

McDonough Community Garden

5th District Mini Farm

NORTH CHESTERFIELD

Arco Iris

Broad Rock Community Garden

La Milpa

Broad Rock Sports Complex

Jeff Davis Flea Market

CHESTERFIELD

James R.

HOPEWELL

Virginia State University

Appomattox R

Petersburg Grows! Urban Farm

PETERSBURG

5 miles

**LA MILPA** (6925 Hull Street, Chesterfield County) restaurant and market has served as a cultural center since its opening in 2000. Recently, its owners started an eight-acre garden and revived the La Plaza Farm-

ers Market. **BROAD ROCK SPORTS COMPLEX** (4802 Warwick Road) has been an important site for Latino community gatherings for decades, and was the initial site of La Plaza when it opened as the area's first Latino farmers market in 2012. **JEFF DAVIS FLEA MARKET** (5700 Jefferson Davis Highway) is a vibrant and diverse hub of over one hundred Latino, Afro-Latino, and Caribbean vendors who sell everything from orchids to electronics to wedding supplies.

Continue south on Route 1 to **VIRGINIA STATE UNIVERSITY** (1 Hayden Street, Petersburg), the state's oldest public Historically Black University. Its Small Farm Outreach Program has enabled many local farmers of color to begin sustainable agricultural production.

Cross the Appomattox River to **PETERSBURG GROWS! URBAN FARM** (145 Halifax Street), where a group of community urban farmers have transformed a former vacant space into a community gathering space.

# Recommended Reading

Abbott, Karen. *Liar, Temptress, Soldier, Spy: Four Women Undercover in the Civil War.* New York: Harper Perennial, 2014.

Adams, Mikaëla. *Who Belongs? Race, Resources, and Tribal Citizenship in the Native South.* Oxford: Oxford University Press, 2016.

Adkins, Elaine and Ray. *Chickahominy Indians–Eastern Division: A Brief Ethnohistory.* Xlibris, 2007.

Alexander, Ann. *Race Man: The Rise and Fall of the "Fighting Editor," John Mitchell Jr.* Charlottesville: University of Virginia Press, 2002.

Allen, Jody, and Brian Daugherity. "Recovering a 'Lost' Story Using Oral History: The U. S. Supreme Court's Historic *Green v. New Kent County* Decision." *Oral History Review* 33, no. 2 (2006): 25–44.

Atkins, Ashley. "Pamunkey Pottery and Cultural Persistence." College of William and Mary thesis, 2009.

Barbee, Matthew. *Race and Masculinity in Southern Memory: A History of Richmond, Virginia's Monument Avenue, 1948–1996.* Lanham, MD: Rowman and Littlefield, 2013.

Barnes, Diane. *Artisan Workers in the Upper South: Petersburg, Virginia, 1820–1865.* Baton Rouge: Louisiana State University Press, 2008.

Belsches, Elvatrica Parker. *Black America Series: Richmond, Virginia.* Mt. Pleasant, SC: Arcadia, 2002.

Berta, Ruth, and Amanda Pohl. *Building Power, Changing Lives: The Story of Virginia Organizing.* New Orleans: Social Policy Press, 2015.

Besch, Edwin. *U. S. Colored Troops Defeat Confederate Cavalry.* Jefferson, NC: McFarland, 2017.

Bluestone, Daniel. "Charlottesville's Landscape of Prostitution, 1880–1950." *Buildings & Landscapes: Journal of the Vernacular Architecture Forum* 22, no. 2 (Fall 2015): 36–61.

Bond, Patrick, and Laura Browder. "Deracialized Nostalgia, Reracialized Community, and Truncated Gentrification: Capital and Cultural Flows in Richmond, Virginia and Durban, South Africa." *Journal of Cultural Geography* 36, no. 2 (2019): 211–45.

Broth, Mickael, and Ed Trask. *Murals of Richmond.* Richmond: Chop Suey Books, 2018.

Brown, Elsa Barkley. "Womanist Consciousness: Maggie Lena Walker and the Independent Order of St. Luke." *Signs* 14, no. 3 (Spring 1989): 610–33.

Brown, Elsa Barkley, and Gregg Kimball. "Mapping the Terrain of Black Richmond." *Journal of Urban History* 21, no. 3 (March 1995): 296–346.

Brown, Kathleen. *Good Wives, Nasty Wenches, and Anxious Patriarchs: Gender, Race, and Power in Colonial Virginia.* Chapel Hill: University of North Carolina Press, 1996.

Bruder, Anne, Susan Hellman, and Catherine Zipf. "Notes from the Road: Documenting Sites Listed in The Negro Motorist Green Book." *Arris: Journal of the Southeast Chapter of Architectural Historians* 29 (2018): 52+.

Brundage, Fitzhugh. *Lynching in the New South: Georgia and Virginia, 1880–1930.* Bloomington: University of Illinois Press, 1993.

Butler, August. "Making a Home Out of No Home: Colored Orphan Asylums in Virginia, 1867–1930." College of William and Mary thesis, 2018.

Campbell, Ben. *Richmond's Unhealed History.* Richmond: Brandywine, 2011.

Campbell, James. *Slavery on Trial: Race, Class, and Criminal Justice in Antebellum Richmond.* Gainesville: University Press of Florida, 2007.

Catsam, Derek. *Freedom's Main Line: The Journey of Reconciliation and the Freedom Rides.* Lexington: University of Kentucky Press, 2011.

Catte, Elizabeth. *Pure America: Eugenics and the Making of Modern Virginia.* Cleveland: Belt, 2021.

Chesson, Michael. "Harlots or Heroines? A New Look at the Richmond Bread Riot." *Virginia Magazine of History and Biography* 92, no. 2 (April 1984): 131–75.

Cohen, Adam. *Imbeciles: The Supreme Court, American Eugenics, and the Sterilization of Carrie Buck.* New York: Penguin, 2017.

Coleman, Arica L. *That the Blood Stay Pure: African Americans, Native Americans, and the Predicament of Race and Identity in Virginia.* Bloomington: Indiana University Press, 2013.

Custalow, Linwood "Little Bear," and Angela "Silver Star" Daniel. *The True Story of Pocahontas: The Other Side of History.* Golden, CO: Fulcrum, 2007.

Dabney, Virginius. *Richmond: The Story of a City.* Charlottesville: University of Virginia Press, 1990.

Daugherity, Brian. *Keep On Keeping On: The NAACP and the Implementation of* Brown v. Board of Education *in Virginia.* Charlottesville: University of Virginia Press, 2016.

Daugherity, Brian, and Brian Grogan, eds. *A Little Child Shall Lead Them: A Documentary Account of the Struggle for School Desegregation in Prince Edward County, Virginia.* Charlottesville: University of Virginia Press, 2019.

Davis, Scott. *The World of Patience Gromes: Making and Unmaking a Black Community.* Seattle: Cune Press, 1999.

Deetz, Kelley. "Slabtown: Yorktown's African-American Community, 1863–1970." College of William and Mary senior honors thesis, 2002.

Department of Community Planning Advisory Board and the University of Virginia. *From Porch Swings to Patios: An Oral History of Charlottesville Neighborhoods, 1914–1984.*

Devlin, Eric. "Colonial Williamsburg's Slave Auction Re-Enactment: Controversy, African American History and Public Memory." College of William and Mary thesis, 2003.

Digital Scholarship Lab and the National Community Reinvestment Coalition. "Not Even Past: Social Vulnerability and the Legacy of Redlining." In *American Panorama: An Atlas of United States History,* edited by Robert K. Nelson and Edward L. Ayers, 2022.

Dussias, Allison. "Protecting Pocahontas's World: The Mattaponi Tribe's Struggle against Virginia's King William Reservoir Project." *American Indian Law Review* 36, no. 1 (2011).

Edds, Margaret. *We Face the Dawn: Oliver Hill, Spottswood Robinson, and the Legal Team That Dismantled Jim Crow.* Charlottesville: University of Virginia Press, 2019.

Edwards-Ingram, Ywone. "Before 1979: African American Coachmen, Visibility, and Representation at Colonial Williamsburg." *Public Historian* 36, no. 1 (2014): 9–35.

Egan, Maureen, and Susan Winiecki. *Richmond's Culinary History: Seeds of Change.* Mt. Pleasant, SC: History Press, 2017.

Egerton, Douglas. *Gabriel's Rebellion: The Virginia Slave Conspiracies of 1800 and 1802.* Chapel Hill: University of North Carolina Press, 1993.

Eisenfeld, Sue. *Shenandoah: A Story of Conservation and Betrayal.* Lincoln: University of Nebraska Press, 2014.

English, Beth. "'I Have . . . a Lot of Work to Do': Cotton Mill Work and Women's Culture in Matoaca, Virginia, 1888–95." *Virginia Magazine of History and Biography* 113, no. 3 (2006): 226–53.

Eskridge, Sara. "Virginia Pupil Placement Board and the Practical Applications of Massive Resistance." *Virginia Magazine of History and Biography* 118, no. 3 (2010): 246–76.

Ethridge, Harrison. "The Jordan Hatcher Affair of 1852: Cold Justice and Warm Compassion." *Virginia Magazine of History and Biography* 84, no. 3 (1976): 446–63.

Fairfax, Colita, ed. *The African Experience in Colonial Virginia: Essays on the 1619 Arrival and the Legacy of Slavery.* Jefferson, NC: McFarland, 2021.

Fausz, Frederick. "An 'Abundance of Blood Shed on Both Sides': England's First Indian War, 1609–1614." *Virginia Magazine of History and Biography* 98, no. 1 (1990): 3–56.

Fausz, Frederick. "Opechancanough: Indian Resistance Leader." In *Struggle and Survival in Colonial America,* edited by David Sweet and Gary Nash. Berkeley: University of California Press, 1981.

Foltz, Caitlin. "Race and Mental Illness at a Virginia Hospital: A Case Study of Central State Asylum for the Colored Insane, 1869–1885." Virginia Commonwealth University thesis, 2015.

Gallavin, Martin. *The Powhatan Landscape: An Archeological History of the Algonquian Chesapeake.* Gainesville: University Press of Florida, 2018.

Gellman, Erik. *Death Blow to Jim Crow: The National Negro Congress and the Rise of Militant Civil Rights.* Chapel Hill: University of North Carolina Press, 2012.

Gleach, Frederic. *Powhatan's World and Colonial Virginia: A Conflict of Cultures.* Lincoln: University of Nebraska Press, 2000.

Goerman, Patricia. *The Promised Land?: The Lives and Voices of Hispanic Immigrants in the New South.* New York: Routledge, 2006.

Gordon-Reed, Annette. *The Hemingses of Monticello: An American Family.* New York: W. W. Norton, 2009.

Grant, Nicole. *The Selling of Contraception: The Dalkon Shield Case, Sexuality, and Women's Autonomy.* Columbus: Ohio State University Press, 1992.

Greenspan, Anders. *Creating Colonial Williamsburg.* Washington, DC: Smithsonian University Press, 2002.

Hall, Simon. "Civil Rights Activism in 1960s Virginia." *Journal of Black Studies* 38, no. 2 (2007): 251–67.

Halloran, Sybil. "Fear, Funding, and Ambiguity: The Policy Dilemmas of Undocumented Students in Virginia Institutions of Higher Education." Virginia Commonwealth University thesis, 2015.

Handler, Richard, and Eric Gable. *The New History of an Old Museum: Creating the Past at Colonial Williamsburg.* Durham, NC: Duke University Press, 1997.

Hantman, Jeffrey. *Monacan Millennium: A Collaborative Archeology and History of a Virginia Indian People.* Charlottesville: University of Virginia Press, 2018.

Harris, Travis. "Lost Tribe of Magruder: The Untold Story of the Navy's Dispossession of a Black Community." College of William and Mary dissertation, 2019.

Hayter, Julian. *The Dream Is Lost: Voting Rights and the Politics of Race in Richmond, Virginia.* Lexington: University Press of Kentucky, 2017.

Henderson, William. *Gilded Age City: Politics, Life, and Labor in Petersburg, VA: 1874–1889.* Lanham, MD: Rowman and Littlefield, 1980.

Hoffman, Stephen. *Race, Class, and Power in the Building of Richmond, 1870–1920.* Jefferson, NC: McFarland, 2004.

Holden, Vanessa. *Surviving Southampton: African American Women and Resistance in Nat Turner's Community.* Champaign: University of Illinois Press, 2021.

Holloway, Pippa. *Sexuality, Politics, and Social Control in Virginia, 1920–1945.* Chapel Hill: University of North Carolina Press, 2006.

Holton, Woody. *Forced Founders: Indians, Debtors, Slaves, and the Making of the American Revolution in Virginia.* Chapel Hill: University of North Carolina Press, 1999.

Horn, James. *A Land as God Made It: Jamestown and the Birth of America.* New York: Basic Books, 2006.

Horton, James and Lois. *Slavery and Public History: The Tough Stuff of American Memory.* Chapel Hill: University of North Carolina Press, 2008.

Howard, Amy, and Thad Williamson. "Reframing Public Housing in Richmond, VA: Segregation, Resident Resistance, and the Future of Redevelopment." *Cities* 57 (September 2016): 33–39.

Jones, Chip. *The Organ Thieves: The Shocking Story of the First Heart Transplant in the Segregated South.* New York: Gallery Books, 2020.

Key, Leslee. "From Desegregation to Desexigration in Richmond, Virginia, 1954–1973." Virginia Commonwealth University thesis, 2011.

Kierner, Cynthia, and Sandra Treadway, eds. *Virginia Women: Their Lives and Times, Volumes 1 and 2.* Athens: University of Georgia Press, 2015.

Kimball, Gregg. *American City, Southern Place: A Cultural History of Antebellum Richmond.* Athens: University of Georgia Press, 2003.

Kiracofe, David. "The Jamestown Jubilees: 'State Patriotism' and Virginia Identity in the Early Nineteenth Century." *Virginia Magazine of History and Biography* 110, no. 1 (2002): 35–68.

Kollatz, Harry, and Anne Soffee. *Richmond Ragtime: Socialists, Suffragists, Sex, and Murder.* Charleston: History Press, 2008.

Kupperman, Karen. *The Jamestown Project.* Boston: Harvard University Press, 2007.

Lassiter, Matthew, and Andy Lewis. *The Moderates' Dilemma: Massive Resistance to School Desegregation in Virginia.* Charlottesville: University of Virginia Press, 1998.

Lauterbach, Preston. *The Chitlin' Circuit and the Road to Rock'n'Roll.* New York: W. W. Norton, 2012.

Lebsock, Suzanne. *The Free Women of Petersburg: Status and Culture in a Southern Town, 1784–1860.* New York: W. W. Norton, 1985.

Lee, Lauranett. *Making the American Dream Work: A Cultural History of African Americans in Hopewell, VA.* New York: Morgan James, 2008.

Lindgren, James. *Preserving the Old Dominion: Historic Preservation and Virginia Traditionalism.* Charlottesville: University Press of Virginia, 1993.

Link, William. "The Jordan Hatcher Case: Politics and 'A Spirit of Insubordination' in Antebellum Virginia." *Journal of Southern History* 64, no. 4 (1998): 615–35.

Link, William. *Roots of Succession: Slavery and Politics in Antebellum Virginia.* Chapel Hill: University of North Carolina, 2004.

Lombardo, Paul. *Three Generations, No Imbeciles: Eugenics, the Supreme Court, and Buck v. Bell.* Baltimore: Johns Hopkins University Press, 2010.

Love, Richard. "In Defiance of Custom and Tradition: Black Tobacco Workers and Labor Unions in Richmond, Virginia, 1937–1941." *Labor History* 35, no. 1 (1994): 25–47.

Mahoney, Shannon. "Community Building after Emancipation: An Anthropological Study of Charles' Corner, Virginia, 1862–1922." College of William and Mary dissertation, 2013.

Marlowe, Gertrude. *Right Worthy Grand Mission: Maggie Lena Walker and the Quest for Black Eco-*

*nomic Empowerment*. Washington, DC: Howard University Press, 2003.

Marschak, Beth, and Alex Lorch. *Lesbian and Gay Richmond*. Mount Pleasant, SC: Arcadia, 2008.

Matthews, Kimberly, and Raymond Hylton, *The Richmond 34 and the Civil Rights Movement*. Mt. Pleasant, SC: Arcadia, 2020.

Maurantonio, Nicole. *Confederate Exceptionalism: Civil War Myth and Memory in the Twenty-First Century*. Lawrence: University of Kansas Press, 2019.

McInnis, Maurie. *Slaves Waiting for Sale: Abolitionist Art and the American Slave Trade*. Chicago: University of Chicago Press, 2011.

McInnis, Maurie, and Louis Nelson, eds. *Educated in Tyranny: Slavery at Thomas Jefferson's University*. Charlottesville: University of Virginia Press, 2019.

McKittrick, Katherine. *Demonic Grounds: Black Women and the Cartographies of Struggle*. Minneapolis: University of Minnesota Press, 2006.

Meier, August, and Elliott Rudwick. "Negro Boycotts of Segregated Streetcars in Virginia, 1904–1907." *Virginia Magazine of History and Biography* 81, no. 4 (October 1973): 479–80.

Mendez, Jennifer Bickham. "Enforcing Borders in the Nuevo South: Gender and Migration in Williamsburg, Virginia, and the Research Triangle, North Carolina." *Gender and Society* 22, no. 5 (October 2008): 613–38.

Minor, Claudia. "The 1886 Convention of the Knights of Labor." *Phylon* 44, no. 2 (1983): 147–59.

Mintz, Morton. *At Any Cost: Corporate Greed, Women, and the Dalkon Shield*. New York: Pantheon, 1985.

Moeser, John, and Rutledge M. Dennis. *The Politics of Annexation: Oligarchic Power in a Southern City*. Rochester, VT: Schenkman Books, 1982.

Moretti-Langholtz, Danielle, and Buck Woodward. *Building the Brafferton: The Founding, Funding, and Legacy of America's Indian School*. Williamsburg: Muscarelle Museum of Art, 2019.

Murray, Paul. "Who Is an Indian? Who Is a Negro? Virginia Indians in the World War II Draft." *Virginia Magazine of History and Biography* 95, no. 2 (1987): 215–31.

Musselwhite, Paul. *Virginia 1619: Slavery and Freedom in the Making of English America*. Chapel Hill: University of North Carolina Press, 2019.

Nelson, Louis. "Object Lesson: Monuments and Memory in Charlottesville." *Buildings & Landscapes* 25, no. 2 (Fall 2018): 17–35.

Nelson, Louis, and Claudrena Harold. *Charlottesville 2017: The Legacy of Race and Inequity*. Charlottesville: University of Virginia Press, 2018.

Newby-Alexander. Cassandra. *Virginia Waterways and the Underground Railroad*. Charleston: History Press, 2017.

Oast, Jennifer. *Institutional Slavery: Slaveholdings Churches, Schools, Colleges, and Businesses in Virginia, 1680–1860*. Cambridge: Cambridge University Press, 2016.

Odem, Mary. "Our Lady of Guadalupe in the New South: Latino Immigrants and the Politics of Integration in the Catholic Church." *Journal of American Ethnic History* 24, no. 1 (Fall 2004): 26–57.

Ooten, Melissa. *Race, Gender, and Film Censorship in Virginia, 1922–1965*. Lanham, MD: Rowman and Littlefield, 2014.

Parkhurst, Kathryn. "Expansion and Exclusion: A Case Study of Gentrification in Church Hill." Virginia Commonwealth University thesis, 2016.

Potterfield, T. Tyler. *Nonesuch Place: A History of the Richmond Landscape*. Charleston: History Press, 2009.

Pratt, Robert. *The Color of Their Skin: Education and Race in Richmond, 1954–1989*. Charlottesville: University of Virginia Press, 1992.

Pula, James. "Fact vs. Fiction: What Do We Really Know about the Polish Presence in Early Jamestown." *Polish Review* 53, no. 4 (2008): 477–93.

Rachleff, Peter. *Black Labor in Richmond, 1865–1890*. Champaign: University of Illinois Press, 1989.

Rainville, Lynn. *Hidden History: African American Cemeteries in Central Virginia*. Charlottesville: University of Virginia Press, 2016.

Randolph, Adah. "'It's Better to Light a Candle Than to Curse the Darkness': Ethel Thompson Overby and Democratic Schooling in Richmond, Virginia, 1910–1958." *Educational Studies* 48, no. 3 (2012): 220–43.

Randolph, Lewis, V. P. Franklin, and Gayle Tate. *Rights for a Season: The Politics of Race, Class, and Gender in Richmond, Virginia*. Knoxville: University of Tennessee Press, 2003.

Richardson, Selden. *Built by Blacks: African American Architecture and Neighborhoods in Richmond*. Charleston: History Press, 2008.

Rountree, Helen. *Before and After Jamestown*. Gainesville: University of Florida Press, 2002.

Rountree, Helen. *Pocahontas' People: The Powhatan Indians of Virginia through Four Centuries*. Norman: University of Oklahoma Press, 1996.

Rountree, Helen. *Pocahontas, Powhatan, Opechancanough: Three Indian Lives Changed by Jamestown*. Charlottesville: University of Virginia Press, 2006.

Rountree, Helen. *The Powhatan Indians of Virginia: Their Traditional Culture*. Norman: University of Oklahoma Press, 1992.

Rountree, Helen. "The Indians of Virginia: A Third Race in a Biracial State." In *Southeastern Indians since the Removal Era*, edited by Walter Williams. Athens: University of Georgia Press, 1979.

Ruggles, Jeffrey. *The Unboxing of Henry Brown*. Richmond: Library of Virginia Press, 2003.

Ryan, James. *Five Miles Away, A World Apart: One City, Two Schools, and the Story of Educational Opportunity in Modern America*. Oxford: Oxford University Press, 2011.

Saunders, James, and Renae Shackleford. *Urban Renewal and the End of Black Culture in Charlottesville, VA: An Oral History of Vinegar Hill*. Jefferson, NC: McFarland, 2005.

Schechter, Patricia. "Free and Slave Labor in the Old South: The Tredegar Ironworkers' Strike of 1847." *Labor History* 35, no. 2 (1994): 165–86.

Schleef, Debra, and H. B. Cavalcanti. *Latinos in Dixie: Class and Assimilation in Richmond, Virginia*. Albany: SUNY Press, 2010.

Schuyler, Lori. *The Weight of Their Votes: Southern Women and Political Leverage in the 1920s*. Chapel Hill: University of North Carolina Press, 2006.

Sebree, Chet'la. *Mistress*. Kalamazoo, MI: New Issues Poetry & Prose, 2019.

Shockley, Megan. *Creating a Progressive Commonwealth: Women Activists, Feminism, and the Politics of Social Change in Virginia, 1970s–2000s*. Baton Rouge: Louisiana State University Press, 2018.

Shockley, Megan. *We, Too, Are Americans: African American Women in Detroit and Richmond, 1940–1954*. Champaign: University of Illinois Press, 2003.

Sidbury, James. *Ploughshares into Swords: Race, Rebellion, and Identity in Gabriel's Virginia, 1730–1810*. Cambridge: Cambridge University Press, 1997.

Silver, Christopher. "The Racial Origins of Zoning in American Cities." In *Urban Planning and the African American Community: In the Shadows*, edited by Thomas Manning et al. Thousand Oaks, CA: Sage, 1997.

Silver, Christopher. *Twentieth Century Richmond: Planning, Politics, and Race*. Knoxville: University of Tennessee Press, 1984.

Silver, Christopher, and John Moeser. *The Separate City: Black Communities in the Urban South, 1940–1968*. Lexington: University of Kentucky Press, 1995.

Smith, J. Douglas. *Managing White Supremacy: Race, Politics, and Citizenship in Jim Crow Virginia*. Chapel Hill: University of North Carolina Press, 2002.

Smith, Ryan. *Death and Rebirth in a Southern City: Richmond's Historic Cemeteries*. Baltimore: Johns Hopkins University Press, 2020.

Stanton, Lucia. *"Those Who Labor for My Happiness": Slavery at Thomas Jefferson's Monticello.* Charlottesville: University of Virginia Press, 2012.

Takagi, Midori. *Rearing Wolves to Our Own Destruction: Slavery in Richmond, Virginia, 1782–1865.* Charlottesville: University of Virginia Press, 2002.

Torkelson, Jacob. "Where Shall We Go?: Race, Displacement, and Preservation at Slabtown and Yorktown Battlefield." University of Pennsylvania thesis, 2019.

Trammell, Jack. *Richmond Slave Trade: The Economic Backbone of the Old Dominion.* Charleston: History Press, 2012.

Trammell, Jack, and Guy Terrell. *A Short History of Richmond.* Charleston: History Press, 2017.

Twitty, Michael. *The Cooking Gene: A Journey through African American Culinary History in the Old South.* New York: HarperCollins, 2017.

Tyler-McGraw, Marie. *At the Falls: Richmond, Virginia and Its People.* Charlottesville: University of Virginia Press, 1994.

Urofsky, Melvin. *Commonwealth and Community: The Jewish Experience in Virginia.* Richmond: Virginia Historical Society, 2000.

Utsey, Shawn, dir. *Meet Me in the Bottom: The Struggle to Reclaim Richmond's African Burial Ground.* Virginia Commonwealth University and Burn Baby Burn Productions, 2010.

Utsey, Shawn, dir. *Until the Well Runs Dry: Medicine and the Exploitation of Black Bodies.* Virginia Commonwealth University and Burn Baby Burn Productions, 2011.

Varon, Elizabeth. *Southern Lady, Yankee Spy: The True Story of Elizabeth Van Lew, a Union Agent in the Heart of the Confederacy.* Oxford: Oxford University Press, 2005.

Wallenstein, Peter. *Blue Laws and Black Codes: Conflict, Courts, and Change in Twentieth-Century Virginia.* Charlottesville: University of Virginia Press, 2004.

Wallenstein, Peter. *Race, Sex, and the Freedom to Marry: Loving v. Virginia.* Lawrence: University Press of Kansas, 2014.

Watkinson, James. "William Washington Browne and the True Reformers of Richmond, Virginia." *Virginia Magazine of History and Biography* 97, no. 3 (1989): 279–310.

Waugaman, Sandra, and Danielle Moretti-Langholtz. *We're Still Here: Contemporary Virginia Indians Tell Their Story.* Richmond: Palari, 2000.

Wood, Karenne, ed. *The Virginia Indian Heritage Trail.* Charlottesville: Virginia Foundation for the Humanities, 2008.

## Journalistic Sources

*Chesterfield Observer*

*Commonwealth Times*

*C-ville Weekly*

*The Daily Press*

*The Daily Progress*

*Daily Beast*

*Henrico Citizen*

*Huffington Post*

*The New York Times*

*The New Yorker*

*National Public Radio*

*The Progress-Index*

*Richmond Free Press*

*Richmond Magazine*

*RVA Magazine*

*Richmond Planet*

*Richmond Times-Dispatch*

*Roanoke Times*

*Smithsonian Magazine*

*Style Weekly*

*Time Magazine*

*Virginia Cavalcade*

*Virginia Gazette*

*Virginia Living*

*Virginia Mercury*

*The Virginian-Pilot*

*Washington Post*

# Acknowledgments

This book had its genesis back in 2012, when Melissa stumbled upon *A People's Guide to Los Angeles* while visiting the city. In 2015, a fortuitous meeting at the Imagining America conference in Baltimore connected us with Amie Thurber, who kindly introduced us to the series editors. That's to say that this lengthy project is a result of serendipitous connections, and one that has challenged and rewarded us in ways we could not have imagined at the outset.

While we will attempt to thank individuals and recognize institutional support to the extent that space and memory allow, this book has been shaped, rethought, and reworked based on numerous conversations with activists and scholars, lectures and community meetings we attended, a poignant question asked in a working group, and leads to follow given to us by someone whose name we may not have known. This guide, then, is the product of deep collaboration and generosity on the parts of many people who make Richmond and Central Virginia their home, and we are so grateful for that support.

We started brainstorming with others nearly a decade ago about what a potential guide might include. Every part of the manuscript has been reviewed by multiple people, often a number of times, but we know that we could never completely capture the full depth and nuance of the region's rich community histories, stories, and spaces. Each time we spoke to a scholar, activist, or community member about a specific site, we returned to that entry with new knowledge as well as increased concern that we could not fully relay every dynamic of that story as part of a short guidebook entry. Those gaps and lapses are the authors' alone.

We have many people to thank. First, we want to express our deepest gratitude to two people who made this book what it is. Photography and cartography are as important to a guidebook as the writing, and for those contributions we thank Kim Lee Schmidt and Rebecca Wrenn. Kim traveled hundreds of miles during a global pandemic and took on this project with nothing but enthusiasm and support. Her keen eye for the sites at times reshaped how we positioned and wrote about a space, and we cannot thank her enough for taking a chance on us when our initial outreach included few details about the project's scope. The wonderful maps were created by Rebecca Wrenn. A professional cartographer and historian, Rebecca has been a friend to us for more than two decades, and again she readily agreed to provide maps when we were still woefully short on details and timelines.

For critical funding and resources without which this project would not have been possible, we thank the *will* program and Westhampton College at the University of Richmond, with particular gratitude to Mia Reinoso Genoni and Holly Blake, and Laura Barraclough at Yale University. Melissa also received a Virginia Humanities fellowship in fall 2022 that aided in the project's completion, and Jason received funding support from the Old Dominion University.

So many people generously donated their time and expertise. Some sat for hours-long interviews, while others connected us with a key person or piece of information that we did not even know we needed. Some read and reread site entries or directed us to a conference or community event that led us to new paths for interpreting sites. We know this list is likely incomplete, for which we apologize.

In alphabetical order, we want to express our thanks to: Niya Bates, Mikael Broth, Laura Browder, Alexandra Byrum, Duron Chavis, Benita Cotman-Lewis, Monti Datta, Brian Daugherity, Kim Dean-Anderson, Alicia Diaz, Terry Dolson, Shelby Driskell, Steve J. Earle, Ana Edwards, Ywone Edwards-Ingram, Colita Fairfax, Sylvia Gale, Jack Gieseking, Hamilton Glass, Tanya Gonzalez, Vinnie Gonzalez, Cheryl Groce-Wright, Euan Hague, Susan Hellman, José "Tito" Henríquez, Wanda Hernandez, Patricia Herrera, Erin Holloway Palmer, Amy Howard, Yuki Hubben, Glyn Hughes, Meg Hughes, Emma Ito, Freda "Corliss" Johnson, Jeannine Keiffer, Kelly Kerney, Harry Kollatz Jr., Beth Kreydatus, Juliette Landphair, Lauranett Lee, Yanet Limon-Amado, Katie Logan, Beth Marschak, Nicole Maurantonio, Lucretia McCulley, Del McWhorter, Mariela Mendez, Leisa Meyer, Derek Miller, Rob Nelson,

Jennifer Oast, Brain Palmer, Erin Holloway Palmer, Patrice Rankine, Benjamin Ross, Helen Rountree, Nicole Sackley, Chet'la Sebree, Queen Shabazz, Andrea Simpson, Julietta Singh, Nathan Snaza, Richard Stewart, Vanessa Stout, Amie Thurber, Sarah Trembanis, Suzie Weng, Cathy Woodson, Eric Yellin, and Michel Zajur. The late Karenne Wood and the late John Moeser were invaluable mentors in the early years of building the foundation for this guide.

Melissa would like to acknowledge a series of collaborative groups that helped shape and form this project. At the University of Richmond, the inaugural Arc of Racial Justice Institute, the Bonner Center for Civic Engagement's East End Collaboratory, and the 2021–22 Institutional History cohort generated important conversations and connections. As well, being part of the 2017 National Endowment for the Humanities institute cohort on "Recognizing an Imperfect Past: History, Memory, and the American Public" at the Georgia Historical Society in Savannah has proven to be invaluable in ways too numerous to name. Finally, many thanks to co-author Jason Sawyer, who took on her passion for this project as his own.

Jason thanks his many community colleagues, mentors, assistants, and guides; without their help, this work would not have been possible. The passion and intellectual discipline of Melissa Ooten drove this project into existence. Her calm, grounded leadership made working with her a joy. Additionally, Mary Katherine O'Connor, F. Ellen Netting, and David Fauri in the School of Social Work at Virginia Commonwealth University allowed him to work alongside them as a student researching local activist and organizational histories. Their mentorship and guidance built the practical and intellectual foundation that led to co-authoring this project. Jason would also like to thank the resident community leaders and skilled community practitioners whom he worked alongside for many years across Richmond, particularly in Greater Fulton and the East End; they provided him with some of the best education he ever received. Thanks to Rosa Coleman, Spencer E. Jones III, Corliss "Freda" Johnson, Linda Sutton, Mary Ellen Otto, Carl Otto, Kara Zinchuck, Annette Cousins, Angie Carey, Ty Carey, Penny Ferris, Rebecca Fralin, Lafayette Harris, Thelma Martin, Cynthia Newbille, Veronica Fleming, Sarah Kim, Cheryl Groce-Wright, Blue Clements, and many others. Their example consistently demonstrated how to put people and community first, always.

Additional organizational and institutional support came from Old Dominion University, including exceptional help from doctoral research assistants Angela Johnson and Shelby Dillingham.

Without the specialized work of librarians and archival professionals, many of these stories would remain untold. Thanks to staff members at The Valentine, the Library of Virginia, the Black History Museum and Cultural Center of Richmond, the Library of Congress, the Virginia Museum of History and Culture, UVA Special Collections, VCU Special Collections, the Boatwright Memorial Library at the University of Richmond, the Pamunkey Indian Museum and Cultural Center, the Jefferson School African American Heritage Center, the Albemarle Historical Society, and the Colonial Williamsburg Foundation. We also want to thank all of the folks at UC Press, especially Kim Robinson, Chad Attenborough, Summer Farah, and Paul Tyler, who transformed this book into the beautiful work that it is.

# Credits

### COVER

Emancipation Day Celebration ca. 1905, Library of
Congress; Lorna Pinckney mural; view of Downtown
Richmond from the Slave Trail.

### FRONTISPIECE

(Clockwise from top left) See page 103; see page 74;
March for Black Trans Lives, Melissa Ooten; see page
149; see page 117.

### CHAPTER 1

Cover photo: Looking toward Downtown Richmond
from the T. Tyler Potterfield Memorial Bridge.

Main Street 1905, Library of Congress.

Tobacco Row, Richmond Chamber of Congress
Photograph Collection, The Valentine.

Sixth Street Market Vendors 1908, Library of Congress.

Virginia Civil Rights Coalition, Tommy Price, *Richmond
Times-Dispatch* Photograph Collection, The Valentine.

Lumpkin's Excavation, J. Maurice Duke Photograph
Collection, The Valentine.

Tobacco Factory Interior, Cook Collection, The
Valentine.

First African Baptist Church Sketch, Library of Congress.

Old City Hall, Library of Congress.

Thanksgiving Ceremony, Lindy Keast Rodman,
*Richmond Times-Dispatch* Photograph Collection, The
Valentine.

Raleigh Hotel, Library of Congress.

ERA at Capitol Square, Bob Brown, *Richmond Times-
Dispatch* Photograph Collection, The Valentine.

Thalhimers Protest, Anderson Collection, The
Valentine.

Tredegar 1865, Library of Congress.

"Bread Riots" Sketch, Library of Congress.

### CHAPTER 2

Cover photo: Bike Riding at Woodcroft, Jay Paul,
Oakwood Arts, Maggie L. Walker Memorial and Plaza
Dedication Photograph Collection, The Valentine.

Fulton Vista, Lindy Keast Rodman, *Richmond Times-
Dispatch* Photograph Collection, The Valentine.

East End Improvement Association, Michael O'Neil,
*Richmond Times-Dispatch* Photograph Collection, The
Valentine.

Belle Bryan Day Nursery, Cook Collection, The
Valentine.

White Female Tobacco Workers, Cook Collection, The
Valentine.

Van Lew Mansion, Library of Congress.

Fulton Gasworks Flood, Finnegan Photograph
Collection, The Valentine.

Trolley Track Removal, Carl Lynn, *Richmond Times-
Dispatch* Photograph Collection, The Valentine.

Creighton Draw-In, *Richmond Times-Dispatch*
Photograph Collection, The Valentine.

## CHAPTER 3

Cover photo: Emancipation Day Celebration ca. 1905, Library of Congress.

First Toll Road, *Richmond Times-Dispatch* Photograph Collection, The Valentine.

VUU Students, Don Long, *Richmond Times-Dispatch* Photograph Collection, The Valentine.

Jackson Ward 1938, Dorothea Lange, Library of Congress.

*Richmond Planet* Newsroom, Library of Congress.

Hippodrome, Scott L. Henderson, Independent Order of St. Luke Photograph Collection, The Valentine.

True Reformers Hall, W. Palmer Gray Collection, The Valentine.

Navy Hill Barber Shop, Edith K. Shelton Photograph Collection, The Valentine.

Navy Hill Students, Carl Lynn, *Richmond Times-Dispatch* Photograph Collection, The Valentine.

Richmond Colored Normal School, Cook Collection, The Valentine.

St. Luke Children, The Browns, Independent Order of St. Luke Photograph Collection, The Valentine.

Walker Statue Unveiling, Oakwood Arts, Maggie L. Walker Memorial and Plaza Dedication Photograph Collection, The Valentine.

Clearing for Toll Road, *Richmond Times-Dispatch* Photograph Collection, The Valentine.

Overby-Sheppard Students, Lindy Keast Rodman, *Richmond Times-Dispatch* Photograph Collection, The Valentine.

Robins Construction, Jack Turner Photography, Richmond Chamber of Commerce Photograph Collection, The Valentine.

## CHAPTER 4

Cover photo: View of Monument Avenue from Marcus-David Peters Circle.

AIDS Vigil, Bruce Parker, *Richmond Times-Dispatch* Photograph Collection, The Valentine.

Triangle Players Playbill, Jason Sawyer.

Women's Festival, Don Pennell, *Richmond Times-Dispatch* Photograph Collection, The Valentine.

## CHAPTER 5

Cover photo: Brown Girls Narrative mural created by Austin Miles and Kristal Brown, Hull Street.

Men Working Quarry, Cook Collection, The Valentine.

Women Tobacco Laborers, Library of Congress.

La Fiesta Latino, Humberto Macaiza Photograph Collection, The Valentine.

## CHAPTER 6

Cover photo: Fort Lee Protestor, Don Long, *Richmond Times-Dispatch* Photograph Collection, The Valentine.

City Point 1861, Library of Congress.

Petersburg Old Towne, 2019, Library of Congress.

La Siesta menu, The Valentine.

Colombo-American Association at La Siesta, Humberto Macaiza Photograph Collection, The Valentine.

Colbrook Motel, Susan Hellman.

Wilcox Lake Postcard, Authors' collection.

Matoaca Millworkers 1911, Library of Congress.

## CHAPTER 7

Cover photo: Downtown pedestrian mall in Charlottesville.

Garrett Street, Holsinger Studio Collection, Albert and Shirley Small Special Collections Library, University of Virginia.

Vinegar Hill, Rip Payne Collection, Albemarle County Historical Society.

Students Gather at Rotunda, University of Virginia Visual History Collection, Albert and Shirley Small Special Collections Library, University of Virginia.

Living Wage Protest on Lawn, Dan Heuchert, University of Virginia Visual History Collection, Albert and Shirley Small Special Collections Library, University of Virginia.

## CHAPTER 8

Cover photo: Yorktown Beach 1941, Library of Congress.

DOG Street 1902, Library of Congress.

USCT at Dutch Gap 1864, Library of Congress.

Black Coachmen at Colonial Williamsburg, *Richmond Times-Dispatch* Photograph Collection, The Valentine.

Formerly Enslaved at Slabtown / Yorktown, 1862, Library of Congress.

Pamunkey Indian School, May 31, 1937, Library of Virginia.

Federal Encampment at Pamunkey River 1862, Library of Congress.

## CHAPTER 9

Cover photo: African American Gothic mural, downtown Richmond.

# Index